MATCH
OF THE DAY
50
YEARS

10 9 8 7 6 5 4 3 2 1

Published in 2014 by BBC Books, an imprint of Ebury Publishing.
A Random House Group Company.

Main text by Nick Constable

The Random House Group Limited Reg. No. 954009

Addresses for companies within the Random House Group can be found at www.randomhouse.co.uk

A CIP catalogue record for this book is available from the British Library.

ISBN: 9781849908139

The Random House Group Limited supports the Forest Stewardship Council® (FSC®), the leading international forest-certification organisation. Our books carrying the FSC label are printed on FSC®-certified paper. FSC is the only forest-certification scheme supported by the leading environmental organisations, including Greenpeace. Our paper procurement policy can be found at www.randomhouse.co.uk/environment

Commissioning editor: Albert DePetrillo
Editor: Charlotte Macdonald
Project editor: Rod Green
Designers: Two Associates
Picture researcher: Claire Gouldstone
Production: Phil Spencer

Printed and bound in Germany by Mohn Media GmbH

To buy books by your favourite authors and register for offers visit
www.randomhouse.co.uk

MATCH
OF THE DAY

YEARS

BOOKS

1990s

2000s

2010s

Foreword

The *Match of the Day* theme tune has been the soundtrack to everything I've achieved in football. As a schoolboy in Leicester taking my first steps towards a professional career, the show was essential viewing in the Lineker house on a Saturday night.

It's easy to forget but in the days before the Premier League – yes the beautiful game did exist then – it was the only consistent football fix available to the nation.

I'll never forget my first appearance on *Match of the Day* as I missed a sitter at Aston Villa but throughout my time as a player with Leicester, Everton and Spurs it was always a thrill to appear on the programme.

Then, to take over from the legendary Des Lynam, and still to be in the hot seat 15 years later, is an achievement of which I'm incredibly proud.

But it's not just me ... you only have to look at the reaction we get every Saturday night to realise just how much *Match of the Day* means to football fans across the country. Almost all of them believe their team is on last each week!

Premier League Chief Executive, Richard Scudamore, has described *Match of the Day* as a 'phenomenon' and, in an era where more live games are televised than ever before, it remains the most watched football programme in the country with up to 10 million tuning in every weekend.

The programme itself has evolved dramatically in the time I've been presenting. The biggest change was introducing extended highlights of every Premier League game across the weekend.

In recent years, the introduction of new graphics, statistics, manager interviews and social media voting has helped keep the show fresh and relevant. We've also added some new faces in the studio from Vincent Kompany to Thierry Henry and Roy Hodgson to Russell Brand!

One familiar face who sadly won't be sat alongside me on Saturdays in the future is Alan Hansen, for so long the king of the pundits. When Hansen speaks, people listen.

Being a pundit on *Match of the Day* is one of the toughest jobs on TV.

Not only do you have to digest up to eight games most Saturdays, but then you have to deliver genuine insight in perhaps two or three minutes maximum. It's a tough skill, so those like Alan, who master it, really stand out. But goals are our business and we never lose sight of the fact that the action remains at the heart of the programme.

That's been the philosophy for 50 years and long may it continue ... with that theme tune remaining an integral part of all our Saturday nights.

Gary Lineker

Introduction

It was never supposed to become a sporting icon. In fact, when *Match of the Day* **was first screened on 22 August 1964, the attendance inside Anfield outnumbered BBC2's audience two to one. For the Corporation it was a one-off series, a trial run for the 1966 football World Cup.**

MotD's first presenter could hardly have expected the show to enjoy such longevity.

No one expected those grey, grainy images, barely distinguishable team strips and Kenneth Wolstenholme in his best bib and tucker to be the genesis of a national obsession. Clubs didn't want it, outside broadcast technology wasn't really ready for it and fans seemed happy just to cheer from the terraces. Football on TV? For the next half-century? Surely not.

To survive in those early days, *Match of the Day* needed all the breaks it could get. It helped that the first game was a cracker – Liverpool beat Arsenal 3-2 – and that the film crew performed miracles from a makeshift studio in the Anfield boardroom. There was also the kind of off-the-ball incident beloved by viewers and editors alike; a cat emerging from the stands to cut inside the six-yard box, body-swerve through the Liverpool defence and dart down the right wing. As commentator John Motson would observe in his inimitable style for an *MotD* anniversary programme years later: 'The black cat that crossed the BBC's path that day brought luck and longevity.'

It was just as well. Within a year, league clubs were joining forces to try to strangle the fledgling programme at birth. They feared a switch to the more accessible BBC1 channel would hit ground receipts and were only mollified when TV executives promised not to reveal the featured Saturday game until full-time whistles had blown across the country. It would be the first of many dogged battles between television and the football authorities. Yet, as the sixties swung on, it was clear that *Match of the Day* had momentum.

That was partly down to the afterglow of England's World Cup triumph. But there were other factors giving the programme a fair wind, not least the affordability of televisions and a surge in technological advances. By 1968

it was pulling in five million viewers, a year later the first colour broadcasts appeared and in 1970 the much-loved theme tune was launched. This was *Match of the Day* as we now know it – lacking a few bells and whistles perhaps but essentially the same simple, accessible format.

Season by season, this book charts the 50-year history of the programme through the fate of England's greatest clubs, the classic matches, the legendary players and the defining moments of league and cup campaigns. There's the extraordinary theatre of big European nights, penalty shoot-outs, giant-killing shocks, derby bragging rights, World Cups to remember (and forget) and, inevitably, those controversial refereeing decisions. Alongside the action shots and Player Of The Year profiles we've also ensured there's a healthy sprinkling of nostalgic images for football-lovers who cut their teeth in the sixties, seventies and eighties.

Match of the Day has always been a football show but it has never ducked the big, sometimes traumatic, stories of the day. So we include some of English football's darkest hours – the rampant hooliganism which bedevilled so many grounds, the disaster at Heysel, the exile of English clubs in Europe and, of course, Hillsborough, the tragedy which claimed 96 lives and continues to cast a long shadow today.

Jimmy Hill's opinions often sparked debate but his dedication to football was never in question.

The thread through all of this, of course, is *Match of the Day* itself; presenters such as Wolstenholme, Jimmy Hill, Des Lynam and Gary Lineker, pundits who've played the game at the highest level (step forward Hansen, Shearer and Lawrenson) and top-drawer commentators like David Coleman, John Motson, Barry Davies and Clive Tyldesley. Through exclusive interviews with members of the *MotD* team, Premier League stars such as Thierry Henry, Patrick Vieira and Peter Schmeichel and an eclectic range of football-loving celebrities, you'll find insights and anecdotes into a truly captivating era of the English game

So we discover how Des Lynam fretted over replacing Jimmy Hill as presenter, why Hill and Terry Venables could never stop arguing, how David Coleman coped with slow motion replays, and the mischievous antics of Tony Gubba as he sometimes led viewers to believe he really did have a sixth sense about imminent goals.

Other contributors include former Tottenham chairman Lord Sugar, who gives his verdict on a classic TV rights battle, Arsenal legend Ian Wright on how Alan Hansen ruined his greatest goal, Patrick Vieira on the great Gooners' penalty bungle and Paolo di Canio explaining why sporting conduct should be easy. And as for that famous Hansen comment about Manchester United winning nothing with kids, Paul Scholes admits he would have agreed at the time.

There are also some typically forthright and colourful takes on *Match of the Day* from celebrities such as Piers Morgan and Russell Brand. Morgan tells how he instantly equates the first bars of the theme tune with passion and argument, while Brand argues that the show has become the last, great, British TV social event – a Saturday night ritual that unites the nation.

And perhaps that's the secret of its enduring success. Des Lynam certainly thinks so – the one piece of advice he gave to his successor, Gary Lineker, was to make the viewer part of the show. 'The only simple thing I said to him,' Des recalled later, 'was never to tell the viewer "thank you for joining me". Because they're not joining you. They're joining us – the programme, the pundits, everyone in the backroom. They're joining us. Gary always does that.'

Here's to the next half-century.

MotD's main presenter, Gary Lineker, found making the jump from professional footballer to professional broadcaster a daunting challenge.

LIVERPOOL

EVERT...

FOOTBALL LEAGUE
DIVISION I.

LIVERPOOL 3
V

A TY-PHOO SERIES OF 24

FOOTBALL LEAGU...

TOTTE
HOTS...
v
CRYS...
PAL...

Official P...

Price Si...

1969. június 11. ★ 20 óra
Megyeri úti Dózsa Stadion

ÚJPESTI
DÓZSA –
NEWCASTLE
UNITED

VVK-döntő   Ára: 2,— forint

No. 4 GEORGE BEST

INTERNATIONAL
FOOTBALL STARS

GEORGE BEST
(Manchester United & Northern Ire...

Signed as a professional for his present cl...
his 17th birthday in 1963, Georg. Best p...
an important role in his team's 5–1 wir...
Benfica (Lisbon) in February 1966 and the...
christened him 'El Beatle'. Voted third
'Footballer of the Year' Award in May 19...
already has 13 full Northern Ireland
national caps to his credit and is hailed...

Best Wishes f...
a Happy and Prosp...
New Year
FROM
THE CHAIRMAN, DIRECTOR...
AND PLAYERS OF THE S...

...OMWICH ALBION FOOTBAL...

...OTBALL LEAGUE CUP, 5th ROUND

BROMWICH ALB...
v.
ASTON VILLA
...ESDAY, 17th NOVEMBER, 19...
...AWTHORNS ◆ WEST BROM...
KICK-OFF 7-30 p.m.
ENTRANCE: TURNSTIL...
WOODMAN CORNER

SEASON 1969–70   **Friday, 26th Dec...**

Vol. 62   No. 27   KICK-OFF ...nd early in their own interest

MATCH OF THE DAY

1960s

Greaves

Banks

Hurst

Hunt

Cohen

Ball

Moore

Eastham

Jackie Charlton

Wilson

Stiles

Jairzinho

Gilmar

Rinaldo

1964-65

For Matt Busby's Manchester United this was a pivotal season. It had been six years since the Munich air disaster had taken the lives of so many exciting young players and fans were desperate to see a reborn team capable once more of major honours.

Above: Denis Law in action for Manchester United, displaying his characteristic, sleeve-gripping concentration.

A longing for success lurks in the DNA of every supporter yet at Old Trafford it now meant so much more. Winning the FA Cup in May 1963, the first silverware since Munich, had been a great start but the First Division title was the real prize. It would serve both as a tribute to the Flowers of Manchester and a statement to the footballing world that while United had been broken, they remained unbowed.

And what a title race it was. Since the end of November Busby's side had been vying constantly with Chelsea and Leeds for top spot and as the season rolled into April it was clear these three were the only contenders. When newly promoted Leeds entertained the Red Devils at Elland Road on 17 April it was off the back of a 25-match league and cup unbeaten run – including a confidence boosting 1-0 FA Cup semi-final replay victory over Man Utd.

But this was a Manchester side in which Denis Law was scoring for fun (28 league goals in 36 appearances), George Best had established himself and Bobby Charlton was, well, Bobby Charlton. They were hungry for revenge and they got it through a single goal from winger John Connelly. Two days later Leeds lost again to Sheffield Wednesday.

Still, the race continued. Although Chelsea's challenge fizzled out Don Revie's team went into their final match away at bottom of the table Birmingham a point clear. Their problem was that Man Utd had a game in hand and an unassailable goal average (see season 1967–68).

At St Andrew's the Whites had a lack-lustre first half and missed several clear chances. By the 51st minute they were 3-0 down while at Old Trafford visitors Arsenal had conceded a wonder goal from Best and a second from Law. By now Revie had accepted the title was gone and was madly signalling his players to 'take it easy' ahead of an FA Cup final five days away. But the message was misunderstood.

Below: Liverpool's FA Cup heroes, with Gerry Byrne standing, far right, favouring the broken collar bone with which he had played most of the match.

Incongruously Leeds came to life, pulling back three goals in the final 25 minutes. It was not enough however; their cross-Pennine rivals eventually beat Arsenal 3-1 and only an impossibly freakish result at Aston Villa could have stopped the trophy heading to Old Trafford. As it turned out United lost to Villa 2-1 although their goal average of 2.282 proved more than enough to deliver.

Match of the Season
Liverpool 2 Leeds United 1

Leeds went into this FA Cup final as firm favourites although, given the disappointment of allowing their title challenge to expire at lowly Birmingham the previous Monday, it was hard to see why. They were playing their sixth match in 15 days and the energy sapping Wembley turf had taken heavy rain. That said, Liverpool had also endured a heavy end of season programme with ten league matches in April.

Whether it was from tiredness or tension the Leeds attack struggled for fluency. In contrast Liverpool, with Tommy Smith playing as an additional centre half enforcer and Willie Stevenson in sublime form in left midfield, controlled much of the play. Yet it wasn't until the third minute of extra time that Roger Hunt guided home a low header from left back Gerry Byrne – later the hero of the hour when he was found to have played virtually the whole game with a broken collarbone.

Leeds responded quickly and well with Bremner thrown full tilt into the attack. And it was the diminutive Scot who brilliantly volleyed home Jack Charlton's nod-down from Hunter's hopeful lob to bring them back into the game. It was not enough. A week that had dangled the double in front of the First Division's new boys ended in heartache when, with nine minutes left, Ian St John met Callaghan's cross with a bullet header to beat Gary Sprake.

Welcome to *Match of the Day*

He couldn't have known he was launching a British institution so Kenneth Wolstenholme's opening words on that very first *Match of the Day* followed the basic rules of broadcasting: keep it brief, clear and simple.

With the Beatles' 'She Loves You' blasting out of Anfield's PA system, Wolstenholme told viewers: 'Welcome to *Match of the Day*, the first of a weekly series coming to you every Saturday on BBC2. As you can hear we're in Beatleville ...'

That evening, Saturday 22 August 1964, some 20,000 people tuned in to watch highlights of Liverpool's 3-2 win over Arsenal with Red's striker Roger Hunt scoring the first goal – a clever lob-volley from Ian Callaghan's delicate right-wing chip. The TV audience was less than half the attendance but within four years five million would watch Alan Ball score twice for Everton in their season opener against Manchester United.

It had all been made possible through technological advances in electronic cameras and videotape. This allowed outside broadcasts to be wired to a central editing suite and trimmed to fit scheduled time slots before transmission.

But not everyone was celebrating. In 1965 several clubs tried to block *MotD*'s move to BBC1 (a channel available to many more viewers) for fear it would hit ground receipts. Eventually a compromise was reached: the BBC agreed not to reveal the televised Saturday match until all games had ended.

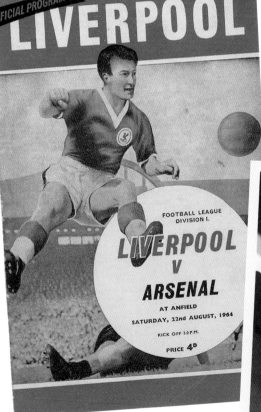

Opposite top: Bobby Collins fits some new studs to his boots with a little help from his son.

Opposite bottom: Captain Collins introduces the Leeds United team to the Duke of Edinburgh prior to the 1965 FA Cup Final.

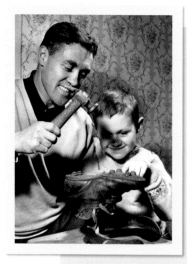

Player of the Year
Bobby Collins, Leeds United

When Bobby Collins arrived at Elland Road in March 1962, a £25,000 signing from Everton, Leeds were facing the ignominy of Third Division football. When he departed five years later Don Revie's outfit was among the most feared in Europe. That turnaround was driven by Collins who was renowned for his boundless energy, technical skills and accurate long-range passing.

The Scottish international's tendency to leave imprints – both physically and mentally – on his opponents was part of the package but he also knew the importance of honest hard work and team spirit. In one interview he recalled: 'Don knew that good pros had good habits and I think that's what he was hoping to instil when he signed me.

'One of the great things about the boss was the way he built up a comradeship. We all loved him because he treated us properly and commanded our utmost respect. He also knew how to build a team.' For his part Revie described Collins as 'the best signing I ever made', adding, 'Leeds can never thank him enough for the transformation he brought to the club.'

1965-66

The run-up to the 1966 World Cup produced a season dominated by the first of Bill Shankly's great Liverpool sides. They hit the top in late November and rarely faltered, conceding only 34 goals and terrorising opposition defences through their formidable strike duo of Roger Hunt and Ian St John.

Above: The Manchester United squad in front of Lisbon's Discoveries Monument prior to the Benfica match.

Opposite: 19-year-old George Best was nicknamed 'El Beatle' by the Portuguese fans.

Hunt's rich vein of form seemed unending – his 30 goals ensured he was the Reds' top scorer for the fifth successive year – and he owed much to the service provided by wingers Ian Callaghan and Peter Thompson. But it was Liverpool's settled first team that proved their ace card, providing a cohesion and consistency unrivalled anywhere else in the division. Their best players seemed impervious to injury and they effectively played out the entire season with only 12 men; the other two notched up just four appearances between them.

The cult of the 'big club' was already surfacing in the English game as fans drawn to *Match of the Day*'s highlights package realised there was no law forcing them to support their home-town team. The most exciting players were becoming national celebrities and successful clubs realised they could develop a national fan-base with all the potential that promised for the sale of souvenirs and club memorabilia. The idea of clubs as a 'brand' had been born – even if nobody really noticed.

The one player who epitomised this glamorous new face of football was George Best. He announced himself on the world stage in a jaw-dropping opening 12 minutes as Benfica entertained Manchester United in the second leg of a European Cup quarter-final (see Match of the Season). Best would go on to become a world footballing icon during the sixties and early seventies but fame, fortune and God-given ability wouldn't be enough to stop his career – and, indeed, his life – eventually spiralling downwards into alcoholism.

As the second half of the 1965-66 season drew on so the thoughts of players and fans alike turned to the imminent World Cup. But in late

March there was the very real possibility of having no Jules Rimet Trophy to win after it was stolen while on display at a stamp exhibition in London's Westminster. Police arrested a petty thief but the 1.8 kg gold trophy was only recovered when a mongrel dog called Pickles sniffed it out under a suburban hedge during a walk with his owner. Pickles duly achieved celebrity status and ended six days of hand-wringing embarrassment for the FA.

Match of the Season
Benfica 1 Manchester United 5

Man Utd went into this game with a 3-2 lead from the first leg – not enough in the eyes of many critics. For one thing Benfica had an excellent European Cup home record and in the 1960s had already twice finished as competition runners-up. Then there was the small matter of Eusebio and his fellow giants of the Portuguese game, Germano and Coluna.

Understandable, then, that Matt Busby should order his team to play a holding game for the first 20 minutes, quietening the crowd and frustrating their opponents. However, as the manager later dryly pointed out, George Best 'must have had cotton wool in his ears'. Best, the 19-year-old with the Beatle haircut, tore into Benfica like a player possessed, putting his side two up inside 12 extraordinary minutes.

The first of these was an exquisite looping header, the second a breathtaking run through the Benfica defence that prompted commentator Kenneth Wolstenholme to observe, '... what a player this boy is'.

United went on to win 5-1 with further goals from John Connelly, Paddy Crerand and Bobby Charlton – one of the greatest away performances of any side in Europe before or since.

Above left: England captain Billy Wright is carried from the pitch after earning his 100th cap in a 1959 victory over Scotland.

Opposite top: Charlton clashes with Chelsea's Peter Osgood.

Opposite bottom: Charlton leaves goal-keeper Tony Waiters floundering as he scores against Blackpool.

Billy Wright and the Manager's Curse

It is a football truism that great players rarely make great managers and Billy Wright is a case in point. Here was a man who became the first player in the world to earn 100 international caps, who captained England at three World Cup Finals, who won three league titles and whose defensive abilities ensured living-saint status at his only professional club, Wolverhampton Wanderers.

After a brief stint managing England's youth team he became Arsenal's manager at the start of the 1962–63 season, guiding them to a respectable seventh. But over the following three years the Gunners went into decline, finishing 8th, 13th and 14th and failing to progress past the FA Cup fifth round. Ahead of the World Cup Wright parted company with the club to pursue a successful career as a TV pundit, eventually rising to Head of Sport with Central Television.

There have been many theories over the years as to why Wright never cut the mustard as manager. These range from a lackadaisical attitude to training to the fact that he was married to one of the singing Beverley Sisters (and supposedly burned the candle at both ends). But then, maybe he just couldn't understand why so few of his players were as naturally talented as him.

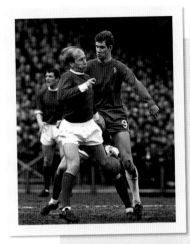

Player of the Year
Bobby Charlton, Manchester United

In the pantheon of Old Trafford greats, nobody embodies the spirit of Manchester United quite like Sir Bobby Charlton. The successful sides under Sir Matt Busby – and later Sir Alex Ferguson – were born from his incisive approach play, combined with an insatiable appetite to win. A survivor of the 1958 Munich air disaster, he was the centrepiece of the Red Devils' resurgence.

Charlton signed for Manchester United in 1955 and the following year scored twice on his debut, as chance would have it against Charlton Athletic. Although he began his top-flight career as a winger-cum-inside forward he soon developed his signature role as a deep-lying centre forward characterised by thrusting drives from midfield.

By the mid-sixties he had really captured the hearts and minds of football fans across the UK. Having banged in 18 goals in United's title-winning season the year before, he again contributed 18 strikes in 1965–6, and put in a series of performances – including an impressive hat-trick in a 6-2 mauling of Northampton Town – that attracted plaudits from across the world of football. Yet despite a team that also featured Denis Law and George Best, United finished fourth and narrowly missed out in European and domestic cup competitions.

Charlton will always be remembered as a gentleman of the game; in a 20-year career he picked up just a single, bizarre, booking for time-wasting while his team was losing. Anyone who witnessed his never-say-die attitude might suspect the ref got that one wrong.

WORLD CUP – ENGLAND 1966

The euphoric response to England's 1966 World Cup victory – which other countries sometimes feel has gone on too long – makes it easy to forget the air of disenchantment among fans and pundits ahead of the tournament.

Opposite top: World
Sports *magazine
front cover.*

*Opposite bottom: The
clash that never came -
Brazil didn't make it to
the quarter finals.*

Below: World Sports
*chart showing the route
to the final.*

In the mid-fifties and early sixties, England were little short of parlous. Home and away friendlies against Hungary, for instance, left manager Walter Winterbottom's players nursing an aggregate defeat of 13-4, while the 1962 Chile World Cup quarter-final exit to Brazil did little to inspire confidence.

In fairness, losing to the eventual '62 winners was hardly a disgrace, but Winterbottom had run out of chances and the FA turned to former England player Alf Ramsey who, as Ipswich Town manager, had guided his team from Division 3 (South) to the Division 1 title inside three years. Ramsey took the job on condition that he alone picked the team. The FA selection panel that had been imposed on his predecessor was axed.

Never short on chutzpah, Ramsey declared that 'we will win the World

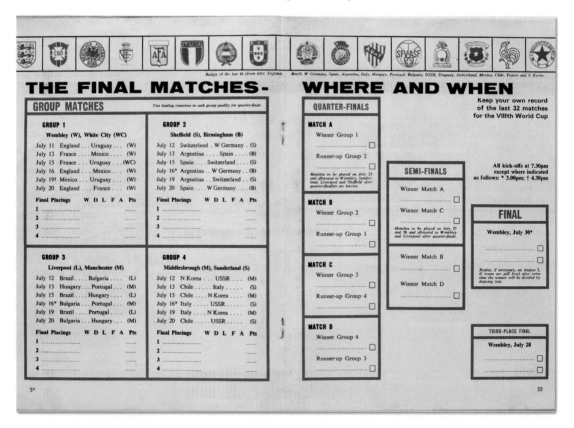

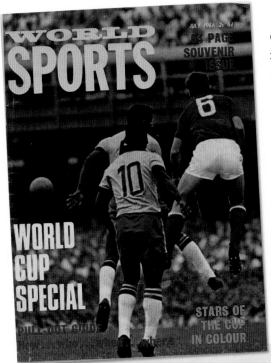

Cup in 1966.' Regular England-watchers weren't so sure. The new manager's first match in charge, a 5-2 defeat to France, ended hopes of European Championships qualification and was described as 'pathetically fumblefooted' by the *Daily Mirror*. England's 1-1 home draw with Brazil in May 1963 left *The Times* thundering that 'Ramsey's men slip even further from world class.'

When England were booed off in a 3-2 home defeat against Austria barely eight months before the start of the World Cup, things looked bleaker than ever. But within two months, the manager's fightback had begun. He unveiled a new tactical formation – the wingless wonders – and wooed sceptical fans with a 2-0 victory over European champions Spain.

Ramsey's new approach ensured a key midfield role for the tireless Alan Ball, then in the form of his life, and pushed Bobby Charlton into a more central attacking

Above: Second choice striker Geoff Hurst dismisses Argentina's 'animals'.

position. Nobby Stiles took on ball-winning duties as a lone wolf ahead of the centre backs and both full-backs doubled as overlapping wide men. This all translated into a loose, and unfamiliar, 4-1-3-2 formation.

England progressed serenely to the quarter finals through a dour 0-0 draw with Uruguay and 2-0 victories over Mexico and France. But Ramsey lost first-choice striker Jimmy Greaves to a shin injury in the French game which meant rookie Geoff Hurst got his chance in the quarter-final against Argentina.

That encounter had almost a Sunday League flavour such was the bookings count. The South Americans' captain, Antonio Rattin, was sent off for, as the referee delicately put it, 'violence of the tongue' and a late Hurst header gave England a 1-0 win. At the final whistle a furious Ramsey stopped George Cohen swapping shirts. He later branded the Argentinians 'animals'. Sporting, it wasn't.

Fortunately the semi-final was the antithesis. Indeed, almost an hour passed before the ref awarded a foul. England eventually beat Portugal with a brace from Charlton (a successful penalty from Eusebio coming too late to turn the match around) and with West Germany defeating the USSR 2-1, one of football's oldest international rivalries was again centre stage.

What more can be said of the final? The first four goals – Haller's for Germany after 13 minutes, Hurst's for England after 19, Martin Peters' effort in the 78th minute and Weber's dying seconds equaliser – are barely remembered. The final was all about that extra-time Hurst strike and the debate over whether it did or didn't cross the goal-line (most now accept it didn't). Oh, and, of course, Hurst's glorious hat-trick for 4-2 accompanied by Kenneth Wolstenholme's equally glorious commentary as Moore floated a killer pass to his West Ham team-mate: 'Some people are on the pitch ... they think it's all over. It is now ... it's four.'

Easily worth five decades of euphoria.

Below: Wembley victory parade - Banks, Wilson, Ball, Charlton, Moore and Cohen.

The aftermath of World Cup glory could easily have led to an anti-climax in the First Division. Yet the season was marked by a competitive title race from some exciting, entertaining sides. Manchester United took their second championship in two years with 60 points but were pushed all the way by an unfashionable, and hitherto underperforming, Nottingham Forest.

Forest manager Johnny Carey had served 17 years as a player at Old Trafford and wanted to embrace the same traditions of free-flowing football. His squad included the likes of versatile skipper Terry Hennessey and explosive winger Ian Storey-Moore – considered one of the greatest finishers in Forest's history. Storey-Moore produced a famous hat-trick in the 3-2 FA Cup quarter-final win over Everton, later voted by fans the greatest game ever at the City Ground.

Below: Joe Kinnear and Jimmy Greaves celebrate Spurs' 1967 FA Cup final victory against Chelsea.

United's other main rival for the title were Tottenham Hotspur, a side that now bore little resemblance to the double-winners of 1960-61. Since 1964 manager Bill Nicholson had brought in the likes of Mullery, Venables, Gilzean, Kinnear, England and Knowles to create a formidable attacking line-up. Although United proved four points too good in the league, Spurs would comfortably triumph in the FA Cup with a 2-1 victory over Chelsea, the first all-London final of the century.

The big upset of the season came in the League Cup. Until now this competition, largely the creation of Football League secretary Alan Hardaker, had been derided by the media as 'Hardaker's Horror'. Not all leading clubs contested it while many supporters regarded it as a joke. However, moving the final to Wembley in March 1967 added credence and the crowd of 97,952 was 28,000 more than all previous finals combined. They were not disappointed as rank underdogs QPR fought back from 2-0 down to beat West Bromwich Albion (see Match of the Season).

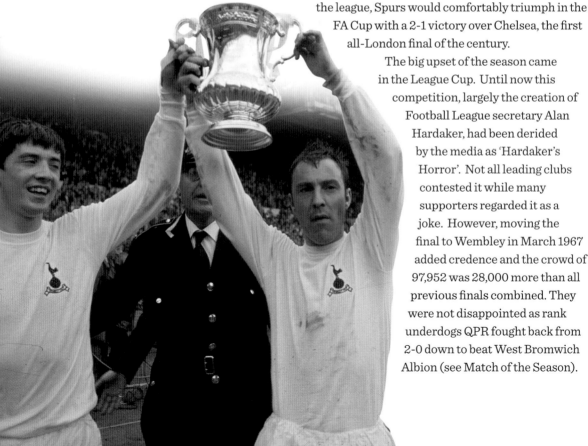

Below: Programme for the 1967 League Cup final in which underdogs QPR claimed a surprising victory over West Brom.

The boost to English football generally from the World Cup also left a legacy in the transfer market. At the start of the 1966–7 season Alan Ball moved from Blackpool to Everton for £112,000 – the first £100,000-plus transfer between British clubs. Initially it seemed like good business for Blackpool who on 22 October showed their attacking credentials with a 6-0 thrashing of Newcastle. Unfortunately, that was their only home win of the season. While no player is bigger than a club (especially not when they're only 5 foot 6 inches tall) the loss of Ball was a huge blow to the Seasiders who finished bottom on 21 points, 16 short of their previous tally.

Match of the Season
QPR 3 WBA 2

This League Cup final was billed as a princes v paupers mismatch. West Brom with their feared attacking armoury of Tony 'Bomber' Brown, Jeff 'The King' Astle, Bobby Hope and winger Clive Clark had coasted through five rounds, including a satisfying 6-1 victory over local rivals Aston Villa. As a Third Division side, meanwhile, QPR had played an extra round and scraped through several skin-o'-your-teeth victories.

It was no surprise when Albion found themselves two up at the break, both scored by Clark. The second half though saw the game turned on its head. First Roger Morgan headed one back for Rangers then the outrageously talented Rodney Marsh went on a jinking run from the halfway line to equalise with a low strike. QPR's 81st minute winner was not without controversy since Albion keeper Dick Sheppard lost the ball in a collision with Ron Hunt, allowing Mark Lazarus to pounce. But their players and ecstatic fans cared little. The goal stood.

Were there any justice in the football world Rangers should have qualified for the Inter-Cities Fairs Cup. But that competition's rules stated that teams could only be drawn from their domestic league's top division. Rangers would have to wait two more years to attain such dizzy heights.

THE FOOTBALL LEAGUE

CUP FINAL

QUEEN'S PARK RANGERS
VERSUS
WEST BROMWICH ALBION
(HOLDERS)

SATURDAY MARCH 4th, 1967
Kick-off 3.30 p.m.

EMPIRE STADIUM WEMBLEY
OFFICIAL PROGRAMME — ONE SHILLING
Incorporating Special Cup Final Issue of Football League Review

Kenneth Wolstenholme –
The Consummate Commentator

Opposite: Jack Charlton with his Player of the Year trophy and in the familiar all-white of the only club for which he played professionally – Leeds United.

Below: Kenneth Wolstenholme did not believe in over-analysing football matches or interrupting the on-screen action.

He coined the most famous phrase in British sports broadcasting – 'they think it's all over ... it is now' – but Kenneth Wolstenholme was much more than the doyen of football commentators.

Inherently modest, he rarely talked of his courageous service as an RAF bomber pilot. In fact, Wolstenholme faced death daily during the Second World War, flying 100 missions by the age of 23 (for which he received the Distinguished Flying Cross and Bar).

He was hired by the BBC in 1948, never having watched a TV programme, and delivered his first commentary from Romford, Essex, on a Southern v Northern Counties football trial. He took the microphone for 23 consecutive FA Cup finals and five World Cups, often acting as both presenter and commentator, but was eased aside in favour of David Coleman after Mexico '70. Wolstenholme later admitted he was 'a bit miffed' by the BBC's decision.

He was involved in football broadcasting into his seventies, presenting Channel 4's Italian league coverage, but had little time for TV's emphasis on analysis and punditry. 'Instead of concentrating on the action we have endless people sitting around dissecting every incident in the studio,' he said.

'They overdo it and all the commentators seem to have been told to change to the same style. It bores me. They don't seem to realize that while silence in radio is death – in television it can be golden.' Wolstenholme died in March 2002, aged 81.

Player of the Year
Jack Charlton, Leeds United

A one-club man in his playing days (he earned a living as a miner before turning to football), this season proved to be a frustrating one for Charlton and his beloved Leeds.

The Whites finished the season fourth in the First Division and lost an FA Cup semi-final to Chelsea, a match the defender missed due to injury. Nevertheless it proved to be a successful campaign on a personal level for Charlton who, alongside partner-in-crime Norman Hunter, helped his side to 15 clean sheets. In total they conceded just 42 goals, the second-best defensive record in the league behind runners-up Nottingham Forest.

A tall and strong presence at the back, Charlton carried forward his form from England's 1966 World Cup winning team. Throughout that tournament he was ever-present at the heart of a Three Lions defence that didn't concede a goal from open play until the final.

His popularity among Leeds fans remains. To this day, he holds the appearances record at Elland Road, with 762 competitive outings, and was voted into the club's greatest ever XI by Leeds supporters in 2006.

For Matt Busby's Man Utd it was the bitterest of pills. Going into the last day of the season they stood level on points with a resurgent Manchester City. United had to beat struggling Sunderland and pray that City failed to win at Newcastle. Draws all round were no use to the Red Devils.

That was because City's goal average, the calculation used by the League as first tie-breaker, was bulletproof. Goal average is a division of the number of goals scored by the number conceded and City's stood at 2 (86/43). United's was 1.618 (89/55) meaning a minimum 21-goal margin of victory was required. In the event they couldn't even scrape a draw.

Sunderland's 2-1 win, coupled with City's thrilling 4-3 victory at St James' Park, was a deserved triumph for Joe Mercer, the old warhorse lured out of semi-retirement to take charge in 1965. This was City's first title for 31 years built on the back of shrewd buys such as Francis Lee (£60,000), Colin Bell (£45,000), Mike Summerbee (£35,000) and Tony Book (a snip at £13,500). But Mercer's first buy was probably also his most important – Malcolm Allison as assistant coach.

With the domestic cups going to WBA (FA) and Leeds (League) Busby's team had just one chance of salvation. Three days after the Sunderland defeat they faced Real Madrid in the second leg semi-final of the trophy that

Below: David Sadler heads home that goal that brought the Red Devils back into their European Cup semi-final in Madrid.

Match of the Season
**Manchester United 4
Benfica 1**

For fans and players alike beating Real Madrid so dramatically was a cathartic moment. Somehow, the European Cup had become bound up in the legacy of Munich. In an interview with the *Daily Mail* almost 45 years later David Sadler put it beautifully:

'Nobody ever said "let's go and win the European Cup for the boys we left behind in Munich",' he said. 'Nothing as obvious as that. But it was there … beating Real Madrid that night and going on to win the European Cup didn't change anything about Munich but it tidied it up. That sounds like a daft thing to say because Munich will always be what it is and what it was. It's not like taking a wet cloth to a blackboard. But it wound it up and put it in a place where we could handle it.'

In the Wembley final United beat Benfica – including the great Eusebio – 4-1. It was another thriller with Charlton's opener cancelled by Graca nine minutes from time. Eusebio almost settled it at the last but his close range shot was brilliantly caught by Stepney, a save which, despite the tension, the Portuguese icon stopped to applaud. In extra time Best, Kidd and Charlton all found the net, however, and Manchester United's tribute to the lost Busby Babes was complete.

Below: Brian Kidd jumps for joy after scoring United's third at Wembley – on his 19th birthday.

Above: Bobby Charlton makes the call at the start of the 1968 European Cup Final, with the Red Devils playing in blue.

had eluded them – the trophy many believed would, should, have been won by the Busby Babes but for the tragedy of Munich. The European Cup.

United took a 1-0 home lead to the six-times European champions but found themselves 3-1 down at half-time through Pirri, Gento and Amancio. Only a ludicrous own goal from Zoco was keeping them in touch and Busby knew the dream was fading. David Sadler later recalled him saying calmly: 'Right, sit down lads. That's done and gone. That wasn't Manchester United out there. I can stand losing in the United way, I can take that. Let's be able to hold our heads up when we come off.'

Busby tweaked his tactics, deploying Sadler in attack. Together with his team talk it was a masterstroke. Sadler scored with 15 minutes left then Best cut down the right to cross for the unlikely marauding figure of centre-back Bill Foulkes – a Munich survivor – to convert for a 4-3 aggregate win.

MotD Memories: Dressing up for Ken

Actress Sue Johnston has long been the nation's favourite TV mum through roles such as *Brookside*'s Sheila Grant and Barbara Royle in *The Royle Family*. Growing up on Merseyside meant it was virtually the law to love football; here Reds' fan Sue recalls her memories of *MotD*.

'In the Sixties I was living at home, still in Liverpool. I remember my family bought my grandma and grandpa a telly. Grandpa was delighted because he could see his football – they were both in their eighties – but my

grandma was of the belief that if you could see them they must be in your house ... it was a huge thing.

'So she used to get changed ready to watch it because she absolutely adored Kenneth Wolstenholme. That's my earliest memory [of *MotD*], my grandmother sitting, saying good evening and dimpling up for Kenneth Wolstenholme.

'My dad was totally impressed with Wolstenholme because he had the gift of letting you watch the game. So many commentators had been used to covering games on the radio that they over-described the action. He was always content to sit back and not patronise you.'

Player of the Year
George Best, Manchester United

A trendsetter in every sense of the word George Best's genius had an enduring impact on Manchester United's style of football. In the club's long line of skilful and pacy crowd-pleasing number 7s he was arguably the first and greatest of the lot.

Best's bewitching wing wizardry and penchant for showboating was a key component of United's brand throughout the mid-to-late-sixties and the 1967–68 season saw him at the peak of his powers. He shared top scorer title with Ron Davies of Southampton after knocking in 28 league goals, was voted European Footballer of the Year (in no small part down to superb performances in those games against Real Madrid and Benfica) and was voted the Football Writers' Association Player of the Year.

He hit 32 goals in all competitions during the season, the most by a midfielder for the Red Devils in a single campaign until Cristiano Ronaldo claimed the record in 2008.

This was the year in which all the promise of Don Revie's eight years in charge reached fruition. The Fairs and League Cup double of the previous season had been undeniably impressive but the measure of any top side is to (a) win the league and (b) produce consistently high standards. Leeds ticked both boxes.

Below: Billy Bremner and Gary Sprake celebrate Leeds' League Championship victory on the cover of GOAL magazine, with a Leeds United collectible pennant alongside.

Their tally of 67 points was a record for 22-club divisions, beating by one the Arsenal side of 1931. However, whereas the Gunners' goal haul that year was 127 Leeds managed just 66, making them only the fifth club to win the championship with more points than goals. This inevitably led to ill-informed sniping about the Whites' defensive approach. They certainly had a tight defence – Norman Hunter, Jack Charlton, Paul Reaney, Terry Cooper and keeper Gary Sprake – and conceded just 26 goals. But only two clubs, Everton and Chelsea, outscored them.

Revie's great achievement was to build a powerful, skilful team from almost nothing. Since taking them from the Second Division eight years earlier only Mick Jones (£100,000), Johnny Giles (£35,000) and Mike O'Grady (£30,000) had cost money while the club's youth and scouting policy produced gems such as Eddie Gray, Peter Lorimer and Paul Madeley. Even rivals recognised this and when Leeds secured a 0-0 draw at Anfield in their penultimate game, ending Liverpool's own title hopes, their lap of honour was sportingly cheered by the Kop. The striker's performance of the season went to West Ham's Geoff Hurst who scored a hat-trick in each half at Upton Park during an 8-0 thrashing of Sunderland. This didn't quite equal the First Division record – Ted Drake put away seven for Arsenal at Villa Park in 1955 – and a mischievous Hurst later admitted that his first was handball anyway.

Sunderland at least managed to avoid relegation. That was a fate destined for QPR, chastened after a parlous first season in the top flight, and Leicester, who lost the FA Cup final 1-0 to Man City. It was also a disappointing end to

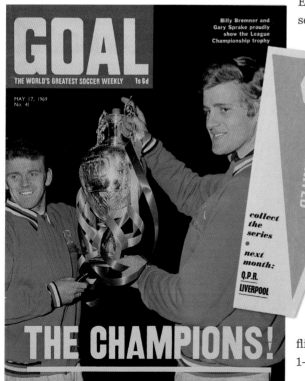

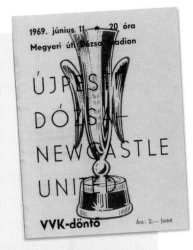

Match of the Season
Ujpest Doza 2 Newcastle United 3 (2-6 agg.)

Newcastle became the butt of rivals' jokes after qualifying for the Fairs Cup by finishing tenth in the First Division. It was a freakish combination of circumstances; England's entry was increased to four clubs, the competition's 'one city, one team' rule disqualified Arsenal, Spurs and Everton and both Man Utd and West Brom were rejected because of other cup commitments in Europe.

But the Magpies did England proud. As Chelsea and Liverpool departed to the toss of a coin and Leeds surrendered tamely to Ujpest, they saw off Feyenoord, Sporting Lisbon, Real Zaragoza, Vitoria Setubal and Rangers, before taking a 3-0 lead in the first leg of the final at St James' Park. To the sound of Toon Army jaws hitting the terraces skipper Bobby Moncur got two of them – his first for seven years.

The return leg in Budapest brought a nightmare start for Newcastle. Revitalised on home turf, and spurred by feared striker Ferenc Bene, the Hungarians pulled back two before half-time. Then Moncur, clearly deciding he should have been a striker himself all along, volleyed home within a minute of the restart. Danish international Ben Arentoft got a second before sub Alan Foggon wrapped up an astonishing 6-2 aggregate victory. Back home the laughing had stopped. This was a European campaign rivalling the very best.

Above right: Match programme for the 1969 Fairs Cup Final in Budapest.

the season for Arsenal who had looked better than their fourth-place league finish. The Gunners suffered the League Cup final embarrassment of losing 3-1 to Third Division Swindon, courtesy of two extra-time goals from winger Don Rogers. Arsenal blamed a flu outbreak and the muddy pitch.

Barry Davies – A Style Apart

There's a temptation when comparing *MotD* commentators to reduce the debate to 'who's better' inevitably followed by the options 'Davies or Motson'.

That's partly because Barry Davies and John Motson were contemporaries across four decades, each keen to cover the biggest games, but also because their styles were very different. Certainly the BBC struggled to decide its main man; after spending much of the early nineties in Motson's shadow Davies was awarded the 1994 World Cup final and got both subsequent FA Cup finals.

Opposite top: Dave Mackay outjumps Liverpool's Ian St John.

Opposite bottom: Man City captain Tony Book puts up a stalwart defence against Notts Forest.

Below: Barry Davies in the commentary box drawing viewers into the game.

Davies, who joined *MotD* in 1969, recalls how commentators were accused of 'putting more women to bed in the country on Saturday nights than anyone else.' The programme even affected the licensing trade: '... the pubs virtually closed at ten minutes to ten so that people could get home to watch *Match of the Day* – it was an extraordinary thing, really.'

For Davies lovers – and there were many – he was simply the best; a rhythmic yet expressive voice, spare yet wonderfully descriptive commentary and the feeling that it was just you and him watching the match. Nor was there any doubt about his feelings for the national team.

One good example came during England's 1986 World Cup group match against Poland. Terry Fenwick lost possession, earning the brutally brief 'Ach...' reproach from Davies, as the Poles broke away. 'England just cannot afford crass errors like that,' he observed. 'We've got away with it twice; we cannot tempt fate further.' You could picture England fans sagely nodding *en masse* from their sofas.

Joint Players of the Year
Tony Book and Dave Mackay
(Manchester City and Derby County)

The first-ever shared Football Writers' Association award – for
Manchester City captain Tony Book and Derby County's Dave Mackay –
was deserved recognition for unsung heroes playing in defence.

Book joined The Citizens from Plymouth Argyle in 1966, was named
captain the following year and went on to become the most decorated
Manchester City skipper of all time. Despite missing the first four
months of the 1968–9 season with an Achilles injury his dedication
and drive remained infectious, particularly during City's FA Cup-
winning run.

Mackay spent nine years at Tottenham, establishing himself as a
fans' favourite, and was all set to wind down his on-field career as
player-manager of his boyhood club Hearts. Instead, Brian Clough
stepped in and brought the Scottish international to Derby in 1968
for £5000, informing the media that his new signing was Spurs'
'greatest ever player'.

It proved to be an inspired acquisition. The energetic Mackay
formed a formidable partnership alongside Roy McFarland at the back,
conceding only 32 goals in 42 games. Derby went on to triumph in the
Second Division and Mackay fully justified his reputation as one of
Clough's shrewdest buys.

1969-70

Fixture congestion can be a cancer to clubs, irrespective of past glories. And so it proved for Leeds United whose brave shot at a debilitating League, FA Cup and European Cup treble collapsed dramatically as they tried to handle nine crucial matches in just 22 days.

The FA had cut the season short by a month to help England acclimatise for the Mexico World Cup. This resulted in a ridiculous schedule in an era when squads were restricted to 20 players and only one substitute was allowed per game (and only then in cases of injury). As a result, some Leeds players logged 62 competitive matches.

Everton, be in no doubt, were worthy winners. Their line-up included scoring sensation Joe Royle with giants of the game Alan Ball, Howard Kendall and Colin Harvey controlling midfield. Harry Catterick's side clinched the title at Goodison on 1 April with a 2-0 win over WBA and went on to finish nine points clear. It's far from a given that Leeds would have successfully defended their title even if they'd collectively climbed into a Tardis and rewritten the fixture list themselves.

Below: Everton's route to the League Championship title was mapped out in a special souvenir brochure.

EVERTON'S TITLE
The match by match march to glory

ARSENAL 0, EVERTON 1
August 9th. Att.: 44,364.
Arsenal: Wilson; Rice, McNab; McLintock, Neill, Simpson; Robertson, George, Gould, Graham, Radford.
Everton: West; Wright, Brown; Kendall (Kenyon), Labone, Harvey; Husband, Jackson, Royle, Hurst, Morrissey.
Scorer: Hurst.

MANCHESTER UNITED 0, EVERTON 2
August 13th. Att.: 60,161.
Manchester United: Rimmer; Brennan, Burns; Crerand, Foulkes (Givens), Sadler; Morgan, Kidd, Charlton, Law, Best.
Everton: West; Wright, Brown; Jackson, Labone, Harvey; Husband, Ball, Royle, Hurst, Morrissey.
Scorers: Hurst, Ball.

EVERTON 2, CRYSTAL PALACE 1
August 16th. Att.: 50,700.
Everton: West; Wright, Brown; Jackson, Labone, Harvey; Husband, Ball, Royle, Hurst, Morrissey.
Crystal Palace: Jackson (J.); Sewell, Loughlan; Hoy, McCormick, Hynd; Taylor (T), Kember, Jackson (C), Queen (Woodruff), Blyth.
Scorers—Everton: Morrissey, Royle (pen). Crystal Palace: Blyth.

EVERTON 3, MANCHESTER UNITED 0
August 19th. Att.: 53,185.
Everton: West; Wright, Brown; Jackson, Labone, Harvey; Husband, Ball (D'Arcy), Royle, Hurst, Morrissey.
Manchester United: Stepney; Fitzpatrick, Burns; Crerand, Edwards, Sadler; Morgan, Kidd, Givens, Best, Aston.
Scorers: Ball, Morrissey, Royle.

MANCHESTER CITY 1, EVERTON 1
August 23rd. Att.: 43,676.
Manchester City: Corrigan, Book, Pardoe; Doyle, Booth, Bowles; Summerbee, Connor, Lee, Bowyer, Coleman.
Everton: West; Wright, Brown; Jackson, Labone, Harvey; Husband, Ball, Royle, Hurst, Morrissey.
Scorers—Manchester City: Bowyer. Everton: Morrissey.

EVERTON 2, SHEFFIELD WEDNESDAY 1
Everton: West; Wright, Brown; Jackson, Labone, Harvey; Husband, Ball, Royle, Hurst, Morrissey.
Sheffield Wednesday: Springett; Branfoot (Fantham), Burton; Young, Ellis, Craig; Pugh, Eustace, Warboys, Ford, Smith.
Scorers—Everton: Ball, Royle. Sheffield Wednesday: Smith.

EVERTON 3, LEEDS UNITED 2
August 30th. Att.: 51,797.
Everton: West; Wright, Brown; Jackson, Labone, Harvey; Husband, Ball, Royle, Hurst, Morrissey.
Leeds United: Sprake; Reaney, Cooper; Bremner, Charlton, Hunter; Madeley, Giles, Jones, Clarke, Gray (Lorimer).
Scorers—Everton: Husband, Royle 2. Leeds United: Bremner, Clarke.

DERBY COUNTY 2, EVERTON 1
September 6th. Att.: 37,728.
Derby County: Green; Webster, Robson; Durban, McFarland, Mackay; McGovern, Carlin, O'Hare, Hector, Hinton.
Everton: West; Wright, Brown; Kendall, Labone, Harvey; Husband, Ball, Royle, Hurst, Morrissey.
Scorers—Derby County: O'Hare, Hector. Everton: Kendall.

EVERTON 2, WEST HAM UNITED 0
September 13th. Att.: 49,052.
Everton: West; Wright, Brown; Kendall, Labone, Harvey; Husband, Ball, Royle, Hurst, Morrissey.
West Ham United: Ferguson; Bonds, Lampard; Peters, Stephenson, Moore; Howe, Boyce, Brooking, Hurst, Cross.
Scorers: Ball, Husband.

NEWCASTLE UNITED 1, EVERTON 2
September 17th. Att.: 36,960.
Newcastle United: McFaul; Craggs, Guthrie; Gibb, Burton, Moncur; Robson, Arentoft, Davies, Elliott, Sinclair.
Everton: West; Wright, Brown; Kendall, Labone, Harvey; Husband, Ball, Royle, Hurst, Morrissey.
Scorers—Newcastle United: Elliott. Everton: Husband 2.

IPSWICH TOWN 0, EVERTON 3
September 20th. Att.: 23,251.
Ipswich Town: Best; Carroll, Mills; Viljoen, Baxter, Bell; Lambert, Charlie Woods, Wigg (Clive Woods), O'Rourke, Brogan.
Everton: West; Wright, Brown; Kendall, Labone, Harvey; Husband, Ball, Royle, Hurst, Morrissey.
Scorers: Ball, Royle, Harvey.

EVERTON 4, SOUTHAMPTON 2
September 27th. Att.: 46,942.
Everton: West; Wright, Brown; Kendall, Labone, Harvey; Husband, Ball, Royle, Hurst, Morrissey.
Southampton: Martin; Kirkup, Hollywood; Kemp, McGrath, Gabriel (Channon); Paine, Stokes, Saul, Byrne, Fisher.
Scorers—Everton: Royle 3 (1 pen), Hurst. Southampton: Stokes, Kemp.

SANDY BROWN . . . our Scottish left back earned his first Championship medal last season and, along with Tommy Jackson (Ireland) and the now-transferred Gerry Humphreys (Wales), was among the only non-Englishmen to appear in the title-winning team.

If nothing else, at least the Whites won the nation's sympathy. They had fought an FA Cup semi-final marathon with Manchester United that was resolved only in the second replay through a superb long-range effort from Billy Bremner. Then, as league defeats mounted, including a 4-1 thrashing at Derby, they lost both legs of their European Cup semi-final against Celtic. Finally, they headed wearily to Wembley only to see a bitterly contested FA Cup final with Chelsea end 2-2.

When that game was replayed at Old Trafford it seemed Mick Jones' brilliant solo opener might finally bring home the bacon. But then Charlie Cooke's teasing cross allowed Peter Osgood to equalise with a diving header and David Webb sealed it for Chelsea in extra time following one of Ian Hutchinson's howitzer throw-ins.

Below: George Best slots home his third of six against Northampton.

Match of the Season
Northampton Town 2
Manchester United 8

It didn't look the likeliest FA Cup shock on paper. But in the run-up to this game Fourth Division Northampton's fans had begun to believe it possible. Hadn't they been in the top flight themselves just four years earlier? Hadn't they beaten Manchester United back in the 1930s? And wasn't George Best coming back from a month's suspension? After all, he was only *human*.

Unfortunately for the Cobblers it turned out he wasn't human. By the time an almost apologetic Best walked his sixth goal of this game into an empty net it seemed like Northampton's players just wanted to throw themselves to the ground on his approach (actually keeper Kim Book did exactly that for the last one).

Even allowing for the opposition Best's performance in this game proved just why he ranked among the most feared players in the world. The *Match of the Day* clip of his double hat-trick has come to define his football – arguably more so than his incredible performances against loftier challenges in Europe. Best was so good, that the merest flick of a shoulder or swivel of an eye when dribbling was often enough. Defenders who played against him must still be having nightmares.

Below left: Bobby Graham scored one of Liverpool's goals in MotD*'s first colour broadcast.*

Below: Chris Lawler carries the match ball out of the Anfield tunnel.

As Leeds faltered so two rivals, lurking in the realms of mid-table mediocrity, celebrated. Particularly Manchester City who took first the League Cup, beating West Brom, then the Cup Winners' Cup, defeating Polish side Gornik Zabrze – on both occasions by a 2-1 margin. Meanwhile, Arsenal ended their 17-year trophy drought with a 3-0 (4-3 on aggregate) defeat of Anderlecht in the second leg of their Fairs Cup final at Highbury. Goals from Kelly, Radford and Sammels won it on the night but it was a young Ray Kennedy, who had scored at the death in Belgium, who gave Arsenal their lifeline.

MotD's First Colour Broadcast

For years televised football had been almost as challenging to watch as to play. Deciphering which shade of grey represented your team could be agonizing – especially inside a packed penalty area. Often it was easier just to follow the ball and hope.

But on 15 November 1969 all that changed as, for the first time, *Match of the Day* was broadcast in glorious full

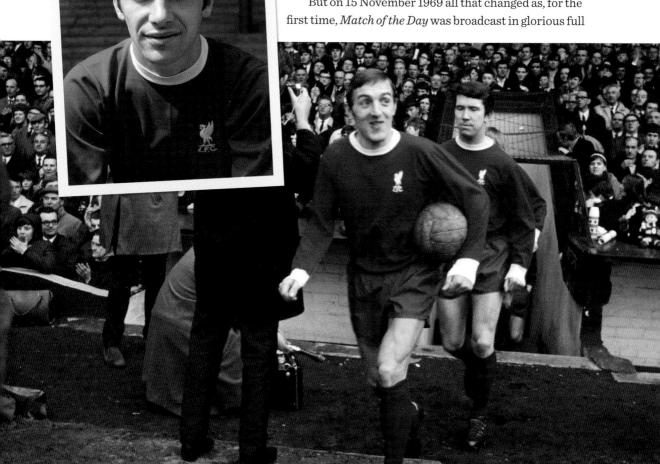

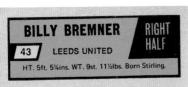

colour. The game was Liverpool v West Ham, a belter by any standards with Bill Shankly's rising stars facing a side still bolstered by England's heroes of '66. Besides, as producer Alan Weeks told the *Liverpool Echo*: 'There's nowhere as colourful as Anfield, both literally and in character, with the Kop and their comments.

'Football in colour is fantastic. Tonight the red and light blue on the green will stand out. Identification of the players is much easier – you can see the colour of their hair, even the blushes if someone is being bawled out.'

The build-up was frenetic for both fans and TV crew alike. Merseyside's electrical retailers reported a surge in demand for colour sets while at Anfield the boardroom was hurriedly transformed into a makeshift studio. Viewers were eventually treated to a 35-minute colour highlights package in which goals from Chris Lawler and Bobby Graham secured a 2-0 home win.

Player of the Year
Billy Bremner, Leeds United

Regarded as one of Britain's most fiery and industrious players of the post-war period, the red-headed Bremner's impact on Leeds United was monumental – so much so that he was recently voted the club's greatest ever player.

A 5 foot 5 inch powerhouse with a crunching tackle, his career spanned 16 years at Elland Road. He helped the club to two league titles, the League and FA Cup and two victories in the Inter-Cities Fairs Cup, as well as a European Cup final.

Bremner was the driving force behind Leeds' historic treble quest, something which had not then been achieved in the English game, and scored in one of the highest stakes matches ever played between British clubs: that European Cup semi-final against Celtic in front of an astonishing 136,505 fans at Hampden Park. Over the season his energetic performances and telling influence ensured he beat a quality field to win the Player of the Year award.

VILLA TOPPED DIVISION THREE IN FINE STYLE, FIGHTING OFF PERSISTENT CHALLENGES BY BOURNEMOUTH AND BY BRIGHTON....

...AND ALSO BY NOTTS COUNTY, WHO OUTPLAYED THEM IN AN EARLY SEASON MATCH AT VILLA PARK. VILLA WON WITH A GOAL BY RAY GRAYDON, BUT ONLY AFTER 'KEEPER TOMMY HUGHES HAD SAVED A PENALTY, AND COUNTY HAD WASTED MANY OTHER CHANCES....

SINCE THEN JIM CUMBES (ABOVE), HAS TAKEN OVER AS VILLA'S GOALIE.

DEFENDERS MICKY WRIGHT (LEFT), AND FRED TURNBULL LOOK GLUM AFTER A GREAT GOAL BY TED MACDOUGALL HAD GIVEN BOURNEMOUTH THE LEAD AT VILLA PARK....

CHARLIE AITKEN (ABOVE), HAS PLAYED 'DS OF GAMES IN VILLA'S 'S, SINCE HIS DEBUT FOR THEM IN 'AST SEASON WAS ONE OF HIS BEST 'PENABLE CHARLIE EVEN GOT HIS NAME SCORESHEET TWO OR THREE TIMES!

TEAM OF THE YEAR

KING STEEL

PAT IS NOW THE NUMBER ONE GOAL- -KEEPER

SAT. 28 JAN. 1978 BLYTH SPARTANS

STOKE Cr
F.A. CUP 4th ROUND

Official Pr

TOP TEAMS ENGLAND

IN APRIL, 1959, BILLY WRIGHT (LEFT), WOLVES CAPTAIN, BECAME THE FIRST ENGLAND PLAYER TO ACHIEVE A CENTURY OF INTERNATIONAL CAPS. HE REACHED A TOTAL OF 105 BEFORE RETIRING, AND WAS ENGLAND'S CAPTAIN IN 90 GAMES. BOBBY CHARLTON HAS BEATEN BILLY'S RECORD OF CAPS AND IT MAY NOT BE LONG BEFORE BOBBY MOORE TAKES OVER AS THE MOST CAPPED ENGLAND CAPTAIN OF ALL TIME.

BILLY WRIGHT CAPTAIN ENGLAND IN THREE WO CUPS (1950-'54-'58). H WAS BOBBY MOORE WHO THE PROUD HONOUR OF MAN TO RECEIVE THE WO CUP... THAT'S HIM ON HOLDING THE TROPHY, WIT ENGLAND. MANAGER W RAMSEY. IN THAT 1965-66 SEASON ENGLAND WERE TH CHAMPIONS OF THE WORL WITH ONLY ONE DEFEAT (3 DRAWS) IN 10 INTER- NATIONALS !

NOW, SIR ALF RAMSEY, WHO A APPOINTED ENGLAND'S MANAG IN 1963 (NEARLY 100 GAMES) IS BUILDING HIS TEAM FOR THE 1974 WORLD CUP FINALS IN MUNICH. ONE OF STARS OF THAT SIDE COULD BE ROY McFARLAND (RIGHT DERBY COUNTY'S CAPTAIN AND CENTRE-HALF, WHO HAS TAKEN OVER FROM BIG JACK CHARLTON.

EUROPEAN NATIONS' CUP FEATURE —INSIDE!

© IPC Magazines Ltd., 1972   Australia 15c., New Zealand 15c., South Africa 12c., Rhodesia 13c., West Africa 1/2d., Malaysia 60c., M

MATCH OF THE DAY

1970s

Mirror

GOAL ACTION REPLAY

No.4

UNFORGETTABLE GOALS BY

WORLD CUP – MEXICO 1970

As holders of the Jules Rimet Trophy, England qualified automatically for Mexico and were seen as joint favourites alongside Brazil. The tournament itself was a classic, although England's disappointing performance is best remembered for two pieces of goalkeeping; one brilliant (Gordon Banks), one bungled (Peter Bonetti).

Above: Francis Lee takes a shot at the Brazilian goal.

Opposite: Bobby Moore praises Gordon Banks' 'miracle' save from Pelé.

Things didn't start well for Sir Alf Ramsey's men when captain Bobby Moore was arrested, allegedly for stealing a bracelet, during acclimatisation training in Bogota, Columbia. Charges were quickly dropped and, while the media brouhaha was unsettling, the team's form remained sound. They beat both Group 3 rivals Romania and Czechoslovakia 1-0 and, despite a second half Jairzinho strike costing them the Brazil game, optimism remained high. The feeling was that this defeat could be turned on its head if both teams made the final.

Banks' big moment came in the first half when Pelé met Jairzinho's cross with a powerful downward header onto a rock-hard pitch. The Brazilian was already screaming 'goal' when Banks, the ball bouncing high and past him, dived backwards to flip it over the bar. To say it was the greatest save in history is hyperbole (who on earth knows?) but revisionist pundits are equally wrong to belittle it. Any Sunday League 'keeper understands the nightmare of a ball bouncing at pace just short of the goal-line. The most absurd argument is that Pelé called the save 'unbelievable' to highlight his impressive header. Really?

Having made his mark, Banks promptly became sick and Chelsea's Peter Bonetti, himself an outstanding goalkeeper, stepped up for a hot and humid quarter final tie against a West German side still smarting from Wembley '66. For more than an hour he had comparatively little to do – England had seized control through goals from Alan Mullery and Martin Peters – but in the 69th minute Beckenbauer's hopeful low shot from distance skidded beneath his diving body.

It was a howler, certainly, but Bonetti wasn't the only architect of the German fightback. Beckenbauer accelerated a little too easily past Alan Mullery, and then came Ramsey's perplexing decision: substituting the

excellent Bobby Charlton for Colin Bell, shortly followed by Peters for Norman Hunter. This attempt to save two key players for the semis was woefully premature as by now, with nine minutes left, the match was swinging dangerously against England.

Barely had Hunter's studs hit the grass when German captain Uwe Seeler's skilful back-header looped over Bonetti. It was nothing to do with the Chelsea man's positioning or ability – Seeler just wanted the ball more than England's defenders. As for Gerd Muller's winner in injury time – few goalkeepers then or since would have stopped a Muller volley inside the six yard box.

West Germany went on to lose 4-3 to Italy in a semi-final thriller while in the final the Italians were beaten 4-1 by Brazil. Ramsey survived the inevitable blame game for three more years but many fans saw that June 14th reverse as the start of a long, slow decline in England's fortunes. Bizarrely, senior politicians even attributed the surprise defeat of Harold Wilson's Labour government in the general election four days later to the result against the Germans.

Labour had enjoyed a healthy opinion poll advantage but in memoirs published later, several former ministers highlighted the World Cup effect. Denis Healey revealed that Wilson asked in April '... whether the government would suffer if the England footballers were defeated on the eve of polling day', while sports minister Denis Howell

Above: Brazil's captain, Carlos Alberto, shows off the Jules Rimet Trophy.

Right: England World Cup souvenir pennant.

recalled how Home Secretary Roy Jenkins was bemused at a Birmingham rally when 'no question concerned either trade figures or immigration but solely the football and whether Ramsey or Bonetti was the major culprit.'

Most outspoken of all was local government minister Anthony Crosland (a passionate Grimsby Town fan) who, in his much-admired diaries, later blamed Labour's failure on 'a mix of party complacency and the disgruntled *Match of the Day* millions.'

Below: Muller shoots past Bonetti to seal England's fate.

The dawn of a new decade brought with it a climax as tense as anything dished up by the Manchester clubs three years earlier. On Monday 3 May, Arsenal had the chance to snatch the title from Leeds at, of all places, White Hart Lane. Fate was also dangling a mouth-watering double; five days later they would face Liverpool in the FA Cup final.

Below left: Arsenal captain Frank McLintock with the FA Cup and League Championship trophies.

Below right: Celebrations at Wembley after Arsenal's FA Cup victory over Liverpool, with hero of the hour Charlie George wearing the cup's lid as a hat.

Leeds had already completed their programme and so tight was it at the top that arithmetic was crucial. Leeds' goal average was 2.4, so a 0-0 draw would be enough to give Arsenal the trophy on 2.413. However, 1-1 would mean a Gunners goal average of 2.36 and a party at Elland Road. Any higher scoring draw only made matters worse. Pity poor Gunners fans in an era before pocket calculators.

The game was a 51,992 sell-out with at least 20,000 more fans locked out. Spurs couldn't win the title themselves but denying Arsenal and killing off their double dream was the next best thing. After all, only one north London club had ever won the double ... and they played in white.

For 87 minutes the match was deadlocked. Then George Armstrong chipped back across goal for Ray Kennedy to nod in off the bar. Bizarrely, Gunners fans still weren't sure how – or even whether – to celebrate. The prospect of home defeat could only encourage Spurs to push harder for the dreaded score draw. Kennedy later admitted: 'As Tottenham came back I remember thinking that perhaps it might have been better had my header

not gone in.' But Arsenal held on and all eyes turned to Wembley.

Where, once again, the Gunners did it the hard way. Having spurned a series of chances, they fell behind to a fine Steve Heighway strike in extra-time. But they equalised with a scrappy effort credited to Eddie Kelly and then, with nine minutes remaining, the influential Charlie George netted from 19 yards, as fitting a double-clinching strike as you could see. His celebration, flat on his back, arms spread, remains an iconic Wembley image.

It meant an unusually barren year for Liverpool but there were consolations for Spurs (a 2-0 League Cup final win over Villa) and Leeds (Fairs Cup final defeat of Juventus on away goals). And Chelsea won the Cup Winners' Cup, beating Real Madrid 2-1 in a replay, with keeper Peter Bonetti at his brilliant best.

 ## Match of the Season
Leed United 1 West Bromwich Albion 2

Rare indeed is the *Match of the Day* highlights package without an offside rumpus. But referee Ray Tinkler's decision in this game, just 16 days before Arsenal's White Hart Lane heroics, is still mourned by Leeds fans as a title-robbing moment.

On paper the game was an odds-on Whites' win. Leeds had lost only seven home matches in five years; the Baggies had not won away in 16 months. Yet Albion were a goal up when, in the 65th minute, Tony Brown intercepted Hunter's pass and kicked the ball out right. The linesman immediately flagged because Colin Suggett was in an offside position near the centre circle. However, after moving towards the ball Suggett turned his back on play.

Tinkler who had raised his whistle to his mouth anticipating a pass to Suggett now lowered it. He judged, correctly, that the player was far from the ball and not interfering. Seeing the flag United's defenders stopped in their tracks but Tinkler had waved play on and Brown, having himself paused, collected and crossed for Astle to score.

Pandemonium ensued. Seven Leeds players surrounded Tinkler, Don Revie stormed over to plead with the linesman and fans invaded the pitch. Leeds eventually lost 2-1 but had the game ended 1-1, their final goal average would have been 2.482, which was $^{34}/_{1000s}$ better than Arsenal. They paid the price for that old schoolboy howler. They didn't play to the whistle.

The *MotD* Theme Tune Makes its Debut

It has been voted the most recognised theme tune on British television, a 44-year-old jewel that defines the BBC's sporting heritage and even English football itself.

Right: MotD *studio for the 1970 World Cup draw with Barry Davies looking after Pickles the dog and the panel of Sir Alf Ramsey, Bobby Moore, Bobby Charlton and Gordon Banks.*

The *MotD* music was commissioned for the programme in 1970 to replace the original theme 'Drum Majorette' by Major Leslie Statham, the former Welsh Guards' Director of Music who wrote under the name Arnold Stock. Penned by Barry Stoller the programme's new theme was titled, predictably, 'Match of the Day'; a later version released as a commercial single was called 'Offside'.

The tune was introduced to freshen up *Match of the Day* in the face of serious competition from ITV's Sunday afternoon show *The Big Match* (launched in 1968 and fronted by Jimmy Hill and Brian Moore). It has remained a constant feature ever since – barring a brief and unpopular re-mix – and in 2010 a survey by the Performing Rights Society for Music placed it top of British TV's most recognisable ditties ahead of *EastEnders*, *Doctor Who*, *Coronation Street* and *Countdown*.

As PRS chairman Ellis Rich said at the time: 'Whether it creates suspense, acts as a cliff-hanger or just wraps the show up neatly, the theme tune plays an indispensable role.'

Below: David Coleman was in the chair when MotD's *classic theme tune was launched.*

FRANK McLINTOCK
Arsenal
69

Player of the Year
Frank McLintock, Arsenal

McLintock arrived at Arsenal from Leicester in 1964 for a then record British transfer fee of £80,000. A lean wing-half, he was signed for his tireless work rate and boundless enthusiasm yet struggled to contribute as expected. After an injury crisis in 1969–70, reserve team coach Don Howe suggested he be drafted into the centre of defence and there McLintock found his true calling. Calm and controlled, he quickly established himself as a natural leader and reader of the game well worthy of the captain's armband.

His status as an undisputed Arsenal legend would never have emerged, however, without the persuasive powers of boss Bertie Mee. After defeats in both the 1968 and 1969 League Cup finals a discontented McLintock submitted a transfer request. But Mee convinced him to stay and in 1971 his loyalty was rewarded in spectacular fashion with that double-clinching campaign.

Above left: Trading card featuring Arsenal legend Frank McLintock.

Left: McLintock battling against Liverpool's John Toshack.

1971-72

For many pros, winning a championship medal is a career highlight. But how much better to win it while sitting with your feet up in the sun? For Derby County players that's exactly how things panned out, although it must have been tense in the bar of the beachside Castell de Mar hotel, Cala Millor, on the evening of Monday 8 May. Once again, the First Division climax was a story not for the nervous.

Above: Kevin Hector and Archie Gemmill congratulate Derby County striker John O'Hare on scoring against Leeds United.

Opposite: Ron Radford's stunning goal for Hereford against Newcastle, recreated step-by-step on Daily Mirror *collectors' cards.*

Typically, County manager Brian Clough had taken the devil-may-care approach. His side sat top following the 1-0 home victory over Liverpool which had completed their fixtures the previous Monday. A foreign holiday would keep the squad together and was no less than they deserved after an astonishing five-year journey from near bottom of the Second Division to flair-packed contenders. Besides, there was now no more Clough could do.

If anything, Leeds United were championship favourites. Having come so close a year earlier they needed only a point at mid-table Wolves to deny Derby. Losing would give Liverpool a tilt at the title, if only they could overcome Arsenal away. Yet there was a further twist; just two days earlier, United had beaten the Gunners 1-0 to win the FA Cup. Both teams were understandably tired while Leeds also had a list of walking wounded. Mick Jones was out following his horrendous dislocated elbow at Wembley and both Eddie Gray and Allan Clarke needed pain-killing injections.

The games at Molineux and Highbury kicked off simultaneously. Leeds found Wolves in inspired form, particularly keeper Phil Parkes, but they were also undone by poor refereeing as two clear penalties were overlooked. When Derek Dougan put the home side up in the 67th minute the Whites looked doomed but Billy Bremner hit back almost immediately and glory was just a goal away.

Meanwhile, at Highbury, with Liverpool fans frantically chanting 'Leeds Are Losing', Shankly's side redoubled their efforts. But they could not break the Gunners down and their agony was crystallised in the 88th minute when John Toshack's 'title winner' was disallowed for a marginal offside. The game ended 0-0, Wolves held on for 2-1 and Derby County were champions.

Match of the Season
Hereford 2 Newcastle 1

For an entire generation outside Tyneside this FA Cup third round replay began a love affair with football. Southern League Hereford United had escaped with a 2-2 draw at St James' Park but most pundits thought the Bulls were now ready for slaughter. Big, big mistake.

In the first hour, Toon did everything but score with Malcolm Macdonald unusually wasteful. Hereford were repeatedly rescued by keeper Fred Potter and, to a lesser extent, the woodwork, but they gradually fought their way into the tie and when Macdonald finally headed in with eight minutes left it was against the run of play. Then Ronnie Radford won a 50-50 ball in the mudbath masquerading as midfield.

John Motson's *MotD* commentary needs no embellishment: 'Tremendous spirit in this Hereford side, they're not giving this up by any means. Radford. Now Tudor's gone down for Newcastle. Radford again ... oh, what a goal! WHAT A GOAL! Radford the scorer. Ronnie Radford ... he got that ball back and hit it from outside the penalty area and no goalkeeper in the world would have stopped that.'

Radford's 30-yard drive won extra-time and then sub Ricky George struck a low, giant-killing winner to ensure a bullish mood in the pubs of Hereford.

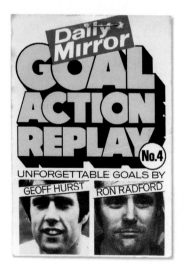

Reproduced from the film *Cup Glory* released by Hemdale Film Distributors Ltd. © Promotion Pictures (John Gregory) Ltd.

GREEN   MONCUR   OWEN   RADFORD

Opposite: England's all-time goalkeeping great, Gordon Banks on the cover of GOAL magazine.

Below: Slow motion technology could highlight incidents such as Jack Charlton and Paul Reaney shutting down Charlie George in the FA Cup Final.

And deservedly so. Any team with McFarland and Todd marshalling the defence, Gemmill in midfield and O'Hare, Hector and Hinton up front was a force to be respected. Clough surely bought them all a Vimto that night in the Castell de Mar.

The Slow Motion Revolution

The dawn of the seventies was an exciting time for TV sport. Previously, studio pundits had been able to show match footage only in real time; now new technology allowed it to be slowed and stopped during key passages of play. Woe betide any referee or linesman who made a mistake.

It may seem strange to non-techies, but showing slow motion, or even still photographs, was for many years a real challenge. Put simply, analogue TV required a stable and continuous signal flow and throughout the fifties and sixties most programmes had to be broadcast live. The transition to videotape, allowing film to be pre-recorded, was a first step but it wasn't

until the American company Ampex produced its HS100 instant slow motion machine in 1967 that sports broadcasters finally got their hands on a shiny new toy.

Even then it took time to roll out. In 1968 the BBC had just a single HS100, a heavy, boxy, behemoth which lurked in the basement of Television Centre, and it was ITV who made the initial running – launching London Weekend Television's *The Big Match* with slow motion clips analysed by Brian Moore and Jimmy Hill. Three years later the Beeb caught up and *Match of the Day* entered a new era of football controversy and debate.

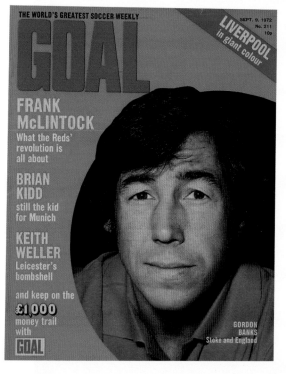

 ### Player of the Year
Gordon Banks, Stoke City

Where to begin? Arguably England's greatest goalkeeper of all time, probably maker of the greatest save of all time – that physics defying tip-over from Pelé's header in the 1970 World Cup – Gordon Banks was in his prime during the early 1970s.

The World Cup winner was signed by Stoke City for £50,000 in April 1967 after being transfer-listed by Leicester City. Curious though this may sound, Foxes' manager Matt Gillies had a young Peter Shilton as his reserve team keeper and believed Banks' best days to be behind him. Fortunately for the Potters they weren't.

In fact, if anything, Banks seemed to improve with age. His agility, accurate distribution and impressive reading of the game as 'sweeper-keeper' helped Stoke win the club's first – and only – major trophy in 1972, beating Chelsea 2-1 at Wembley in the League Cup final (goals from Terry Conroy and George Eastham either side of a Peter Osgood strike).

Sadly, just months after collecting the Player of the Year award, the first keeper to receive the honour since Bert Trautmann in 1956, Banks' playing career was ended by a car crash in which he lost the sight of his right eye.

1972-73

Unquestionably, it was Liverpool's season. Having seen the demise of his old guard in the late 1960s – icons such as Ian St John, Ron Yeats and Roger Hunt – Bill Shankly's re-building plans were now founded on canny signings from the lower leagues.

Players like Ray Clemence, John Toshack, Larry Lloyd and Steve Heighway would form the nucleus of the great Liverpool sides that so dominated English and European football for the coming decade.

A testament to Shankly's '72/'73 squad was the pedigree of their key rivals. Eventual runners-up Arsenal were challenging off an outstanding double the previous year while Leeds remained in their pomp and would have won the the '73 Cup Winners' Cup but for a parlous refereeing performance. Yet Liverpool's title rarely looked in doubt; they bested the Gunners by three points and finished seven ahead of Don Revie's side. And all using just 16 players.

The pivotal day was March 31st. Playing at Anfield against Tottenham, Liverpool went behind to a fine Alan Gilzean goal after 21 minutes. That in itself was not a problem but the form of Pat Jennings, who had assumed colossus status in the Spurs goal, most certainly was.

Below: The Liverpool team with Bill Shankly as featured in GOAL *magazine.*

Jennings pulled off penalty saves against Keegan in the 38th minute and Smith in the 85th, adding brilliant stops from a Cormack six-yard strike

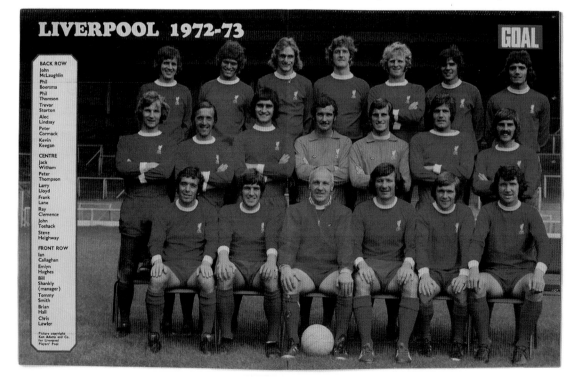

LIVERPOOL 1972-73   GOAL

BACK ROW
John McLaughlin
Phil Boersma
Phil Thomson
Trevor Storton
Alec Lindsay
Peter Cormack
Kevin Keegan

CENTRE
Jack Witham
Peter Thompson
Larry Lloyd
Frank Lane
Ray Clemence
John Toshack
Steve Heighway

FRONT ROW
Ian Callaghan
Emlyn Hughes
Bill Shankly (manager)
Tommy Smith
Brian Hall
Chris Lawler

Picture copyright
Ken Adams and Co.
for Liverpool
Players' Pool

and a close-range Hall header. Liverpool only scraped a draw when Keegan's mishit ballooned over Jennings' head into the net. It was a rare dropped point for Shankly at Anfield but it barely mattered. That same afternoon both Arsenal and Leeds lost.

For Leeds of course it was a season best forgotten. Quite apart from the League, their FA Cup final defeat to underdogs Sunderland (see Match of the Season) smacked of complacency while the 1-0 loss to Milan in the Cup Winners' Cup was a waking nightmare. Lacking the genius of Clarke, Gray, Bremmner and Giles – either through injury or suspension – they had to contend with a dodgy Milan goal and a ref who waved away three clear penalty shouts. No wonder Greek spectators in the Salonika stadium chanted 'shame, shame' at the Italians.

Right: Sunderland manager Bob Stokoe stormed across the pitch to wrap his arms around goalkeeper Jim Montgomery.

Meanwhile Liverpool continued English clubs' domination of the UEFA cup, beating Borussia Mönchengladbach 3-2 on aggregate to take their first European trophy.

Match of the Season
Sunderland 1 Leeds United 0

To a generation of fans it was the game when all those old clichés about the 'magic of the cup' finally delivered. True, Leeds had endured a disappointing year but they were FA Cup holders and Cup Winners' Cup finalists; brimming with talent and physically uncompromising. Second Division Sunderland seemed plucky cannon fodder at best.

And yet, and yet. The Black Cats were no hoofing, kick-and-rush opponents. They played with spirit under Bob Stokoe's management and their huge, inspirational following effectively turned Wembley into Wearside. When Ian Porterfield shot them ahead in the 32nd minute – from their first corner – neutrals across the country shuffled armchairs a touch closer to the TV.

Leeds responded like the class act they were, laying siege to the Sunderland goal. In the 65th minute their fans were already celebrating Trevor Cherry's sweet header as it apparently sailed past 'keeper Jim Montgomery. Montgomery twisted in mid-air to parry superbly... only for the ball to fall perfectly for Peter Lorimer's lethal right foot. Yet, incredibly, Montgomery made a second save. While Sunderland rallied the spectre of doubt loomed over Leeds.

The abiding memory of that day was Stokoe at full time, arms crazily aloft, steaming across the turf to embrace his 'keeper. Porterfield had scored the winner. But it was Montgomery's double save that counted.

*Above: A statue of Best,
Law and Charlton
outside Old Trafford,
commemorates their
contribution to the club.*

*Below: Charlton, Law and
Best pose with Sir Matt
Busby during a break
from training.*

*Opposite top: Pat Jennings
stops a shot from Liverpool's
Brian Hall at Anfield.*

*Opposite bottom: Front
and back of a Pat Jennings
trading card.*

The Reds certainly needed their 3-0 home result because they were outplayed in Germany. But they held on with a dour defensive performance – proving they had character as well as flair.

Manchester United's Holy Trinity

There was an Englishman, a (Northern) Irishman and a Scotsman and simply writing their names on the team sheet was often worth a goal start. How could any Manchester United player not ooze confidence running out with Bobby Charlton, George Best and Denis Law; the so-called 'Holy Trinity'. For most opposition defences the converse was true. It signalled a tough day ahead.

All three spent their best years at United and for those lucky enough to have watched them regularly the statistics matter little. For the rest of us it's worth noting that Charlton scored 249 times in 758 appearances, Best 181 in 474 and Law 237 in 404. Charlton, particularly, the last link to the Busby Babes and the Munich air disaster, was seen as the embodiment of the club's proud fighting spirit.

When he walked off the pitch for the last time in a United shirt, at Stamford Bridge on April 28, the Chelsea crowd rose as one. Yet Charlton knew it was time to go. The Red Devils were a fading force and had climbed out of the relegation zone only a month previously. Law was off for a final swansong at Manchester City and Best's high-maintenance phase, marked by defection threats and unreliability, had begun.

Player of the Season
Pat Jennings, Tottenham Hotspur

His performance in that Anfield game led Bill Shankly to exclaim: 'Did you ever see the likes of that? Did you ever see anything so incredible'. But It wasn't just brilliance against Liverpool that made Patrick Anthony Jennings deserved winner of the 72-73 Football Writers Association award.

The genial Spurs goalkeeper with hands the size of dinner plates kept 24 clean sheets for his club including a 1-0 League Cup final victory over Norwich City. He was undoubtably the form 'keeper of the year; so impressive that he kept both Peter Shilton and Ray Clemence out of Sir Alf Ramsey's British XI to face a select European side in a game commemorating UK entry into the Common Market. One of his great contemporaries, Bob Wilson, believes he created a new style of goalkeeping by using his feet and legs as shot-stoppers; unheard of then but an essential skill today.

Jennings made over 1,000 appearances in top flight football including 119 outings for his country (still a Northern Ireland record). He also managed to transcend North London rivalry; playing for both Arsenal and Tottenham yet remaining popular with both sets of fans.

TOTTENHAM

PAT JENNINGS

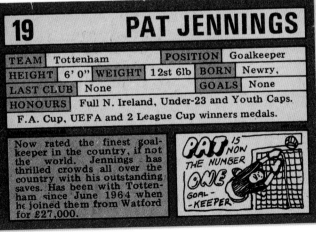

19	PAT JENNINGS		
TEAM	Tottenham	POSITION	Goalkeeper
HEIGHT	6' 0" WEIGHT 12st 6lb	BORN	Newry,
LAST CLUB	None	GOALS	None
HONOURS	Full N. Ireland, Under-23 and Youth Caps. F.A. Cup, UEFA and 2 League Cup winners medals.		

Now rated the finest goalkeeper in the country, if not the world. Jennings has thrilled crowds all over the country with his outstanding saves. Has been with Tottenham since June 1964 when he joined them from Watford for £27,000.

PAT IS NOW THE NUMBER ONE GOAL-KEEPER

It was a season of farewells to familiar stalwarts. Brian Clough and Peter Taylor left Derby, Bill Shankly left Liverpool, Sir Alf Ramsey vacated the England manager's chair ... and Manchester United dropped out of the First Division.

Clough was outspoken and opinionated and even the fervent support of fans could not prevent him being shown the door. Arguably his motormouth kept him out of contention for the England post. Chaotic spells at Brighton and Hove Albion and Leeds United lay ahead before he settled into the manager's chair at Nottingham Forest.

After 15 years in charge, manager Shankly gave way to Bob Paisley, bowing out as Liverpool secured the FA Cup with a 3-0 win over Newcastle United – two goals from Kevin Keegan and another from Steve Heighway ensured a comfortable win.

However, a final First Division title was denied him by a largely dominant Leeds United who were unbeaten for 29 matches until meeting Bristol City, languishing in the lower reaches of the Second Division, in the fifth round of the FA Cup. Bold Bristol put a goal past the hot favourites in the 23rd minute and held on to the lead against all odds.

Below: On an open-topped bus ride through Liverpool, Bill Shankly displays the FA Cup helped by assistant manager Bob Paisley.

That barely broke United's stride in the league as Norman Hunter and company won the title a comfortable five points ahead of second-placed Liverpool and 14 points ahead of Derby, in third. Despite this, a glorious season for the Whites ended in heartbreak for fans as Don Revie left for the England manager's post.

Sir Alf was stung by his sacking, not least because it came a good six months after England failed to qualify for the 1974 World Cup Finals in West Germany. And few could criticize the team he'd picked to win, rather than draw, the crucial match against Poland at Wembley. Instead plaudits went to Polish keeper Jan Tomaszewski whose red-hot form on the night blocked English qualification.

It was a bleak midwinter for Manchester United considering that goalkeeper Alex Stepney was joint top goalscorer at Christmas, with two successful penalties. Former United legend Denis Law, who had transferred to Manchester City, helped nail the coffin lid by scoring in the match that saw them relegated.

Below: Denis Law is mobbed by Man City fans as he leaves the pitch after scoring against his old club.

Match of the Season
Manchester United 0
Manchester City 1

This match gets the nod not for footballing reasons (it was an uninspiring game) but for its extraordinary climax. The myth is that Denis Law's 81st minute back-heel through Alex Stepney's legs relegated his old club. It didn't – they had managed that just fine by themselves over a poor season – and in any case Birmingham and West Ham got the points they needed to stay up at United's expense.

However, the sight of a distraught Law, arms locked to his side, knowing that United could no longer even cling to hope – this was the abiding image of the season. He shrugged off the exuberant celebrations of City defender Mike Doyle (whose *schadenfreude*

extended to running half the length of the pitch) and was immediately substituted on compassionate grounds.

A shameful pitch invasion by United fans then forced the referee to abandon the match and there was initially doubt over whether the result should stand. The League decided that it should, partly because it was irrelevant to any relegation or promotion issues, but it didn't stop outrage across the back pages with some commentators calling for the Stretford End to be closed the following season.

United went down in the company of Norwich and Southampton as, for the first time, three teams departed the top flight. Meanwhile, Spurs left the final of the UEFA Cup as losers in more ways than one. Dutch champions Feyenoord won 2-0 – then baton-wielding police had the final say as Tottenham fans rioted.

Jimmy Hill Joins *MotD*

Above: Jimmy Hill at work off-air in the MotD *studio.*

Opposite top: Ian Callaghan holds the record to this day for the most games played for Liverpool.

Opposite bottom: Callaghan takes the ball past Man City's Francis Lee.

Few can match Jimmy Hill's record of innovation in English football and when he was lured to *Match of the Day* from London Weekend Television's *The Big Match* in 1973 it was a massive coup for the BBC.

Hill had enjoyed a successful playing career with Brentford and Fulham but his biggest contributions to the game came after he hung up his boots. As chairman of the Professional Footballers' Association he successfully campaigned to scrap a £20 per week cap on players' wages, and pioneered all-seater stadia while manager at Coventry City FC during the early 1960s. He was later credited with persuading the Football League to adopt the three-points-for-a-win rule.

Hill's transfer to the BBC came during a revolution in the presentation and editing of football coverage (see 1971-72). At LWT he introduced the first pundits panel for the 1970 World Cup and his natural studio presence, populist approach and much-caricatured bearded chin made him a hit with fans.

He went on to make more than 600 appearances for *Match of the Day* during a 26-year BBC career in which he covered every major domestic and international championship.

Player of the Year
Ian Callaghan, Liverpool

A name synonymous with the great Liverpool teams of the sixties and seventies, Ian Callaghan played an astonishing 857 games for the Reds – a club record to this day.

Bursting on to the scene in the early 1960s as a skilful right winger, the 5 foot 7 inch Callaghan relied on devastating acceleration to get the better of his opponents and became an integral part of Liverpool's 1964 and 1966 championship-winning teams.

He was moved into the centre of midfield by Bill Shankly in 1970 to prolong his career following a knee operation and took to his new role brilliantly, pulling the strings behind the dynamic strike duo of John Toshack and Kevin Keegan. Despite losing out to Leeds United in the race for the 1973–4 title, the Toxteth-born midfielder was instrumental in the Reds' FA Cup-winning run.

It seemed apt that, in Shankly's last season at Anfield, the only player to have been in the first team longer than he had managed it would also become the first Liverpool player to win the FWA award.

Hooliganism – the so-called English disease – was the story on and off the pitch, with Kevin Keegan and Billy Bremner setting the bar low during the Charity Shield at Wembley in August.

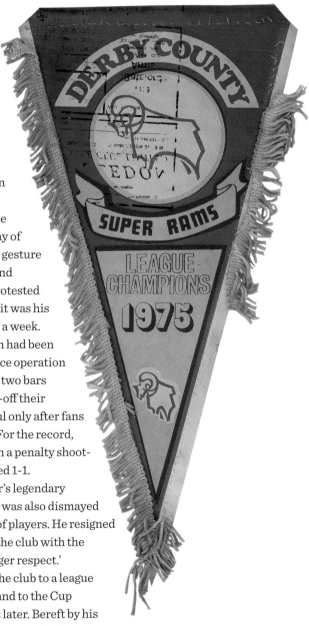

Right: A Derby County souvenir pennant.

Opposite top: Gordon McQueen complains as Billy Bremner and Kevin Keegan become the first British players to be sent off at Wembley.

Opposite bottom: Wimbledon keeper Dickie Guy celebrating after saving a Peter Lorimer penalty.

History was made as the two soccer icons threw punches in the 56th minute. They became the first British players to be dismissed from the hallowed turf in its 51 years, after referee Bob Matthewson intervened.

The brawlers left the field bare-chested by way of protest. Yet the juvenile gesture seemed only to compound their disgrace as they protested innocence. For Keegan, it was his second dismissal inside a week.

Ironically the match had been the focus of a major police operation against hooligans. With two bars smashed up before kick-off their efforts proved successful only after fans entered the turnstiles. For the record, Liverpool won the day in a penalty shoot-out after the match ended 1-1.

Tottenham Hotspur's legendary manager Bill Nicholson was also dismayed by the general conduct of players. He resigned to end a 38-year link to the club with the lament: 'There is no longer respect.'

Nicholson had led the club to a league and cup double in 1961 and to the Cup Winners' Cup two years later. Bereft by his impending departure Spurs made him an honorary president.

There was brighter news for neutrals, however, as teams jostled for the top spot. Indeed the lead changed hands a record 21 times before Derby, now managed by Dave Mackay, finally won it. The Rams' leading goalscorer was Bruce Rioch with a solid 15 to his credit.

But the division's top goalscorer was Newcastle

Match of the Season
Burnley 0 Wimbledon 1

This FA Cup third round classic was the match when Wimbledon gave notice that they were out to bag big beasts. It was the first time since the war that a non-League side had beaten First Division opposition away. But then Wimbledon were rather more than plucky hopefuls – the 1974–75 season returned the first of three consecutive Southern League title wins heralding their election to the Football League.

Mick Mahon scored the only goal, tapping in Ian Stevenson's parried shot, but the man of the moment was goalkeeper Dickie Guy (later made President of AFC Wimbledon) who pulled off a string of blinding saves. The feisty Dons then drew a plum tie

away at high-flying Leeds United and again Guy was the hero securing a replay after saving a Peter Lorimer penalty.

Ticket demand for the replay in south London was unprecedented and the match was moved to Selhurst Park to accommodate 40,000 fans. Unfortunately for Wimbledon the run finally came to an end with a Dave Basset own goal. But the Dons had got a taste for the FA Cup ... as shell-shocked Liverpool would discover 13 years down the line.

United's Malcolm Macdonald with an emphatic 21, not including the five he fired past a dispirited Cypriot goalkeeper in a Wembley international. At the bottom Luton Town, Chelsea and Carlisle United were relegated.

For Leeds a pedestrian season and a ninth-place finish was capped with defeat and ignominy at the European Cup final in Paris. Leeds had looked the better bet, especially after crunching tackles by the men in white saw two key Bayern Munich players limp off. But the referee failed to see two apparent handballs by Franz Beckenbauer.

When a goal by Leeds was disallowed for offside fans in the French stadium rampaged, pursued by baton-wielding riot police. Meanwhile, on the pitch, Bayern sneaked two goals past disconsolate Leeds players who were consequently banned from Europe for three years for the conduct of their supporters.

MotD Memories: For the Love of Arsenal

Opposite top: Mullery battles Johannes Linssen of Duisburg during a friendly at Craven Cottage.

Opposite bottom: Alan Mullery with his Fulham team-mate Bobby Moore.

Former newspaperman and TV chat show host Piers Morgan believes lax parenting and stubborn defiance combined to make him a Gooner. 'My dad's a Spurs fan,' he says. 'It was either terrible parenting or early rebellion – probably a bit of both – but I became an Arsenal fan in 1971.

'I was six years old, we'd won the double and Charlie George scored that remarkable goal in the FA Cup final, that 30-yard screamer. That was it for me. I had a choice; go with my dad's team, Spurs, which seemed like a death sentence, a life of utter misery and unrelenting loss, or go with this glorious, wonderful team just down the road who seemed to win everything. So I went for Arsenal and thank God for that.

'My first game was Arsenal versus Manchester United in April 1972. It was at Highbury, we won 3-0 and Johnny Radford scored, I think Ray Kennedy scored [Peter Simpson got the first] and I just remember this roar, this visceral thing, everyone stood, it was pouring with rain … it was the most exciting thing I'd ever seen.

'Rushed home, watched *Match of the Day*. All I remember is the excitement of going to a game then going back to watch it on *MotD*. From that moment on it was how I spent my weekends.'

 Player of the Year
Alan Mullery, Fulham

The only Fulham player ever to have won an FWA award, Alan Mullery was a tough-tackling, quick, central midfielder who had two spells with the Cottagers either side of an eight-year stint at Tottenham.

After beginning his career at Craven Cottage, Mullery moved to White Hart Lane in 1964 when just one short of 200 appearances. He fully justified the eye-watering £72,500 transfer fee, helping Spurs to FA Cup, League Cup and UEFA Cup triumphs while also forcing his way into the England side (he later earned the unfortunate tag of becoming the first man to be sent off playing in a major international for England).

In 1972 he re-signed for the Cottagers and three years later, alongside his former England skipper Bobby Moore, helped guide the then Second Division club to an FA Cup final. Although they lost 2-0 to Moore's former side West Ham, Mullery's tireless work rate in the midfield boilerhouse showed precisely why he got the nod as FWA Player of the Year.

1975-76

It was one of those momentous matches that changed the complexion of an entire season. On 4 May Liverpool's players were bidding for a record-breaking ninth First Division title; opponents Wolverhampton Wanderers were teetering on the brink of relegation.

Although the terraces at Molineux had turned ominously to red there were no quaking hearts among the Wolves team and dangerously quick striker Steve Kindon notched a 13th minute opener to prove it. Nor was there much sign of Liverpool's class. It wasn't until the 76th minute that Kevin Keegan netted the goal – following a long ball from Tommy Smith and a back header by John Toshack – that took them top of the table. Two more in the last five minutes, from Toshack and Ray Kennedy, put the championship's destination beyond doubt.

Until then tension had been equally rife at Queens Park Rangers who had amassed 27 points in a brilliant 15-match run-in. Having completed their 42-game season Rangers had spent ten anxious days at the top. But their 59 points couldn't stop Bob Paisley claiming his first Anfield title with 60 and two weeks later the Reds clinched their second double in three years with the UEFA Cup. As for Wolves, they departed the division with Burnley and Sheffield United.

Previous bottom: Liverpool legend Emlyn Hughes takes on Steve Daley of Wolves, a club Hughes was later to join.

Below: Liverpool captain Emlyn Hughes keeps the UEFA Cup firmly in his grasp.

Meanwhile, there were glum faces up the East Lancs Road as an uninspiring Manchester United assured a lively Second Division Southampton side of an unexpected FA Cup win. It had been all but three-quarters of a century since Saints were in the running for a cup. But, buoyed by tame opponents, their persistence brought a memorable left-foot strike from Bobby Stokes in the 83rd minute. Curiously Lawrie McMenemy had predicted Stokes would be the match winner – further evidence for The Dell contingent that their manager was heaven-sent.

It was a better year for the light blue half of Manchester as City, fired by their inspirational captain Mike Doyle, beat Newcastle 2-1 to take the League Cup. Doyle played one of his greatest ever games, controlling defence, launching incisive counter-attacks and heading down a free-kick for the precocious Peter Barnes to score a 12th-

Match of the Season
Liverpool 3 Bruges 2 (4-2 agg.)

This UEFA Cup final first leg was one of Anfield's great European nights. With a 50,000 crowd, and the Kop in full voice, expectations were high. But initially this pressure also brought out the worst in an uncharacteristically nervous Liverpool.

Bruges were two up through Lambert and Cools inside 15 minutes and there seemed a strong chance the Reds would not even take a lead into the second leg. But around the hour mark a pulsating seven minutes turned the game on its head. Attacking their favourite Kop end, Liverpool pulled one back courtesy of Ray Kennedy's sweet 20-yard strike. Then Case tapped in a rebound off the post and the ever-reliable Keegan slotted home a penalty after Heighway was brought down.

Although they had home advantage for the return Bruges' players must have realised their chance had passed. Sure enough the game ended 1-1, with Keegan replying quickly to Lambert's 11th-minute penalty. One commentator described the spectacle as 'composed rather than colourful' and the most enduring image of the night came as the cup was placed into the hands of Liverpool captain Emlyn Hughes – who promptly dropped it.

minute opener. Newcastle fought back hard and Alan Gowling's equaliser was the culmination of the best move of the match. But the game was settled with Dennis Tueart's superb bicycle kick from Tommy Booth's headed cross.

The season's award for Most Determined Effort to Hog the Score Sheet went to Aston Villa defender Chris Nicholl who scored four times in a 2-2 draw. Twice Nicholl put Leicester City ahead in a match at Filbert Street, equalising both times for his own side. Although he'd prefer to be remembered as part of the Villa team that twice won the League Cup in the seventies, Foxes wags still revere him as their fifth highest scorer of the 1975–76 season.

Bob on the Beeb

Right: Before becoming a TV presenter or a goalkeeper, Bob Wilson trained as a teacher.

Opposite top: Kevin Keegan enjoying a bath on the front page of the Liverpool Echo.

Opposite bottom: Keegan strikes for Liverpool against Dynamo Dresden.

Bob Wilson first appeared as a *Match of the Day* pundit during the 1970 World Cup – a time when his best years as Arsenal's goalkeeper were arguably still ahead of him.

Wilson was a late arrival in the professional game (his dad had stopped him signing for Manchester United because it wasn't a proper job) and he trained as a teacher before making his Arsenal debut in 1963 aged 21. He was then still an amateur and understudied Jim Furnell until breaking through as first-choice keeper in 1968. From then on he was a fixture and in 1971 was named Gunners' player of the year after appearing in every league and cup game during their double-winning season.

He retired unusually early – many fans would say too early – in 1973 and the following year made his debut as presenter of *Football Focus*, the BBC's lunchtime football highlights and analysis show which became a must-see for viewers who had missed the previous week's *MotD*. He stayed with the BBC until 1994, teaming up with Jimmy Hill, but transferred to ITV Sport following the arrival of Des Lynam. He has remained an occasional guest on both *Football Focus* and *MotD2*.

 Player of the Year
Kevin Keegan, Liverpool

Kevin Keegan was quite simply the footballing superstar of the seventies. With a distinctive style on and off the pitch (his bubble perm captured the nation's imagination) he was a consistent goal-machine for the great Bill Shankly and Bob Paisley sides with exactly 100 over six seasons.

Signed from Scunthorpe as an apprentice in 1968 Keegan was Shankly's choice to replace an ageing Ian Callaghan on the right wing. But such was the threat he posed to opposition defences that he was paired with John Toshack in what would soon become the European game's most feared strike partnership.

In the 1975–76 title-winning season Keegan missed only one First Division game and his crucial goals in both legs of the UEFA Cup final ensured Liverpool reprised their 1973 cup double. He was that rarest of football jewels; a game-changer. For many Reds fans he remains perhaps the most complete footballer ever to have donned the shirt.

As the season closed Liverpool were once again riding high, taking their tenth domestic title with an unprecedented treble clearly in sight. But, at the end of a long season, an FA Cup Final against a Manchester United side still smarting from their previous year's Wembley humbling was always going to be tricky.

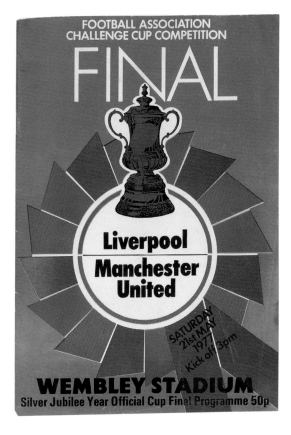

Above: Programme for the 1977 FA Cup Final where an uncharacteristic mistake from Lou Macari gave Manchester United the chance they needed.

Sure enough it was Bob Paisley's men who stumbled first and in a frantic five minutes after half-time United struck through Stuart Pearson. Jimmy Case equalised with one of the great cup final goals, controlling the ball on his thigh before hammering it into the roof of the net, but then a fluke from Lou Macari as he tried to dodge, and unintentionally deflected, Jimmy Greenhoff's shot sealed it for Docherty's side. It is a measure of Liverpool's devastated players that they still picked themselves up to win the European Cup four days later (see Match of the Season).

Despite winning at Wembley the end of Tommy Docherty's career at Manchester United was nigh. Revelations that he was having an affair with the club physiotherapist's wife became public six weeks after his cup triumph and he was promptly sacked.

In the League it was a season of rule-tweaking. Red and yellow cards, the brainchild of referee Ken Aston, were introduced for the first time (although Aston's idea had been adopted by FIFA as early as 1970). And goal difference replaced goal average (see 1967–68) as first tie-breaker to determine placings.

Perhaps this new method, rewarding higher-scoring clubs, was the genesis of some surprisingly meaty scorelines. The biggest home win was recorded by Ipswich – 7-0 against West Brom – in a campaign that left the team third, just a point behind Liverpool. But West Brom also got into the stats book with the highest away win, beating Leicester 5-0 in March. The highest scoring match overall was a ten-goal shot-fest between Derby and Tottenham with the Rams depositing eight in their opponents' net. It was an early indicator of trouble ahead; Spurs were ultimately relegated with a sorry 33 points along with Sunderland and Stoke.

The hardest fought of all the major trophies this year was unquestionably the League Cup which Aston Villa finally won after an epic five and a half hour battle against Everton. Two goals from Brian Little in the second replay at Old Trafford – the winner converted in extra time – proved just enough to edge it for the Villans.

Match of the Season
Liverpool 3 Borussia Mönchengladbach 2

Winning the European Cup for the first time remains arguably the greatest moment in Liverpool's history. Expectations were high among fans – the club had certainly served its apprenticeship with 13 consecutive appearances in European competitions – but the FA Cup Final defeat had knocked their momentum.

Then there was the emotional trauma of seeing two Anfield legends playing in a Reds' strip for the last time, Kevin Keegan bound for Hamburg and Tommy Smith, eventually, for Swansea.

Liverpool commanded the early stages and fully deserved their lead

as Terry McDermott ghosted through to latch on to Heighway's perfect delivery. But Borussia equalised early in the second half when Case's poor pass was intercepted and for a time the Germans took control. Appropriately it was the redoubtable Smith, once described by Bill Shankly as being 'quarried' rather than born, who found space as two defenders panicked over yet another Keegan run. His powerful header from Heighway's corner calmed nerves before Neal's penalty wrapped up the win.

Above: John Motson became the voice of Match of the Day, *especially after his performance at the 1977 FA Cup Final.*

Motty's FA Cup Blinders

If the likes of Lineker, Lynam and Hill became the face of *Match of the Day* then John Motson was its voice. Apart from a brief spell in the nineties when his friend and colleague Barry Davies claimed the senior commentator's mantel, 'Motty' was BBC Sport's go-to man. So far, he has covered more than 1,500 matches for radio and television.

He joined the BBC as a Radio 2 sports presenter in 1968, later wangling his way into *MotD* roles. His big break came in February 1972 while covering the Hereford v Newcastle FA Cup 3rd round replay (see 1971-72) in which Ronnie Radford's equaliser sparked a famous giant-killing win. *MotD* editors had assigned the match a five-minute slot but promoted it – and Motty – to the main event. The commentator's passion and excitement shone through, winning him thousands of armchair fans and the trust of his bosses.

In 1977 his career received another upward nudge. Senior colleague, David Coleman, was bounced out of the FA Cup Final between Liverpool and Manchester United over a contractual dispute and Motson stepped in at short notice. With Liverpool a goal down, he produced this insightful gem as the ball fell to Joey Jones in an innocuous deep position. 'There's a saying in football that Liverpool are at their most dangerous when they're behind,' mused Motty. 'That remains to be seen ... Jones ... Case ... good turn ... OH, YES!' Eleven seconds had passed since the mention of 'dangerous'.

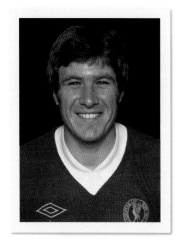

Player of the Year
Emlyn Hughes, Liverpool

A model leader who captained club and country, Emlyn Hughes will always be revered by Liverpool fans for leading their team to a first-ever European triumph in 1977. Signed by Bill Shankly from Blackpool for £65,000 in 1967 he went on to make 665 appearances for the Reds, and helped Bob Paisley establish the most successful side in Europe during the late seventies.

Hughes, a physically imposing figure on the pitch, represented everything Shankly valued in a player. Noted for his stamina and unrelenting passion – attributes that explained his 'Crazy Horse' moniker – as well as his invaluable versatility, he could dominate opponents in whichever position he played, from the back four to the centre of midfield.

His performances were consistently influential, standing out in one of the greatest modern-day sides, and he was an instrumental figure in Liverpool's defence during the final few games of the 1976–77 season.

At international level Hughes was unlucky to figure in an England outfit that endured a long, slow demise from the giddy heights of 1966. After winning the first of his 62 caps against Holland in 1969 he went on to take the captain's armband 23 times but, alas, never featured in World Cup Finals.

Above: Emlyn Hughes' stamina gave him the ability to keep on running, never giving up, and earned him the nickname 'Crazy Horse'.

Left: Hughes on the ball for Liverpool against Leicester.

1977-78

With Liverpool winning the European Cup for a second successive season you'd think nothing could steal Bob Paisley's thunder. But stolen it was by a manager who had once again transformed an unfashionable side into an outstanding outfit. Step forward Brian Clough of Nottingham Forest and, his trusted lieutenant Peter Taylor.

Below: Brian Clough on Notts Forest's League Cup final souvenir booklet.

Bottom: Peter Shilton has a friendly exchange with Kenny Dalglish.

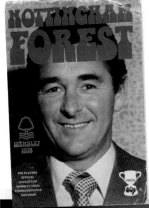

In football's modern era it is all but impossible to imagine a promoted side going on to win the top division in their first season. But that is precisely what Clough and Taylor did ... and with aplomb. Three seasons after taking over at the City Ground they not so much won the First Division as rampaged through it – taking the title with four games to spare and finishing seven points clear. And this against main rivals Liverpool who, although minus Kevin Keegan, had been hugely strengthened by the £400,000 signing of Kenny Dalglish from Celtic. In the four games between the two sides only one ended in a win, for Forest, in the League Cup final replay.

Forest's league goal record – 69 – was good but not remarkable. Everton, Manchester City and Coventry City all scored more. But their defence was positively Scrooge-like. The fact that they conceded just 24 goals, ten fewer than Paisley's side, was in no small part due to Clough's inspired purchase of Peter Shilton from Stoke for £250,000. It was the highest ever fee for a goalkeeper but he more than repaid it in world-class saves. His physical presence, speed and agility was a striker's nightmare and woe betide any Forest defender out of position. Shilton gave the impression that everyone – attackers, defenders, probably the referee as well – should ask permission before moving in his penalty area.

And so to Liverpool, bested at home by upstart East Midlanders, but still indisputably Kings of Europe. Their 1-0 European Cup final defeat of FC Bruges at Wembley (that night basically Anfield on tour) never quite had the quality and passion of the previous year's Rome triumph, but it was a professional performance with Dalglish coolly hitting the winner in the 66th minute.

At the bottom, Ipswich, who had narrowly avoided relegation, dismantled Arsenal at Wembley to

Below: Wrexham later faced Arsenal at the Racecourse Ground and lost 3-2.

take the FA Cup. With Geddis and Woods rampant down the flanks and Mariner and Wark in great form up front, the only real surprise was how late Osborne's 76th-minute winner came.

Match of the Season
Wrexham 1 Blyth Spartans 1

Northern League Blyth Spartans had a deserved reputation as cup giant-killers (FA Secretary Ted Croker once described them as 'the most famous non-league side in the world'). But on 18 February 1978 Spartans came within a heartbeat of a truly incredible achievement – an FA Cup quarter-final tie.

The 11th match of their cup run saw them take on Wrexham away. Terry Johnson put the visitors ahead, jabbing at a poor back pass, and the lead was maintained until the final seconds. With Northumbrian fans now desperate for the final whistle Blyth skipper John Waterson tackled Bobby Shinton. The ball bobbled out of play off the Wrexham forward but referee Alf Grey pointed for a corner, duly taken by Lee Cartwright.

Blyth's Dave Clark punched the ball clear for a second corner and when Cartwright tried again the keeper gathered safely unopposed. A boot upfield and a home quarter-final tie with Arsenal was in the bag.

But referee Grey had spotted that the corner flag had fallen over. He ordered a re-take, Cartwright's third attempt was headed in by Dixie McNeill, and it was back to Blyth for a replay which Wrexham won 2-1. Rarely can a giant-killer have been so cruelly killed.

 ## Player of the Year
Kenny Burns, Nottingham Forest

Bought from Birmingham for £150,000 in 1977, Kenny Burns was one of Brian Clough's more inspired signings, terrorising opposition attacks during Nottingham Forest's golden era.

The gritty Scot, who made 20 appearances for his national team, hit the ground running at Forest, immediately exerting his physical presence at centre-back and forming a strong partnership with Larry Lloyd.

His unflinching and confrontational style of play was supplemented by versatility (he once scored four goals while playing in attack for Birmingham against Derby) and his battering ram role during forays upfront was an attribute that proved invaluable to Clough.

Long after he retired Burns told how he agonised about asking his manager for a pay rise. He decided the time was right after winning Player of the Year and then turning in colossal performances during the club's European Cup heroics of the following season.

After plucking up courage to enter the lion's den of his boss's office, Burns suggested a £350 per week increase on the basis that the manager would beat him down. Clough calmly replied 'OK' and Burns walked away punching the air 'until I realised that I could easily have asked for more.'

MotD Clocks up 500 Shows

Opposite top: Winning the Player of the Year award gave Kenny Burns the courage to ask Brian Clough for a pay rise.

Opposite bottom: Burns holds off Trevor Francis in a Scotland v England match at Hampden.

Below: Children holding photo cards created special images for MotD's *500th show.*

Broadcasting 500 shows is some achievement for any TV programme. And given that, initially, *Match of the Day* wasn't even supposed to be a regular slot (it was a practice run for the 1966 World Cup) the BBC was determined to celebrate in style.

There was a flurry of press, TV and radio coverage, a special edition of *Radio Times* and a new opening titles sequence which saw hundreds of children packed into a football stand with photo cards. This was effectively a huge jigsaw puzzle; each card contained tiny facial details of Jimmy Hill's face and the *Match of the Day* logo. When the cards were simultaneously raised, there was Jimmy's beaming face. It was a masterful piece of production.

The previous 14 years had seen a revolution in TV football coverage, not just in the use of technology and the analytical punditry, but also in the attitude of the game's authorities to the presence of cameras. Indeed, the programme had been almost suffocated at birth when some clubs tried to stop its return to screens in the autumn of 1965. They argued it would hit ticket sales and eventually forced the BBC to agree a 10.00pm 'watershed' for broadcast and a reduced 45-minute show.

Two years later, *MotD*'s new contract with the Football League specified that five matches from Division 2, and two from Divisions 3 or 4, had to be broadcast alongside the 23 plum fixtures from Division 1. And as late as 1973 the programme was required to lead with a Division 2 match at least once, and a Division 3 game twice.

1978-79

Deep within the Forest a fairytale was unfolding. But at first no-one, but no-one, believed it could end happily for Clough and Taylor's extraordinary band of football adventurers. To scramble out of the Second Division, win the First Division title and then lift the European Cup, all in the space of three seasons ... you couldn't make it up.

The fact that Nottingham Forest began the final as favourites against Malmo of Sweden said everything about their character and ability. Their run to Munich began with the toughest-possible challenge – against a Liverpool side that had won the trophy twice on the trot – but they took a 2-0 lead to the second leg at Anfield through Birtles and Barrett and then defended doggedly to earn a 0-0 draw.

There followed comfortable aggregate victories over AEK Athens (7-2) and Grasshoppers of Zurich (5-2) but Forest were almost skewered in the semi-final after going 2-0 down to FC Cologne. They recovered to post a 3-3 draw before pulling off an against-the-odds 1-0 win in Germany.

The final itself was hardly a classic with key players on both teams sidelined. Forest took the lead just before the break, a typically scything run by John Robertson on the left wing culminating in the perfect cross for Britain's first £1 million player, Trevor Francis. With skipper McGovern masterful in midfield the Forest fairytale was always going to end happily.

For Liverpool there was the 'consolation' of taking the First Division title back from Nottingham and they did so in style, a full eight points clear of Clough's team in second place. For Forest it had been a comparatively poor domestic mid-season but their 3-2 League Cup final win over Southampton proved, especially in the second half, that their football was at times on another planet.

Of all the silverware finals, though, none beat the FA Cup showdown between Arsenal and Manchester United. With five minutes to go and their team 2-0 down thousands of United fans had already streamed through the exits. Then goals from McQueen and McIlroy in the 86th and 88th minutes brought the scores level only for man of the match Liam Brady's teasing cross to find Alan Sunderland, who gleefully fired home.

Top: A patriotic souvenir cloth patch.

Above: The Evening Post *celebrates Forest's victory.*

Match of the Season
Man Utd 3 WBA 5

There's many a pointless (though, of course, still worthwhile) bar-room argument over the greatest game ever, but West Brom's 5-3 victory over Manchester United in December 1978 surely has to be up there. Breathtaking goals, saves that defied belief and pure, pulsating, fantasy football, this was a season ticket's worth of action in 90 minutes.

There was Brian Greenhoff's brilliant volley to open United's account, Tony Brown's instinctive strike to draw level, Len Cantello's rocket-fuelled drive to put the visitors 2-1 up, Gordon McQueen's classic header for 2-2 and Sammy McIlroy's jinxing penalty-area run to restore United's lead. The only scrappy goal came just before the break courtesy of Tony Brown. By then Albion manager Ron Atkinson was so flabbergasted he started his half-time talk by telling his players they didn't deserve to be losing. 'Er, boss,' said Brown, 'we're not.'

The second half included two breathtaking saves from United's Gary Bailey – both from the superb Cyrille Regis – and two more collectors' strikes courtesy of Laurie Cunningham and, inevitably, Regis himself. Goals aside, Cunningham on the ball was the enduring memory of the game – shrugging off pathetic racist boos with a performance that oozed class, grace and pace. If ever a winger was art in human form, it was Cunningham that night.

Above: Laurie Cunningham ignored racist taunts to concentrate on playing stunning football.

Right: Trevor Francis heads home the winner against Malmo at the Olympic Stadium in Munich.

David Coleman Bows Out of Live Football

Above: David Coleman as part of the BBC's team covering the World Cup in 1966.

Above right: Coleman combined his role as MotD's main presenter with that of the BBC's se nior football commentator.

Opposite top: Dalglish takes on Arsenal defender David O'Leary.

Opposite bottom: Graham Souness and Alan Hansen give Kenny Dalglish a hand with the FA Charity Shield.

David Coleman emerged into TV sport at a time when the BBC appeared almost to have a God-given right to broadcast it. He helped launch *Grandstand* in 1958 and went on to front other classics such as *Sportsnight With Coleman* and *A Question Of Sport*.

He first appeared on *Match of the Day* with Kenneth Wolstenholme in 1968 and took over as sole presenter the following year. Coleman combined this with his role as the BBC's senior football commentator, delivering a classless, concise yet passionate style of commentary which, though often parodied by impressionists, was grudgingly admired by rivals. He rightly saw himself as a hard-nosed journalist for whom brevity was crucial – the tone of his trademark 'one nil' comment to greet an opening goal suggested he always knew it was coming.

His ITV rival Brian Moore – himself a masterly commentator – said of him: 'His hard edge made him as formidable a journalist as he was an opponent. He knew he was the best and professionally, all said and done, we knew he had set the standard.'

Coleman's run as *MotD* presenter ended in 1973 and his last live football commentary was for International *Match of the Day* in May 1979 as England beat Scotland 3-1. He died in December 2013.

 Player of the Year
Kenny Dalglish, Liverpool

Bob Paisley once said of Kenny Dalglish: 'Of all the players I have played alongside, managed and coached in more than forty years at Anfield, he is the most talented.' Some compliment from one of the greatest managers of all time – particularly given the pedigree of that particular footballing stable.

Dalglish was a technically gifted and instinctive striker blessed with lightning pace and the ability to turn defenders at will. Signed from Celtic in 1977 for £400,000 – then a British transfer record – he lived up to his promise straight from the off, scoring four times in his first seven appearances before going on to strike 31 goals in 62 games including that winner in the 1978 European Cup final. And to think Liverpool fans had mithered over whether he was truly worthy of Kevin Keegan's number 7 shirt.

Dalglish continued his fine form into the 1978–9 season, scoring 21 league goals and appearing in every league match. During his Liverpool playing career he found the net 172 times in 515 appearances but he was as much a master of the assist as the scoring shot. His great strike partnerships – first with Ian Rush and later John Aldridge and Peter Beardsley – remain the stuff of sweet dreams on Anfield.

1979-80

Once again Bob Paisley's Liverpool were the standout league team of the season although they needed every precious point of an impressive mid-way tally as Manchester United stormed into contention late on. But hopes of any double were dashed; quickly in the European Cup (a first-round defeat to FC Dinamo Tbilisi) and agonisingly in the FA Cup (after a third semi-final replay against Arsenal).

Domestic cup glory went to two famous old teams - Wolverhampton Wanderers and West Ham United – while Forest shrugged off inconsistency at home to successfully defend the European Cup. That final, against an SV Hamburg side counting Kevin Keegan among its stars, saw Forest assert tactical guile rather than trademark flair; with both Francis and Bowles missing they had to combine patient defence with the occasional rapier-like break. It was one such attack, inspired by Frankie Gray's run from deep, which produced the game's only goal – a 20-yard Robertson shot in off the far post.

At home the FA Cup was won by Second Division West Ham who must surely have profited from Arsenal's semi-final marathon. That said, John Lyall's team fully merited a 1-0 win founded on the Gunner's own tried and trusted formula: score early, defend tight and counter-attack fast. Trevor Brooking's 15th-minute goal (a rare header) got things moving and the Hammers were rarely troubled thereafter.

Below middle and right: Trading card featuring Peter Shilton, one of the heroes of Hamburg.

Below left: Shilton made 202 appearances for Brian Clough's Forest and won 125 England caps.

![MATCH OF THE DAY]

Match of the Season
Liverpool 4 Aston Villa 1

The game in which Liverpool regained their First Division crown coincided with the afternoon Avi Cohen's personal angel popped down to Anfield to see how the lad was doing. Good news you might think and Avi was delighted to hear he'd made the starting line-up, on his home debut, with a tilt at championship glory. Except this angel had a mischievous streak.

All was tickety-boo when David Johnson put the Reds ahead after only four minutes. But then Cohen put the ball into his own net to level for the Villans and a frisson of nervousness swept Anfield. At half-time second-placed Man Utd were still in with a shout. Had Avi availed their bitter rivals of a trophy?

Fortunately Cohen's chance of redemption was not long coming. In the 50th minute the Israeli international met Dalglish's low cross with a peachy drive into the far corner. Anfield duly erupted, Liverpool rallied with a second from Johnson plus one from Kennedy and the title was back home. Quizmasters still love asking which Liverpool player scored for both sides on his home debut on the afternoon his club won the championship.

Above right: Israeli international Avi Cohen made a unique contribution to the Match of the Season.

The League Cup final was a dour affair with Wolves' Andy Gray sealing victory over Forest. Far more memorable was the manner of his goal, that rarest of football spectacles, a Shilton goalkeeping clanger.

When Peter Daniel floated over a hopeful cross it seemed as though centre-back Dave Needham would calmly chest the ball away. But Shilton was already committed, first clattered, then bounced off, his defender and the ball bobbled between them. Wolves manager John Barnwell had just shelled out £1,469,000 to bring Gray from Villa to Wolves – almost ten times the club's previous record fee – but the Scottish international can never have poached a simpler goal. Shilton must have had a word with himself; his performance in that Hamburg game a few weeks later was outstanding.

The season ended with a reminder to all of the fragility of success. Only five years earlier Brian Clough had taken Derby to the First Division title. Now they were relegated alongside Bolton and Bristol.

Snatch of the Day

Above: Michael Grade
poses with an LWT
football after announcing
that London Weekend
Television had signed
a secret football
broadcasting deal.

Opposite top: Terry
McDermott outstrips
West Ham's Trevor
Brooking at Anfield.

Opposite bottom:
McDermott representing
England against Scotland
at Hampden Park.

It was among the most audacious coups in the history of British television. And, for *Match of the Day*, many observers really did think it was all over.

For years ITV and the BBC had adopted a 'joint negotiating strategy' with the Football League over broadcast rights – an attempt to avoid being played off against each other – but in November 1979 it was revealed that London Weekend Television's Director of Programmes, Michael Grade, had signed a secret £5 million deal with the League to acquire exclusive rights to games for three years from 1980-81.

The story was broken by the *London Evening News* and perfectly summed up in the headline 'Snatch of the Day'. It seemed that Auntie (the Corporation's long-standing nickname) had been 'caught with her knickers down', as one former BBC Sport executive put it. ITV commentator Brian Moore described it as 'the coup of the century.'

The BBC hit back, obtaining a ruling from the Office of Fair Trading that blocked the deal. However, the OFT's compromise pleased nobody. It meant ITV could take over Saturday nights for its highlights programme *The Big Match* (previously aired on Sunday afternoons) for the 1980-81 season. After that, the rival channels would have to share the coveted Saturday slot on alternate years.

 ## Player of the Year

Terry McDermott, Liverpool

Terry McDermott was one of Bob Paisley's first signings as Liverpool boss, arriving from Newcastle United after a football league apprenticeship at Bury.

He initially struggled to hold his place and there was even speculation about his future at the club. But he gradually established himself as one of the most eye-catching and thrilling midfielders of his generation and the 1979–80 season encapsulated his enormous worth to Paisley's talented team.

McDermott scored 16 goals from 37 appearances in all competitions to help the Reds safely to their 12th league title. His impressive haul included several 'goal of the season' contenders including one effort – during an FA Cup quarter-final against Tottenham – which characterized his ability to conjure something from nothing. Receiving to the right of the penalty area, some 30 yards from goal, McDermott nonchalantly flicked the ball up in the air with his right foot before smashing home an unstoppable strike.

As well as his Football Writers' Association Player of the Year award he also won the Players' Player award – the first professional to win both accolades in the same season. He stayed at Liverpool until 1983, finishing with 81 goals in 329 appearances, before returning to Newcastle to wind down his career.

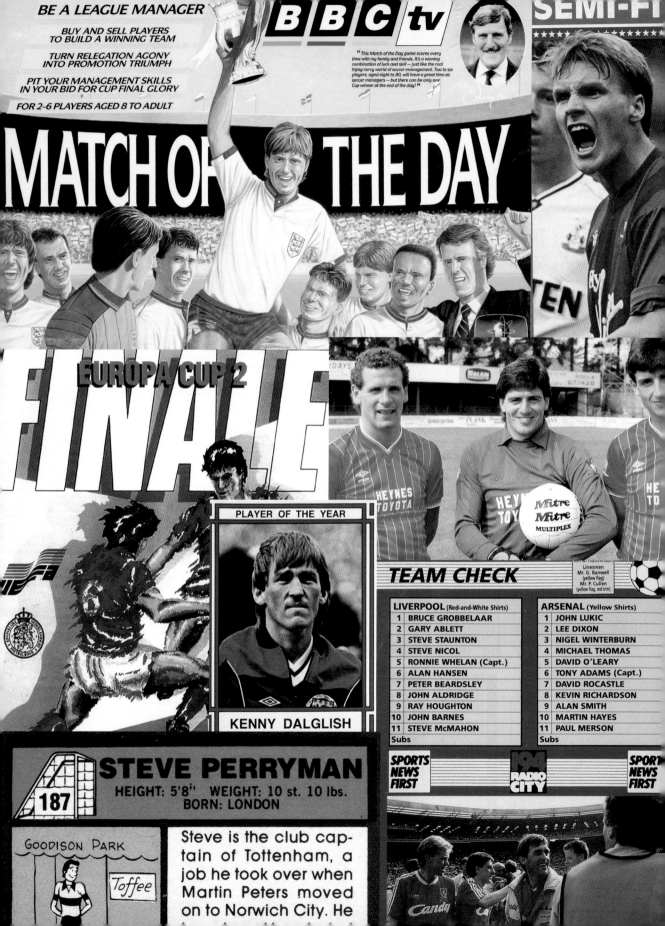

BBC tv

SEMI-FI

" *This Match of the Day game scores every time with my family and friends. It's a winning combination of luck and skill — just like the real topsy-turvy world of soccer management. Two to six players, aged eight to 80, will have a great time as soccer managers — but there can be only one Cup winner at the end of the day!*"

MATCH OF THE DAY

EUROPA CUP 2
FINALE

PLAYER OF THE YEAR

KENNY DALGLISH

TEAM CHECK

Linesmen
Mr. G. Banwell (yellow flag)
Mr. P. Cullen (yellow flag, red trim)

LIVERPOOL (Red-and-White Shirts)		ARSENAL (Yellow Shirts)	
1	BRUCE GROBBELAAR	1	JOHN LUKIC
2	GARY ABLETT	2	LEE DIXON
3	STEVE STAUNTON	3	NIGEL WINTERBURN
4	STEVE NICOL	4	MICHAEL THOMAS
5	RONNIE WHELAN (Capt.)	5	DAVID O'LEARY
6	ALAN HANSEN	6	TONY ADAMS (Capt.)
7	PETER BEARDSLEY	7	DAVID ROCASTLE
8	JOHN ALDRIDGE	8	KEVIN RICHARDSON
9	RAY HOUGHTON	9	ALAN SMITH
10	JOHN BARNES	10	MARTIN HAYES
11	STEVE McMAHON	11	PAUL MERSON
Subs		Subs	

SPORTS NEWS FIRST

194 RADIO CITY

SPORT NEWS FIRST

STEVE PERRYMAN

187

HEIGHT: 5'8"   WEIGHT: 10 st. 10 lbs.
BORN: LONDON

GOODISON PARK

Toffee

Steve is the club captain of Tottenham, a job he took over when Martin Peters moved on to Norwich City. He

Candy

MATCH OF THE DAY

1980s

WIN
two seats
at
Wembley

1980-81

Settled top-flight sides – especially good ones – are always going to be in the mix come silverware distribution and by the spring of 1981 it was clear Aston Villa qualified on both counts. Using just 14 players all season they had evolved steadily since winning promotion six years earlier.

Opposite top: Trading cards featuring some of the Aston Villa stars.

Opposite bottom: Argentinian striker Ricardo Villa makes history for Spurs.

Below: A souvenir patch celebrating Ipswich's European Cup title.

Plain-speaking manager Ron Saunders had balanced his team with both flair and firepower. In midfield skipper Dennis Mortimer formed a redoubtable axis with the likes of Des Bremner and Gordon Cowans, while up front Peter Withe and Gary Shaw were worthy target men for winger Tony Morley. Here were players who created space apparently effortlessly and few neutrals outside the West Midlands would have grudged them the title. But could they still blow it?

As Villa travelled to Arsenal for their last game they were top on 60 points. Their last and only challenger was Ipswich Town, four behind, but Ipswich still had a game in hand and a slight advantage on goal difference. Jimmy Hill's revolutionary three points for a win was not due to start until September so a draw at Highbury would be enough. Villa lost 2-0.

Among the 16,000 travelling fans the only sound was of transistor radios on full blast as they tried desperately to hear the commentary from Ayresome Park. Arsenal fans didn't help – after all they were loudly celebrating a UEFA Cup place – but when Middlesborough's 2-1 defeat of Ipswich at last became clear both sets of supporters invaded the pitch. For once, it was the most joyous of confrontations.

Fifth-placed Liverpool's attentions were focused elsewhere. Their 1-0 European Cup final victory over Real Madrid was the third time they had won the competition in five years and the fifth on the trot for an English club. They also remedied some unfinished trophy-hunting business by winning the League Cup in a replayed final against West Ham. It was the one major domestic cup that had eluded them.

After running Villa so close Ipswich could easily have suffered an anti-climax. Facing Dutch champions AZ '67 Alkmaar in the final of the UEFA cup they posted a 3-0 home lead – not quite enough for fans well aware of some flaky European away form. In the second leg Frans Thijssen's early opener settled the visitors' nerves but Alkmaar hit back twice and it was left to John Wark to score a record equalling 14th European goal of the season to restore the cushion. Ipswich eventually ran out deserved 5-4 winners.

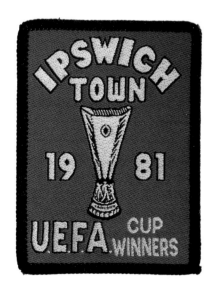

DENNIS MORTIMER   KENNY SWAIN   KEN McNAUGHT   JIMMY RIMMER   DES BREMNER   GORDON COWANS

Match of the Season
Tottenham Hotspur 3
Manchester City 2

The 100th FA Cup final and what a goal to settle it. For Ricardo Villa it was at once the defining moment of his career and a step up to the pantheon of White Hart Lane's heroes.

Days earlier Villa had been in tears as he was substituted at Wembley with his side behind. But Spurs fought back to 1-1 and manager Keith Burkinshaw put him straight back into the team for the replay. The bearded Argentinian responded by giving Spurs a seventh-minute lead and this potboiler of a final then bubbled away beautifully. Steve MacKenzie levelled with a marvellous volley, Reeves put City ahead from the spot and then a glimpse of trademark Glenn Hoddle genius allowed Garth Crooks to make it 2-2.

With seven minutes to go Ricky Villa began a powerful run down the left.

It was pure South American magic. Villa cut inside, dribbling past one flailing defender after another, until it seemed that deep in the penalty area he had tried to do too much. But with one last flick of the shoulder he belted the ball past Joe Corrigan to the adulation of half north London.

Pullover Punditry – That Sunday Afternoon Look

The previous season's bust-up over TV rights, and the Office of Fair Trading's ruling requiring the BBC and ITV to share Saturday night highlights on alternate seasons, marked a sea-change in *MotD*'s brand.

For the first time in 16 seasons the programme switched to a Sunday afternoon and it was felt this required a more casual look. Out went the formal jackets, shirts and ties and instead Jimmy Hill and Bob Wilson donned pullovers. The message was: you've had the roast, you've washed up, now sit down and relax with your favourite uncles.

Below: John Hollins scored two of Arsenal's five against Leeds while the MotD *cameras were elsewhere.*

Nonetheless, Sundays presented a problem, not least because football fans are creatures of habit. They like their pre-match drink in the same pub, their half-time pie from the same stall, their lucky underpants for the big game. *Match of the Day* on a Sunday? Sacrilege.

The other difficulty was more practical. If *MotD* had exciting games fans would switch on. But producers then had to select their three chosen fixtures weeks in advance, making it difficult to follow form teams. Viewers could be served up 0-0 draws, 24 hours old, only to then hear Bob on the 'newsdesk' inform them that '... elsewhere, there was a six-goal thriller ...' 8 November 1980 was a case in point – *MotD* screened two 0-0s (Liverpool-Forest and West Brom-Villa) while 'elsewhere' Arsenal thumped five past Leeds at Elland Road and Southampton and Ipswich drew 3-3.

Player of the Year
Frans Thijssen, Ipswich

Only the third foreign player to pick up the award (and the first of three Dutchmen) diminutive midfielder Frans Thijssen arrived at Ipswich from FC Twente in 1979 for a fee of £220,000.

Foreign transfers were rare in this era and overseas players who did make the move to England often struggled to adapt. Thijssen, though, had no such problems and thrived under the tutelage of Bobby Robson. He joined an Ipswich team which embraced a technical style of play – a strategy markedly different from the traditionally direct approach of English football.

Thijssen later told one interviewer: 'Bobby Robson changed the style of football; he told the defenders to play it to the Dutch guys in the midfield [himself and Arnold Mühren] – that style suited the team very well.'

Blessed with an abundance of skill and trickery Thijssen bagged six goals in 52 appearances over the 1980–81 season – capping a fantastic campaign by scoring in each leg of that memorable 5-4 aggregate UEFA Cup final victory over AZ '67.

Following a four-year spell at Ipswich he spent a season at Nottingham Forest, and a somewhat less inspiring period of his career, before moving on to the Vancouver Whitecaps, Fortuna Sittard, FC Gronigen and Vitesse. He retired from playing in 1991.

Above: Thijssen playing for Ipswich in a UEFA Cup match against Widzew Lodz.

Left: Ipswich Town's Flying Dutchman Frans Thijssen leaves Sunderland's Iain Munro floundering.

1981-82

The spring of 1982 saw two managers at the opposite ends of football's hall of fame earning their corn. One was Bob Paisley, mastermind of three European Cup wins and a flurry of league titles at Liverpool, the other Tony Barton at Aston Villa.

The problem for Paisley was that, for all the Reds' success, team re-building was overdue. But that also meant new players gelling, an often protracted process, and time was running out. Liverpool were languishing in 10th place at the New Year, already written-off by the pundits. In the famous Anfield Boot Room Paisley and his coaches put on their thinking caps.

By the start of March minds were made up. Ray Kennedy, a midfield fixture for years, would make way for the fledgling Irish international Ronnie Whelan while in attack 20-year-old Ian Rush would be fully unleashed to see if he could fulfil the promise of his £300,000 signing from Chester City. Turned out he could.

Rush would go on to net 30 times in 49 appearances across all competitions. Crucially, 17 of these were in the league, a performance which re-ignited Liverpool's fire. They posted 11 straight wins between March 9 and May 1 to overtake Ipswich and seal the club's 13th League title –

Opposite: Front cover of the programme for the European Cup clash between Villa and Bayern Munich.

Below : The team line-ups as shown inside the programme.

BAYERN MÜNCHEN

.....AUGENTHALER, Klaus
.....BEIERLORZER, Bertram
.....BÖCK, Rudolf
.....BREITNER, Paul
.....DEL'HAYE, Karl
.....DREMMLER, Wolfgang
.....DÜRNBERGER, Bernhard
.....GÜTTLER, Günther
.....HERBST, Dieter
.....HORSMAN, Udo
.....JUNGHANS, Walter

.....KRAUS, Wolfgang
.....MATHY, Reinhold
.....MÜLLER, Manfred
.....NIEDERMAYER, Kurt
.....PFLÜGLER, Hans
.....RUMMENIGGE, Karl-Heinz
.....SCHEHL, Stefan
.....SIGURVINSSON, Asgeir
.....WEINER, Hans
.....WINKLHOFER, Helmut

Referee/Schiedsrichter: Georges Konrath
Linesmen/Linienrichter: Joel Quiniou — René Lopez
(France/Frankreich)

16

ASTON VILLA

.....BREMNER, Des
.....BLAKE, Noel
.....BULLIVANT, Terry
.....COWANS, Gordon
.....CROPLEY, Alex
.....DEACY, Eamon
.....EVANS, Allan
.....DONOVAN, Terry
.....GEDDIS, David
.....GIBSON, Colin
.....HEARD, Pat
.....LINTON, Ivor
.....LITTLE, Brian
.....McNAUGHT, Ken

.....MORLEY, Tony
.....MORTIMER, Dennis
.....PEJIC, Mike
.....ORMSBY, Brendan
.....READY, Kevin
.....RIMMER, Jimmy
.....SHAW, Gary
.....SHELTON, Gary
.....SWAIN, Kenny
.....WILLIAMS, Gary
.....WITHE, Peter
.....YOUNG, Willie

17

according to Paisley, the toughest of his reign. Rush got the headlines but other new boys were equally important; Mark Lawrenson – now a regular *MotD* pundit - at centre back, Australian Craig Johnston as super-sub and of course Whelan himself. After a shaky start even the mecurial Bruce Grobbelaar found safer hands.

And so to Barton, thrust into the Villa job with just three months left in the season. He had the unenviable task of trying to follow title-winning Ron Saunders (who had suddenly and surprisingly quit) but in reality Villa were never in the running. The European Cup was their one, optimistic, hope and they somehow fought their way to the final against Bayern Munich. Massive underdogs, their 1-0 victory may have been founded on Saunders. But it said much for the man-management qualities of Barton – a journeyman player who in just 105 days won the respect and confidence of his team.

Elsewhere Spurs won the FA and lost the League Cup final (against QPR and Liverpool respectively). Their blossoming squad now included Graham Roberts, plucked from non-league obscurity the previous year and converted from striker to central defender. Old habits die hard though. In the League Roberts scored a hat-trick against his home town team Southampton, one of the clubs who had rejected him.

Match of the Season
Aston Villa 1
Bayern Munich 0

Perhaps Tony Barton never expected to actually reach the European Cup final. But having got to Rotterdam he must have allowed himself to dream. Even against mighty Bayern there was a chance and this Villa side possessed no mean talent. Things could hardly have started worse.

In the 9th minute Jimmy Rimmer realised the shoulder injury he'd sustained in training was too severe to continue. On came 23-year-old reserve 'keeper Nigel Spink for only his second senior game (the first had been two years earlier). Now, who was it who said you win nothing with kids?

It was a towering performance from the youngster. Against the cream of German midfield talent - the likes of Karl-Heinz Rummenigge and Paul Breitner - he pulled off a string of brilliant saves just as it seemed Villa were crumbling. His confidence inspired his team-mates and re-enthused the travelling Holte End. When in the 67th minute Tony Morley, twisting and tormenting down the left, crossed for Peter Withe to shin home you just knew it was Villa's night.

MotD and the No-Goal Controversy

It seems incredible that goal-line technology deciding whether or not a ball had crossed the line didn't emerge in English football until August 2013 – because *Match of the Day* was providing this service 32 years earlier.

It may not have been as fancy or accurate as the computer graphics of Hawk-Eye's Goal Decision System but the slow motion replays of the early eighties were often perfectly capable of proving a team had been wronged. And on 6 September 1980, Crystal Palace were clear victims.

Playing away at Coventry, the Eagles were 2-1 down when a free-kick nudged to Clive Allen was ferociously despatched into the top right corner of the net. So ferociously, that when it hit the supporting stanchion it bounced out like a bullet. In fairness, John Motson was initially fooled '... Clive Allen hammered that and it came back off the woodwork. Palace say it was over the line ... and the referee says no goal. Well, there's a talking point.'

Palace manager, Terry Venables, was certainly keen to talk. 'There's not a doubt in my mind that that went in and hit the iron stanchion at the back,' he said afterwards. 'Now, if he's saying we've got to hit some particular part of the net to get a goal – that's different.'

MotD's slow motion replays proved the point and many clubs decided to re-design their goals – a move initiated, almost inevitably, by Jimmy Hill.

Player of the Year
Steve Perryman

Steve Perryman was a fully paid-up Tottenham legend who made a club record 854 appearances and in the process won more honours than any other player in its history. His combative and bellicose presence in midfield, and later defence, was evident from the moment he made his Spurs debut at the tender age of 17.

By the time he was 20 he had become club captain and went on to experience massive highs – winning the League Cup twice in 1971 and 1973 and the UEFA Cup in 1972 – and crushing lows in the form of 1977 relegation. By the early Eighties he was leading what many consider to be the greatest Tottenham side of all time.

Perryman captained a squad boasting the glittering talents of Osvaldo Ardiles, Ricardo Villa and Glenn Hoddle to back-to-back FA Cup triumphs in 1981 and 1982. He also won the UEFA Cup for the second time his career in 1984, beating Real Madrid on penalties, although he was suspended for the second leg of the final. He was made an MBE for services to the game in 1986.

1982-83

When Bob Paisley became the first manager in history to lead his League Cup winners up to the Royal Box it marked the end of a career unrivalled in any era of the British game and confirmed his status as an Anfield legend.

Both Bill Shankly and Sir Alex Ferguson achieved extraordinary managerial feats but in his nine years at Anfield Paisley brought home three European Cups, six championships, one UEFA Cup, and three League Cups, plus a host of second-tier trophies. Never is a long time but, over that period, it's hard to see another manager ever coming close.

Paisley's team beat Manchester United 2-1 in that last Wembley final (a controversial game enlivened by superb Whiteside and Kennedy goals but tarnished by Grobbelaar's professional foul to deny Gordon McQueen a winner at the death). The affable Geordie then saw his team through to another title before bowing out of the club he'd served loyally as player, coach and manager for 44 years.

There will always be those who question the quality of his rivals. But with the likes of Brian Clough's Forest and Bobby Robson's Ipswich hungry for honours, and recovering giants Manchester United and Everton in his backyard, the Paisley Years were a bear pit not for the faint-hearted. And, fortunately for Liverpool FC, Bob wasn't.

Below: Arnold Mühren of Bobby Robson's Ipswich beats Arsenal's Graham Rix.

Football though can be a cruel master. While one ex-Reds player-turned-manager was signing off on a high, another was enduring the fickle nature of life in the top-flight. John Toshack, whose partnership with Keegan was instrumental to Liverpool's success in the seventies, had taken

Match of the Season

Manchester United 2
Brighton and Hove Albion 2

For Brighton fans the prospect of a return to the Second Division was no real surprise. But they had remained chipper all season thanks to a great FA Cup run which almost produced one of the shocks of the decade.

With three minutes on the clock at Wembley they were 2-1 down to Manchester United. It had been a classic final, despite the boggy pitch, with the underdogs holding their own against a side which had finished third in the league. Gordon Smith's header had put Brighton in front but goals from Stapleton and Wilkins had given United the edge. Then Gary Stevens struck a fine equaliser and the final moved into extra time.

With seconds left the Seagulls' Michael Robinson and Smith found themselves through on goal with only a defender to beat. Robinson threaded the ball perfectly to his fellow striker but tired legs brought a tame shot from Smith, Bailey saved, United won the replay 4-0 and another cup dream sadly died.

Above: Gary Stevens slots Brighton's second past United keeper Gary Bailey.

Swansea on an incredible ride from the Fourth to the First Division in four seasons. In 1981–82 they had for months even been serious title contenders. Yet now they were relegated with Man City and Brighton, relatively big money signings were moved on and the following season the Swans suffered a second successive dose of the drop.

The most important appointment of the season, at least for English fans, was Bobby Robson as England manager. Robson's tenure at Ipswich had impressed the FA not least because of the way players such as John Wark, Alan Brazil, Paul Mariner and Terry Butcher had blossomed under him. He also had a natural eye for imports that could make a good team outstanding – his Dutch midfield duo of Frans Thijssen and Arnold Mühren proved that – and to bring Ipswich major European honours on a frugal budget was some achievement.

Robson's predecessor at England, Ron Greenwood, was a good and talented international coach who brought stability at a time his country most needed it. He resigned two days after England were knocked out of the 1982 World Cup in Spain; his squad promising much but failing to deliver.

Jimmy Hill and the Professional Foul

The notion of the professional foul – denying a clear goal-scoring opportunity – remains controversial. It became a key part of the referee's armoury after the uproar surrounding the 1980 FA Cup final ... and, once again, Jimmy Hill was at the centre of things.

The closing minutes of that final saw Arsenal's Willie Young cynically hack down West Ham's 17-year-old Paul Allen as he was clean through on goal. As the laws stood, referee George Courtney could award only a free kick.

Although West Ham went on to lift the cup the teenager was in floods of tears as he collected his medal – he knew Wembley goals were career rarities. In armchairs across the nation you could picture a million mums torn between wanting to cuddle him and shout at someone.

The Football League subsequently appointed a sub-committee to look at ways of improving football as a spectacle. Chaired by Jimmy Hill, and with Bobby Charlton and Sir Matt Busby as consultants, it recommended making the professional foul – including deliberate handball to deny a goal – a sending-off infringement. This was rejected by the International Football Association Board but the League got its way ahead of the 1982-3 season by instructing referees to interpret professional fouls as serious foul play, already a red card offence.

Below: Jimmy Hill remained totally involved in football matters when not appearing on the nation's TV screens.

PLAYER OF THE YEAR

KENNY DALGLISH

Player of the Year
Kenny Dalglish

Kenny Dalglish began the 1982-83 season slowly, taking two months to bag his first goals of the campaign – a brace in the League Cup tie against Brighton & Hove Albion. He was now adjusting to a new position 'in the hole' behind the Ian Rush goal machine.

However, the Scot was a masterful reader of the game and he soon kicked on to fashion a dead-eye partnership with Rush. Together the pair shared 51 goals between them across all competitions.

Dalglish started all but one of Liverpool's 59 games in this, Bob Paisley's final, season and he was unquestionably the architect of the Reds' championship success. His instinctive knack of delivering the right weighted pass at the right time was the perfect foil for Rush's poaching instincts. Rare indeed was the defensive lock they didn't pick.

This was Dalglish's second Player of the Year award – an achievement no other Scot has matched – and it was no great surprise when two years later he was named as Liverpool's first-ever player-manager.

Above: Kenny Dalglish
Player of the Year
trading card.

Left bottom: Dalglish
on the ball for Liverpool
against Arsenal.

101

1983-84

If any club was going to challenge Anfield's dominance of the early eighties you might have thought Man Utd would be top of the queue. And, after 7 April's games, so it seemed; Liverpool on 69 points were leading United by two with Forest (60) heading the chasing pack. No one really noticed an outsider coming up on the rails.

That April Saturday Southampton had scraped a 2-2 draw with Leicester on the back of two away defeats. The Saints hardly looked serious contenders on 56 points but they had a game in hand and a promising fixtures run-in. Unbeknown to them, their loftier rivals were also about to get a touch of the collywobbles.

Liverpool won just three and drew five of their last eight games. United fared even worse, with a win, four draws and three defeats. Southampton, however, hit the throttle winning six and drawing three of their remaining games to finish second, a tantalising three points off the pace. Fans must have looked back on two of those away draws – against struggling Stoke and Birmingham – and pondered what might have been. Certainly, fixture congestion cost them dear; they had to play the last five matches inside 12 days.

This was unquestionably a Southampton side worthy of respect.

Below: Mick Mills of Southampton controlling the ball in a Division One clash against Spurs.

Apart from Shilton, still masterful in goal, their line-up included veteran defensive quality in the form of Mick Mills and Reuben Agboola and a future England international in Mark Wright. With midfielder David Armstrong contributing 15 league goals, and two exciting young strikers in Steve Moran and Danny Wallace, they won the admiration of almost every fan outside Portsmouth.

None of which is to denigrate another vintage season for Liverpool for whom Ian Rush, with 47 goals in 65 games, was in magisterial form. The Reds became only the third club in Football League history (after Huddersfield in the 1920s and Arsenal in the 1930s) to win a hat-trick of championships. But they also clinched the League Cup, beating Everton in a replay, and the European Cup, defeating AS Roma in Rome following the first penalty shoot-out in the competition's 28-year history. And all this in manager Joe Fagan's first season at the helm since stepping out of Bob Paisley's shadow.

Below: Spurs keeper Tony Parks with his captain Graham Roberts and the UEFA Cup.

Despite the anguish of losing a cup final to their arch-rivals, Everton at least had the satisfaction of winning the FA Cup, beating a fine Watford side 2-0. More importantly, Howard Kendall's team had sent out a clear message. Silverware was no longer the prerogative of Anfield.

Match of the Season
Tottenham Hotspur 1
Anderlecht 1 (4-3 agg.)

The second leg of this UEFA Cup final was beautifully set up for Keith Burkinshaw's farewell to the Lane. Spurs looked to have done the hard work in Belgium by restricting the cup holders to 1-1. However, when Alex Czerniatynski scored on the hour it seemed the visitors were more than capable of defending their lead.

Then in the 83rd minute, Ossie Ardiles' firecracker of a shot hit the bar, the ball was only partially cleared and a second cross found acting captain Graham Roberts. He controlled the ball on his chest, half stumbled into the penalty area and stabbed in an equaliser. Extra time came and went; the cup's destiny fell to a penalty shoot-out.

Which, in the usual scheme of things, would have left the home fans quietly confident. Goalkeeper Ray Clemence was among the world's best and a three-times European Cup-winner with Liverpool. Trouble was, he had missed the tie through injury. It was all down to young understudy Tony Parks.

With the penalty count at 4-3, Gudjohnsen stepped up needing to score to keep Belgian hopes alive. His low shot was heading just inside the left post but Parks guessed right, brilliantly palmed clear, performed an acrobatic double-roll and, in the same movement, sprinted into the arms of his team-mates. Parks won no other major honours ... but what a way to win this one.

So you'd like to be a football commentator . . . says John Motson

'It's exhausting work but there's nothing like being paid for following your hobby!'

MotD's First Live League Game

Above: Motty featured on duty in a Match of the Day Annual.

Opposite top: Rush causing problems for the Yugoslavian defence while playing for Wales.

Opposite bottom: The unstoppable Rush taking on Manchester United's Ray Wilkins.

Negotiations to get live league football on TV had proved long, hard and testy for broadcasters. The only regular live domestic football had been the FA and European Cup finals and England versus Scotland.

So, when camera manufacturers Canon announced a £3 million sponsorship of the Football League, beginning in August 1983, it seemed that at last the walls would come down. This was by far the biggest sponsorship deal in British sporting history; the only caveat was that it must include TV coverage. You'd have thought cutting a deal would have been straightforward. And you'd have been wrong.

When the League rejected the channels' offer of £5.4 million over two seasons, to include limited shirt advertising and four live matches each weekend, the BBC and ITV stormed out of talks in disgust. Their joint statement issued later stated that '... the Football League are strangling themselves to death. They have shown this with the Chester Report [on future football finances, published 1983] and the television negotiations. They are in chaos.'

Despite the tears and tantrums, a deal was eventually struck. The BBC and ITV each got seven live matches a year, ITV opting for Sunday afternoons, the BBC trying a Friday evening experiment alongside its usual *MotD* Saturday night highlights. But for *MotD* there was a last, frustrating twist when strike action led to the show's cancellation for four weeks. John Motson eventually took the microphone for the first live game on 16 December 1983 – a 4-2 home win for Manchester United over Spurs.

Player of the Year

Ian Rush, Liverpool

Two enduring images spring to mind whenever Liverpool goal-machine Ian Rush is mentioned. One is that distinctive bushy moustache; the other is him wheeling away as another shot finds the back of the net.

Yet when he first arrived at Anfield from Chester in 1980 for £300,000 – a British transfer record for a teenager at the time – Rush looked gawky, thin and somewhat ungainly. He took time to make his mark, with Paisley ensuring he 'learnt the Liverpool way' in the reserves before playing regularly for the firsts, but after hitting his first goal in a European tie against Oulun Palloseura in 1981 he was rarely out of the team.

Rush combined electric pace and eagle-eyed anticipation with intelligent positioning and an excellent reading of the game. He hit 346 goals in 660 appearances for the Reds either side of an ill-fated and mercifully brief spell in Italy with Juventus. It is a club record tally unlikely to be broken any time soon.

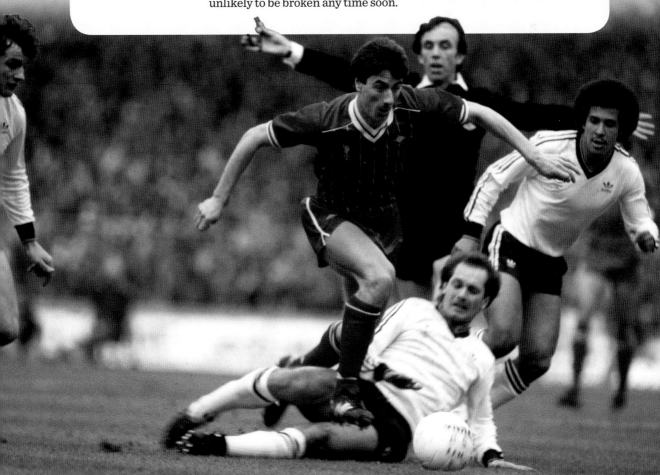

This was the season results mattered little in comparison to two horrendous football tragedies just 18 days apart. The loss of 56 people in the Bradford City fire, and a further 39 in the Heysel disaster, sent shock waves across Europe, reminding fans that, actually, life or death is more important than football. Juventus's 1-0 European Cup final victory over Liverpool at Heysel was an irrelevance.

Above: Programme for Everton's glorious win over Rapid Vienna in Rotterdam.

On the field it had been 15 years since Everton last won the championship. Then Howard Kendall had helped make it happen. Now manager, he was running a side that had flirted with success (twice placed seventh; once eighth during his three seasons in charge) but had never quite cut the mustard.

Fortunately Everton's board kept faith and Kendall's rebuilt team came good. Young players like Trevor Steven and Peter Reid proved revelations while Neville Southall emerged as a genuinely world-class goalkeeper. Kendall's big early buy, for £250,000 from Wolves, was Andy Gray and his strike partnership with fellow Scot Graeme Sharp grew stronger as the season progressed. The Toffees finished on 90 points – a whopping 13 clear of nearest rivals Liverpool – and on course for a historic treble. Meanwhile, at the bottom Stoke were relegated on 17 points; the lowest First Division tally ever under the three-points-for-a-win rule.

Everton secured the league title on 6 May with a 2-0 win over QPR and 11 days later completed the second leg of the treble with a largely untroubled 3-1 Cup Winners' Cup victory over Rapid Vienna (the club's first European honour). A win against Manchester United in the FA Cup final would mean a bumper Brasso order to cope with the glittering Goodison trophy cabinet.

That match finally jerked into life 12 minutes from the end of normal time. United defender Kevin Moran brought down Peter Reid on the break with Gray and Sharp both unmarked and clear. He was dismissed for a 'professional foul', the first-ever red card of the competition's 104 finals. But it wasn't Moran's disappointment that so riled his team-mates. An attempt by the FA to make such fouls a sending-off offence had been pretty much shelved amid disapproval from FIFA. No one had expected Moran to walk.

The result was a ten-man United re-energised by a sense of injustice. They created two more good chances before the whistle, then grabbed the winner five minutes into the second period of extra time through Norman Whiteside's fabulous curled strike. For Everton there was only sympathy... and a sense of what might have been.

Below: Chris Waddle bagged a hat trick in 24 minutes in a high-scoring match against QPR.

Match of the Season
QPR 5 Newcastle 5

The scoreline isn't the half of it. Alan Mullery's QPR had gone into this game on 22 September with some decent early-season form, winning and drawing two. The Toon, meanwhile, had won three but lost their previous three on the trot, conceding ten goals in the process. Unsurprisingly, Newcastle manager Jack Charlton's team selection was designed to shore things up at the back. He hadn't expected Chris Waddle to fire a 24-minute hat-trick; nor to be 4-0 up come half-time.

In the home dressing room Mullery was seething and it clearly had an effect. Rangers scored three without reply – a fortuitous 49th minute header from Gary Bannister, a bizarre own goal (a clearance deflected in off the unwitting Kenny Wharton) and a 74th minute strike from John Gregory. With six minutes left United looked to be safe as Wharton converted a great Beardsley–Waddle move but then Steve Wicks' set-piece header immediately made it 4-5 and with 90 minutes Gary Micklewhite calmly chipped the equaliser.

It was great for the fans; not so much the managers. A furious Charlton called it 'a total embarrassment, absolutely diabolical' while Mullery admitted: 'These kind of games give managers heart attacks.'

English Clubs in Exile - and Football Pays the Price

Opposite top: Trading card featuring Player of the Year Neville Southall.

Opposite bottom: Southall introduces John Motson to his domain prior to the 1985 FA Cup final against Manchester United.

Below: Trouble spills onto the pitch during a Wimbledon/Man City match.

The tragedy of Heysel and the hooliganism bedevilling English clubs cast a long shadow over football. *MotD* took its share of the hit in several ways – not least the disenchantment of viewers at the way the national game had degenerated.

This was reflected in ratings for live Friday night matches, although the BBC pointed out that this scheduling had been experimental. Jonathan Martin, Head of Sport at the time, conceded: 'We only got six or seven million viewers on a Friday night which was poor for the slot. So we moved to Sundays in the following year.' Waning interest wasn't just a problem for TV, ground attendance figures were also declining.

There were other factors contributing to the general malaise. UEFA's ban on English clubs in Europe meant that, over the next five years, there was a drift of talented players to continental clubs. TV was in the entertainment business, it needed big stars, and football no longer had a monopoly on live action – other sports were increasingly pushing for live coverage as a lever to encourage sponsorship and participation.

With a new round of TV rights negotiations already underway, this was to be the last season for seven years that *Match of the Day* would contain weekly league highlights.

NEVILLE SOUTHALL
EVERTON

Player of the Year
Neville Southall, Everton

A former bin-man who spent his formative years in the game as a semi-professional at clubs such as Bangor City, Conwy United and Winsford United, Neville Southall's journey to becoming one of European football's greatest goalkeepers makes for heart-warming reading.

Signed from Bury by Howard Kendall after impressing in his first full professional season at Gigg Lane, he went on to help Everton win the League Championship (twice), the FA Cup (twice) and the European Cup Winners' Cup. Some of his saves have since passed into folklore and two, particularly, come to mind from the 1984–5 vintage. There was his stunning tip-over from Mark Falco's header in the final minute of Everton's game against title rivals Tottenham, then an extraordinary, scrambling, save to the disbelief of Sheffield Wednesday's Imre Varadi.

That game at Hillsborough was one of the finest performances by any goalkeeper, anywhere, over 90 minutes. 'I don't think I've ever seen such intense pressure applied by a football team,' said commentator Barry Davies of Sheffield Wednesday. Everton won the game 1-0 and two days later wrapped up the title.

Surprisingly nimble for a man of 6 foot 1 inch, Southall may have been blessed with natural ability but he never relied on it. He was a notorious perfectionist and would spend hours on the training pitches at Bellefield to fine-tune his positioning and reaction saves. He still holds the Everton appearance record, turning out for the Toffees 751 times, and also has a record 92 caps for Wales.

1985-86

Everton's exciting team mounted a strong defence of their title. Although Andy Gray had been controversially shipped out to former club Aston Villa, Kendall had signed a sharp 24-year-old replacement from Leicester City in the close season. His name was Gary Lineker and he would go on to become the league's top scorer with 30 goals.

Below: West Ham's Frank McAvennie was the second-highest goal scorer in the league behind Gary Lineker.

But it wasn't enough. Across Stanley Park Kenny Dalglish had taken the job of Liverpool player-manager, replacing Joe Fagan who had announced his retirement before Heysel. Dalglish didn't see himself as automatic first-choice striker and was happy to let the blossoming Ian Rush–Paul Walsh partnership continue to strengthen. He was also desperate to restore bragging rights on Merseyside.

For much of the run-in this seemed highly unlikely. Liverpool trailed their local rivals by 11 points, needed to win their last seven games (five away) and hope those around them faltered. Everton certainly obliged

by losing 1-0 away to lowly League Cup winners Oxford United but West Ham fought doggedly to win eight of their last nine, including an 8-1 evisceration of Newcastle. They eventually finished third, their best-ever league placing, and owed much to consistent performers such as Alvin Martin, Tony Cottee and, particularly, Frank McAvennie whose league goal tally of 26 was second only to Lineker.

On the final day Liverpool needed a win at Stamford Bridge to secure their eighth title in 11 seasons. This was a tough call – Chelsea were themselves a strong side – and Alan Hansen later admitted he wasn't convinced the title was going to Anfield until the final whistle sounded. Almost inevitably it was Dalglish who sealed it; chesting down a hopeful lob into the penalty area to dispatch a perfectly placed first-time volley. Everton, who had beaten Southampton 6-1 at Goodison, were powerless though they still had the chance of revenge in the first all-Merseyside FA Cup final.

Below left: Souvenir badge commemorating Liverpool's double.

Below right: Gary Lineker shoots past Mark Lawrenson.

At the bottom it was a bad year for the Midlands with both West Brom (24 points) and Birmingham City (29 points) hopelessly adrift. On the last full day of fixtures the final relegation place could have sucked down any one of four clubs but when Leicester and Coventry both won at home, and Ipswich lost at Hillsborough, it was left to Oxford to decide matters. Two days later they beat Arsenal 3-0 to send Ipswich into the Second Division, the culmination of a steady decline from the heady Robson years.

Match of the Season
FA Cup Final
Liverpool 3 Everton 1

Five days after an exquisitely tense season climax Liverpool faced Everton in the FA Cup final. The Reds were chasing their first-ever double, a tantalising prospect given that this prize had always eluded Messrs Shankly, Paisley and Fagan. Yet for the first hour of the game it seemed the newly crowned champions had blagged their way to the title, so dominant were Howard Kendall's side.

Lineker put them ahead after 28 minutes and it would have been all over with a Graeme Sharp header but for Grobbelaar's brilliant save. But in the second half Liverpool dusted themselves down and class began to tell. Particularly in the form of Danish international Jan Molby who played perhaps the most

imperious 45 minutes of his career to shrug aside Everton's dynamic midfield engine of Reid and Bracewell. He laid an angled pass for Rush's 57th minute equaliser then a low cross for Craig Johnston to snatch a second. With six-minutes to go he found Whelan on the left, the Irishman centred for Ian Rush and it was all over. Winning Liverpool's first double in his first year as manager – destroying Everton's own double bid in the process – Dalglish must have wondered what was so hard about being the boss.

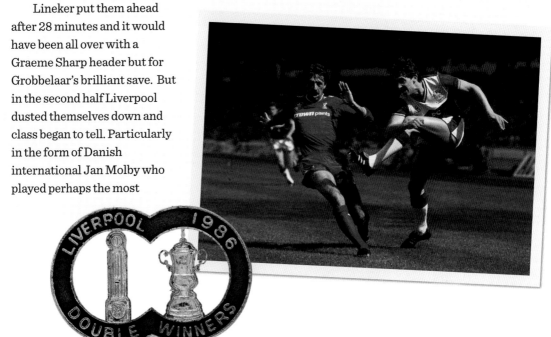

The Great Autumn TV Blackout

With the prospect of a new player in the rights market – satellite TV – clubs were determined to screw down the best possible deal with terrestrial channels. Equally, BBC and ITV executives were mindful of the League's weak negotiating position post-Heysel. Both sides played hard-ball. Perhaps a little too hard.

In early 1985, the joint TV negotiating team wooed the League with a £16 million bid covering four years. It would include 19 live games per season plus a weekend highlights package. The clubs, however, were unimpressed with their suitor's offer and – you can see where this is going – rejected it during a Valentine's Day meeting. The result of the tiff – no *Match of the Day* and a lot of cross football fans.

The Great Autumn Blackout lasted until 20 December and benefited no one. TV had lost viewers (and advertising); the League had to settle for less money per match and a short two-and-a-half year contract. Rights for the remaining six months of the season were agreed at £1.3 million with a £6.2 million two-year contract extension confirmed in June.

For *Match of the Day*, the deal heralded bleak years ahead. The programme now focused on FA Cup highlights with the occasional Sunday afternoon live game when possible. For loyal viewers it felt like the end of an era.

GARY LINEKER

Player of the Year
Gary Lineker, Tottenham Hotspur

Arguably England's finest finisher, *MotD*'s very own Gary Lineker was a prolific goalscorer wherever he played.

He began his career at home-town club Leicester City, helping the Foxes win promotion to the First Division twice in 1980 and 1983. When he first broke through at Filbert Street opposing barrel-chested centre-halves would queue up to batter the young whippersnapper; their only problem was how to catch him.

Lineker made up for his slight build with lethal acceleration and, inside the penalty area, anticipation verging on a sixth sense. He scored 103 goals in 216 games for City before securing an £800,000 move to Goodison in 1985.

It was with Everton that he won the first of his two Player of the Year awards, scoring three league hat-tricks en route to an impressive tally of 40 goals in 57 games. After just one season, and a wonderful World Cup at Mexico '86 where he won the Golden Boot, he was transferred to Barcelona for £2.8 million and later joined Tottenham (see 1991–92).

WORLD CUP – MEXICO 1986

Every football team suffers the occasional shocker – but when the ref doesn't spot the ball being punched into the net by a 5ft 4in player jumping against a 6ft goalkeeper, the shockwaves rumble on for years.

When that goal proves the decider in an England v Argentina World Cup quarter final, three decades of rumbling is surely the least you can expect. Cheating is sadly part of the modern game and refereeing blunders are inevitable. But what really rankled about the 'Hand of God' incident is that the man responsible, Diego Maradona, was so naturally gifted that he didn't need to cheat. As he showed to devastating effect when, four minutes later, he beat Peter Shilton again – this time legally – after dribbling effortlessly past four England players.

Until that point, Mexico '86 had begun to look promising for England, despite a shaky start. They lost their first game 1-0 to a distinctly ordinary Portugal, then ground out a dire 0-0 draw against Group F surprise package Morocco. In that second game, talismanic skipper Bryan Robson bravely played in a shoulder harness (another of the injuries which plagued his career) although afterwards it was clear his tournament was over. Manager Bobby Robson was also without Ray Wilkins, sent off after he angrily, and uncharacteristically, threw the ball at the ref.

Opposite: Gary Lineker scored a hat-trick against Poland in Mexico.

Right: England captain Peter Shilton shakes Argentina captain Diego Maradona's innocent hand.

Without these trusted internationals the must-win final group game against Poland looked tricky. Robson went for broke and in addition to the two forced changes dropped striker Mark Hateley and winger Chris Waddle. In came the excellent Peter Beardsley as Gary Lineker's strike partner while Peter Reid, Steve Hodge and Trevor Steven also got their chance. The new 4-4-2 formation worked. Lineker bagged a first-half hat-trick, half the tally that won him the tournament's golden boot, and England were through to a second round tie against Paraguay.

In that game the much-mangled line-up really clicked. They cruised past their opponents 3-0 and suddenly there was talk of England as 'contenders'. But Argentina in the quarters was a different matter. Poignantly, these were countries whose soldiers had fought each other in the 1982 Falklands War; a scenario akin to the proverbial elephant in the room (or, perhaps, on the pitch). From a strictly footballing perspective, the South Americans were the tournament's only unbeaten side. It was against this highly-charged backdrop that the teams met in front of 114,580 in Mexico City's Azteca Stadium.

The flashpoint came six minutes after half-time. Steve Hodge's hopelessly ballooning back-pass put Shilton in trouble and as the 'keeper raced out, Maradona beat him to it, cunningly flicking the ball into the goal with his left hand. He later described it as 'a little with the head of Maradona and a little with the hand of God.' It was an obvious handball to everyone but Tunisian referee Ali Bin Nasser, although BBC commentator Barry Davies remained doggedly neutral as he mildly asked: 'Was it the use of the hand England are complaining about?'

Below: Scarves were to be waved rather than worn in the Mexican summer heat.

It's not hard to imagine millions of furious fans back home screaming at their TV words to the effect: 'Yes, actually, Barry that is why they're a touch miffed.' And yet, when Maradona scored his second, picking the ball up in his own half, beating four England players, slotting home with consummate ease, Davies' instinctive, simple summary was bang on: 'You have to say that was magnificent.'

Below: Maradona's guilty hand comes into play against Shilton.

England almost clawed their way back after wingers John Barnes and Waddle were sent on to broaden the attack. Lineker scored with ten minutes to go and would have equalised but for the back of Julio Olarticoechea's head. But it was not to be. England went home feeling cheated and frustrated; Argentina went on to win the World Cup, beating West Germany 3-2 in the final.

1986-87

That old chestnut about league campaigns being marathons not sprints was never better illustrated than by this season. In the opening two months of the season Nottingham Forest got off to a flyer, shrugging off an opening day defeat at Goodison Park to win six and draw one of their next seven games.

Their run included a 6-0 home romp against Villa, a 6-2 annihilation of Chelsea at Stamford Bridge and a 1-0 win over Arsenal. During that Gunners game at the City Ground Brian Clough angrily remonstrated with his own fans as they chanted abuse at injured striker Charlie Nicholas. Clough was clearly at his uncompromising best. But was he on the march to glory?

Er ... no. Over the next two months Forest won only three of their nine games and by 15 November Arsenal had taken top spot after recovering from their own early season woes. They held that position until the end of January but then themselves faltered in the face of a determined Merseyside challenge. With Manchester United hopelessly adrift (Ron Atkinson had been sacked in November to make way for Alex Ferguson) the season was coming down to a Liverpool–Everton shoot-out.

Above: Coventry made a record for their FA Cup final trip to Wembley, and set a record by winning there.

Right: A neat collection of Liverpool team stickers.

Opposite top: The strips were recognisable, even if the players weren't, on the front cover of the League Cup final programme.

Opposite bottom: Charlie Nicholas netted both of Arsenal's goals against Liverpool.

Match of the Season
Arsenal 2 Liverpool 1

When Ian Rush conjured a typically clinical finish to give his side a 23rd minute League Cup final lead Liverpool fans breathed a sigh of relief. They never lost when Rush scored; fact. And what a great way for the maestro to sign off ahead of his much-trumpeted £3 million end-of-season move to Juventus.

They were right to be confident. Jan Molby and Steve McMahon had started as if they held Land Registry deeds proving midfield ownership while Arsenal did a collective impression of rabbits caught in headlights. The Gunners had scored only once in their previous seven, winless, league games.

But then on 30 minutes the mercurial Charlie Nicholas stabbed the ball home through a crowded penalty area and, as so often happens following an equaliser, the balance of the game subtly shifted. Now Paul Davis, David Rocastle and Steve Williams began to get a grip and by midway through the second half it was anyone's cup. Dalglish brought himself on for Paul Walsh while George Graham swapped Niall Quinn for Perry Groves.

And it was Groves who made the difference. In his first attack he slipped past Gillespie and sent a cross to the feet of the unmarked Nicholas. The Scot seemed to shin his shot, diverted by Ronnie Whelan's lunge, but as the ball beat Grobbelaar none of the North Bank faithful cared. Charlie was their darling.

Opposite top: Allen headed home the first goal in the 1987 FA Cup final after just two minutes.

Opposite bottom: Scoring for Spurs in a 4-0 drubbing of Manchester United.

By the middle of March the smart money was on the Reds. Given their proven experience of delivering under pressure it was hard to see Kenny Dalglish's side slipping up – especially with Ian Rush in such scintillating form (40 goals in 57 appearances). But Liverpool could not maintain a consistent pace. Between 28 March and 11 May they won five and lost five of their eleven league games. In contrast, Everton, despite losing the Merseyside derby on 25 April, produced some devastating form to win ten of their last twelve. The 42-game First Division was always a marathon. But Everton's sprint finish made them champions.

If losing the title to the Toffees wasn't bad enough, Liverpool fans had also seen a much cherished bastion demolished. Up until the League Cup final against Arsenal, Liverpool had never lost a game in which Rush scored. The Welshman could point to 144 previous matches that underpinned this particular nugget of terraces wisdom but Arsenal proved no respecters of superstition (see Match of the Season).

Perhaps the most celebrated result of the season – at least for neutrals – was Coventry City's thrilling 3-2 FA Cup final win over Spurs. This was not only the Sky Blues' first final, it was their first major honour since being elected to the League in 1919. For Spurs it was also a first – they had won all seven of their previous FA Cup finals.

MotD Memories – 'World Cups Mess You Up'

Comedian Russell Brand remembers feeling both inspired and confused by England's performances in '86 and '90.

'They're the World Cups that are most indelibly in my mind,' he said. 'Gary Lineker with his arm all bandaged up – I bandaged up my own arm when I was a kid because I liked what he was doing out there – then Ray Wilkins injured, Bryan Robson injured. I loved it. I think '86 was the awakening of my football consciousness.

'And then 1990; that was a gut-wrenching and confusing time. The previous [tournament], going out in the quarter final and the genius of Maradona – even with the Hand Of God you can make sense of it. But '90 – that really messed me up. I don't think people understood what happened.'

So how would he handle a penalty shoot-out? 'I certainly wouldn't do one of those short run-ups. I'd have gone for a proper, long run-up, I'd have trained and practised and said "I'm not going to shoot down the middle of the goal – that's too risky."

'I'd have drilled and drilled and drilled; low, bottom right corner. You've got to have a very clear plan and pursue it. How must it feel? I think you'd need some kind of pharmaceutical support.'

Player of the Year
Clive Allen, Tottenham Hotspur

Clive Allen had big boots to fill when he arrived at White Hart Lane from QPR for £700,000 in 1984 – his father, Les, had been part of Spurs' famous 1961 double-winning side.

He didn't disappoint. Small, stocky and quick, the prolific marksman smashed a staggering 112 goals in 173 games. But it was for his magical Player of the Year season that Allen will best be remembered on the Tottenham terraces.

Thriving from the silver service he received courtesy of Ardiles, Hoddle and Waddle, he hit 49 goals in all competitions for David Pleat's thrilling side as Spurs went chasing – and narrowly missing – a treble on three domestic fronts.

After cementing his status as a Lane favourite, Allen went on to play in France with Bordeaux before spells with Manchester City, Chelsea and West Ham.

In the two main knockout competitions it was a great year for the underdogs. Wimbledon defied all odds to edge Liverpool in a dramatic FA Cup final while Luton beat Arsenal in a truly breathtaking finale to the Littlewoods Cup.

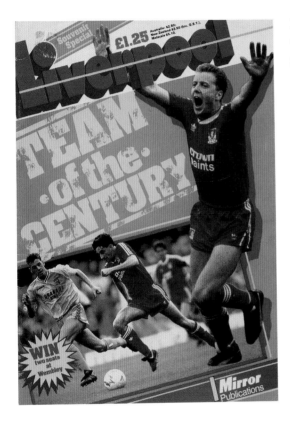

Above: The souvenir magazine front cover said it all ...

It was a different story in the league however where Kenny Dalglish's side resumed normal service, taking the title a full nine points clear of Manchester United. Liverpool's imperious consistency included a 29-game unbeaten run – equalling that of the great Leeds 1973–74 side – and on Sunday 20 March they had a chance to claim the record outright. Only the small matter of a home Merseyside derby stood in their way.

There was a huge amount riding on the game. Liverpool had not forgotten reigning champions Everton's utter domination of the previous season while Everton already knew their title was heading across Stanley Park. Denying Dalglish the record would at least give the Toffees some bragging rights once post-match banter got lively.

The footballing gods have ways of stage-managing games like this and they didn't disappoint. Everton got a 14th-minute lead and defended it desperately, doggedly, to the final whistle. The scorer? Step forward Wayne Clarke whose big brother Allan was the classy striker in that 1973–4 Leeds side. As he watched from the stands, Allan must surely have struggled to hide a smug grin.

Elsewhere there was a nightmare for Chelsea as they succumbed to relegation in the second year of the new play-off system. Up against a good Middlesborough side they lost 1-0 in the second leg at Stamford Bridge, a result that sparked a night of bloody violence. Fans on both sides were beaten up, ambulancemen were stoned and 102 arrests were made. It was hardly an encouraging omen ahead of the European Championships.

Indeed, that 1988 competition was a debacle for English football. England failed to win a single point, losing 1-0 to Jack Charlton's Republic of Ireland side, 3-1 to the USSR and 3-1 to a Dutch side which, inspired by the magnificent Marco Van Basten, went on to beat the Soviets 2-0 in the final.

Below right: Mark Stein hugs his brother, Brian, who scored two of Luton's goals.

Below: How the Luton News *celebrated.*

Far worse for England, though, was the shameful performance of their fans. Riots after the Holland game, and again the following night in Frankfurt, saw more than 200 arrested and a political backlash at home. As Downing Street held an emergency summit on soccer hooliganism, the FA moved quickly, withdrawing their request to UEFA for readmission to European club competitions.

Match of the Season
Luton Town 3 Arsenal 2

Every fan knows the feeling.

It's a vital game, your team is dead and buried, the wake is already looking messy and days of mourning lie ahead. And then, from nowhere, the tiniest sliver of hope appears.

So it was for Luton fans as they gloomily watched Nigel Winterburn preparing to fire home the penalty that would put Arsenal 3-1 up with ten minutes left. Luton had taken a 1-0 lead only to be outplayed and overpowered in the second half. Hatters' keeper Andy Dibble was their last chance.

It was a brilliant save. Luton's tired players suddenly saw the faintest glimpse of extra time while Arsenal's, inevitably, were still mentally popping champagne corks. When the hesitant Gus Caesar miskicked a clearance in front of goal, and Danny Wilson pounced to equalise with seven minutes to go, the momentum was with the underdogs.

Even so, there were just 14 seconds left when Ashley Grimes deceived the Arsenal defence by crossing from the right with the outside of his left foot. The ball was met by Brian Stein who drove it – and himself – into Wembley history, giving Luton fans their first major trophy in 98 years and a celebration worthy of waking the dead.

Branding Football

The season saw the start of Barclays Bank's £4.5 million, three-year sponsorship of the League, a move that football officials hoped would give some much-needed stability and restore credibility to the notion of big-ticket sponsorship. The previous season's deal had turned sour when Eddy Shah's *Today* newspaper pulled out just 12 months into the contract.

Looking at the ever-spiralling value of sports sponsorship today, it's hard to see that either Barclays or the League were taking any kind of risk. Yet in 1987, English football remained mired in a culture of hooliganism. League president, Philip Carter, made clear the deal could be threatened by terrace violence while the bank's chairman, John Quinton, revealed a specific get-out clause, pointing out that Barclays did not want its name linked to anything which 'led to blood running in the streets.'

In fact, Barclays stayed on board despite the disgraceful scenes at Chelsea and across Europe. Although it was outbid by Carling following the formation of the Premier League in 1992–93, it regained rights, first as the 2001 Barclaycard Premiership then from 2004 as the Barclays Premiership and from 2007 as the Barclays Premier League.

Right: Branding from a bygone age on this cheque made out to Spurs player Vivian Woodford in 1929.

JOHN BARNES 63

Player of the Year
John Barnes, Liverpool

In the mid-eighties John Barnes' outstanding performances for Watford – including 65 goals in 233 appearances – sent out a clear 'buy me' signal to big-name clubs. Ahead of the 1987–8 season new Hornets manager Dave Bassett realised his star winger could not be persuaded to stay and so sought to maximise value by giving Manchester United first dibs on a transfer offer.

However Alex Ferguson turned Bassett down. He had just signed Jesper Olsen to a long-term contract and believed United's left-wing requirements were fully covered. In a later interview Ferguson admitted that the decision ranked among his greatest regrets.

Jamaican-born Barnes joined Liverpool from Watford for £900,000 at the start of the season – the first high-profile black player to play for the Reds at a time when racism remained prevalent on the terraces. Together with fellow newbies Peter Beardsley and Ray Houghton he helped create thrilling and effective attacking options and bagged 15 of Liverpool's 87 league goals in his first season – second only to the prolific John Aldridge.

Above: The formidable John Barnes in full flight on a trading card.

Left: Jamaican-born Barnes played 79 times for England, but had also been approached by Scotland.

1988-89

With ten minutes to go before kick-off hundreds of Liverpool fans were still milling around outside Hillsborough's Leppings Lane turnstiles. Fearing they would miss the start of the all-ticket FA Cup semi-final against Nottingham Forest they pressed forward with tragic consequences.

Above: Ian Rush beats Neville Southall at Wembley.

Opposite bottom: Front cover of the Anfield Review *prior to Liverpool's clash with Arsenal.*

Police ordered a gate to be opened, fans poured inside, those ahead become trapped as the crush intensified. At 3.06 a policeman rushed on to the pitch to stop the game. Ninety-six people would never return home.

That terrible day, 15 April 1989, continues to cast a long shadow more than 25 years on. The grief among friends and relatives of those lost has never diminished –not least because their battle to unearth the truth seems unending. As this book goes to press new inquests, inquiries and, perhaps, trials lie ahead. All that can be done here is to acknowledge the strength and determination of the families affected and hope they can find some justice and peace.

So, how to sum up triviality alongside tragedy; mere football against human life? There was the question of whether the competition should be abandoned altogether or the trophy presented to Liverpool. Neither was felt appropriate. In the end it was the city and particularly the players – all of whom were outstanding in the respect they showed the dead – that settled it. The FA Cup would go on. And in an impossibly difficult replay for both sides at Old Trafford Liverpool emerged 3-1 winners to play, of all teams, Everton in the final.

Winning at Wembley became the obsession of both players and fans. Victory would be the club's tribute to Hillsborough victims in a way no memorial service could hope to match. In the end Liverpool managed it but only after one of the most exciting finals of the century; Aldridge's early goal, McCall's last-minute equaliser, Rush four minutes into extra-time, McCall's second and finally Rush's exquisite headed flick from Barnes' cross to seal a 3-2 victory. It meant Liverpool were hunting their second double in four years as they closed the gap on league leaders Arsenal. At the end of February they had been 19 points behind yet at the denouement of a season extended by Hillsborough's aftermath they sat three points clear of the Gunners. No title had been pursued with such zeal. Or lost so dramatically.

Right: Arsenal won the league but the squad's record release didn't help their FA Cup campaign.

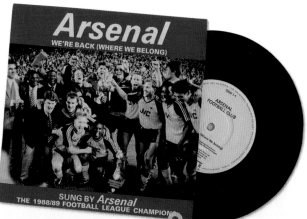

Match of the Season
Liverpool 0 Arsenal 2

So close was the margin between these two sides – both in points and goal difference – that a single mistake, flash of brilliance or lucky bounce might decide the championship. Liverpool could afford to lose but only by a single goal; Arsenal had no choice but to press for a two-goal victory.

All the omens were in the Reds' favour. They were unbeaten since January while Arsenal had not won at Anfield in almost 15 years. But fixture congestion caused by the Hillsborough tragedy had demanded much from the Liverpool players both physically and mentally. They were conscious of their three-point cushion and inevitably played to defend it rather than push for a win. George Graham however had

come to attack, reverting to the sweeper system that allowed full-backs Lee Dixon and Nigel Winterburn to press forward.

Even so it was not until the 52nd minute that Alan Smith headed in Winterburn's free kick and the visitors declared game on. With every passing moment tension was ratcheted up (the last time a title had been won on the final day was in 1952) and fans of both sides sensed history in the making. As the clock ticked into injury time it seemed Liverpool would prevail. Then Arsenal keeper John Lukic bowled the ball out, it fell to Smith and his long, hopeful pass dropped perfectly for 21-year-old midfielder Michael Thomas. Thomas tried to lift the ball over Steve Nicol's head but instead the ball bobbled between them and suddenly Thomas was through on goal. His strike beat Grobbelaar on the right. The title belonged to Arsenal.

While it was hard not to feel sympathy for Liverpool the Gunners won both the game and the championship on merit. Years on, Michael Thomas still couldn't believe it. He once admitted that every time he sees a replay he wonders whether his shot is going in.

Des to the Rescue

Cometh the hour, cometh the man. As *Match of the Day* faced the dreadful reality that, for the first time since its inception it could no longer cover league football, a morale booster was desperately needed. Des Lynam was it.

Lynam came to the programme at a time when TV sport executives were throwing toys out of prams faster than Lineker in the six-yard box. In May 1988, satellite arrivistes British Sky Broadcasting had offered the Football League a juicy £9 million per season over ten years – blowing the joint BBC-ITV bid out of the water. It looked a closed deal ... until Greg Dyke, then chairman of ITV Sport, dumped the BBC and negotiated directly with the League to win a four-year £11 million-per-season contract. This left *Match of the Day* with only the FA Cup and England internationals.

Lynam now had the tricky job both of re-invigorating cup coverage and filling the very large boots of Jimmy Hill, who had just ended his record 15-year stint as main presenter. The new boy's great advantage was a very different, languid, presenting style and a conversational approach to punditry. He was a proven sports broadcaster, having already fronted *Grandstand* and major events such as Wimbledon, the Olympic Games and the Grand National. He was also, TV critics pointed out, useful eye candy in the scramble for women viewers.

With Des in the hot seat *MotD* dusted itself down and relaunched, this time as *Match of the Day – the Road to Wembley*.

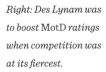

Right: Des Lynam was to boost MotD *ratings when competition was at its fiercest.*

Right: MotD merchandise came to include a board game where you could spend fortunes just like a football manager.

Below: Nicol beats Peter Beardsley to the ball while playing for Scotland against England at Wembley.

Player of the Year
Steve Nicol, Liverpool

Signed by Bob Paisley from Ayr United for £300,000 in 1981, Steve Nicol is regarded as one of the most versatile players English football has ever seen. As adept at right-back as he was on the left wing – or even centre-half – his was a rare quality that would prove crucially important for the Reds during the 1988–9 season.

With Alan Hansen hospitalized for the majority of the campaign (a dislocated left knee) Nicol thrived in a successful spell at centre-back alongside Gary Ablett. However that wasn't his only deployment. Kenny Dalglish used him in no fewer than six different positions during the campaign, giving 'Chico' a chance to showcase his skill and technical prowess going forward.

In total he played 468 matches for the Reds, scoring 46 goals, before leaving in 1995 to take up a player-manager role with Notts County.

The legacy of Hillsborough would haunt a generation of Liverpool FC players, but if any rivals thought it might affect their hunger and professionalism on the pitch then events at Anfield on 12 September 1989 quickly snuffed out that particular notion.

Above: Liverpool stalwart John Aldridge made a surprise move from Merseyside to Spain in a £1 million transfer deal.

Liverpool were simply, ruthlessly, brilliant – scoring nine times against Crystal Palace to post both their club record First Division win and make Football League history as the first team in which eight players scored in a single match. Among the eight was Kop favourite John Aldridge, due to complete a surprise £1 million transfer to Spanish side Real Sociedad the following day.

Aldridge was bustled off the subs bench to take a penalty, jogged straight to the spot as an adoring Anfield rose in tribute, and thumped home the sixth goal. It was the 63rd of his two-year, 104-game career at Liverpool and few football lovers begrudged him his showboating moment in front of terraces where he'd once stood as a supporter. For Crystal Palace it was a humiliating experience. But revenge was not far away.

Although Liverpool were favourites for the title they were pushed hard. At the end of November they were level with Arsenal, Aston Villa and Chelsea on 27 points and Graham Taylor's classy Villa side doggedly remained in touch throughout the season, even briefly going top in mid-March. It was not until the end of April, and successive wins over Chelsea and QPR, that Liverpool finally achieved the points cushion they needed for their 18th championship.

Cup giant-killers of the season were Oldham Athletic whose plastic pitch at Boundary Park helped confound some lofty visitors. In fairness the Division Two club were also an outstanding unit and their 32-match unbeaten run at home included League Cup victories over Arsenal and

Southampton and a 6-0 semi-final first leg pasting of West Ham United. Alas the Wembley turf proved a surface too far for the Latics and a Nigel Gemson goal gave Nottingham Forest a fourth League Cup final win.

It was a similar story in the FA Cup where Oldham beat Everton 2-1 (after two replays) in the fifth round, dismissed Villa 3-0 in the sixth and then drew 3-3 at Old Trafford after extra time in the semis. Although they lost the replay to Manchester United 2-1, the result was mired in controversy after the referee ruled an early Oldham 'goal' hadn't crossed the line.

Below: Crystal Palace's John Salako enjoys his team's FA Cup victory.

Match of the Season
FA Cup Semi-Final
Crystal Palace 4 Liverpool 3

With just 14 minutes on the clock in this FA Cup semi-final at Villa Park it felt like Groundhog Day for a Palace side still smarting from that 9-0 Anfield drubbing. Ian Rush's opener from a typically accurate Steve McMahon pass put the Reds in cruise control and by half-time the tie looked over. But Palace manager Steve Coppell – who as a player became one of the great Manchester United wingers – had other ideas. He sent his team back out breathing fire.

Just 16 seconds after the break Mark Bright volleyed an equaliser and the balance of the match subtly shifted. Liverpool had been forced to substitute Rush during the first half with a bruised rib while Gary Gillespie had not re-emerged from the tunnel after suffering a groin strain. These were key players but this was a Liverpool side chasing the double. They still had quality aplenty.

In the 70th minute Gary O'Reilly put the Glaziers ahead – his first goal of the season – to give Palace a shot of self-belief. Yet when McMahon equalised 11 minutes later, and Barnes converted a penalty awarded for a senseless trip on Staunton, it seemed it was still not enough. Only when Andy Gray headed an equaliser two minutes from time did Palace fans dare to start wondering and after Alan Pardew put them ahead in extra time Wembley dreams finally became reality. Palace, fired by a partially fit Ian Wright, came within seven minutes of winning that final but Mark Hughes pulled it back to 3-3 in extra time and United won the replay by a single goal.

MotD Memories: Aftermath of Hillsborough

Sue Johnston – who played Sheila Grant in the Channel 4 soap *Brookside* – was due to attend the Hillsborough semi-final as guest of the Liverpool players' wives. But she had an editing deadline and instead watched, horrified, at home as the death toll mounted.

'I can remember worrying about my cousin because he was there and some of the kids at Brookie were there,' she said. 'You were just caught like rabbits in headlights, watching this story unfold. Just dreadful. I remember my cousin ringing eventually. They were all queuing outside people's houses – there were no mobile phones – they were stopping and asking to use people's home phones.

'On the Sunday we walked through the streets [of Liverpool] to the cathedral; it was just awful, quiet, everyone walking towards the cathedral, nobody speaking, this terrible atmosphere of sadness and disbelief ... there were people throwing in scarves – Everton as well as Liverpool – that service was just extraordinary.

Below: The Anfield Review's *tribute to the Hillsborough victims.*

Below top: John Barnes storming down the wing during Liverpool's FA Cup match with Palace.

Below bottom: Barnes in action for England against Scotland at Wembley.

'We took flowers down to the pitch. [Someone said] relatives of the deceased are here and they would love to meet you. One woman thought I was Sheila Grant and said: "You know what it's like, Sheila. You've lost a son." I felt totally inadequate but also, well, if she believes that, who am I to say? It was heartbreaking. Heartbreaking.

'The Cup final? No one really wanted to play it but it did seem right that it was Everton and Liverpool and Gerry Marsden would go out and sing 'You'll Never Walk Alone' and the Everton fans would sing it for the first and last time. They were spectacular. There is rivalry between Liverpool and Everton but deep down there is an affinity through the city and through Hillsborough and it had a colossal effect on everyone – the families obviously – but also on the club moving forward.'

Player of the Year
John Barnes, Liverpool

Nobody was keener to abolish the crushing memory of 26 May 1989 than John Barnes. He blamed himself for giving the ball away seconds before the Gunners' last-gasp title-winning goal, admitting he should have trotted off to the corner flag for some time-wasting rather than attempt a mazy run into the penalty area.

The following season Barnes set off on his road to personal redemption with the kind of ruthless efficiency fans had come to expect

from their talismanic winger. Although Liverpool struggled to find early season form he banged in 12 goals in 20 games to keep them in the hunt. And when the Anfield machine was finally cranked up after Christmas he also shifted up a gear, eventually hitting 28 goals in all competitions. That was two more than Ian Rush and only two fewer than Gary Lineker.

Barnes left Liverpool for Newcastle in 1997 as an all-time Kop idol. He'd made 407 appearances for the club, scored 108 goals and, just as importantly, left the fans with wonderful memories of a brave, attacking brand of football.

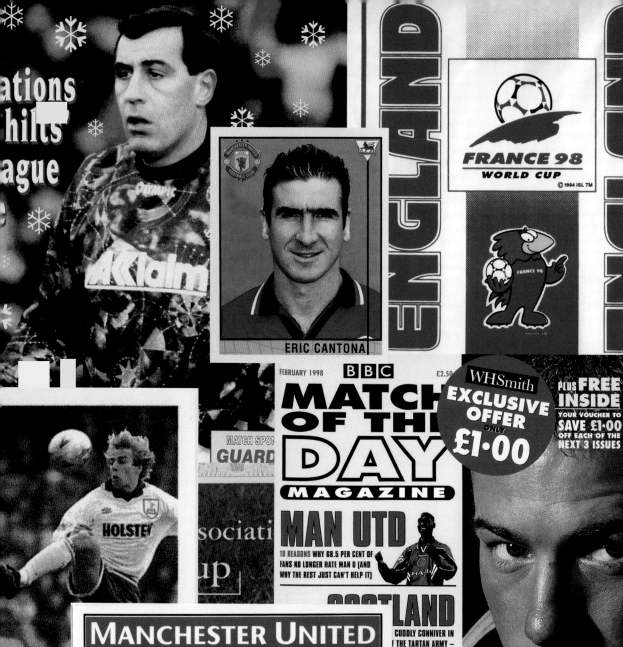

ations
hits
gue

A!Claim
Olympic

ENGLAND

FRANCE 98
WORLD CUP
© 1994 ISL TM

FRANCE 98

ENGLAND

ERIC CANTONA

HOLSTE

JURGEN
Totten

MATCH SPON
GUARD

sociati
up

FEBRUARY 1998 · BBC · £2.50

MATCH
OF THE
DAY
MAGAZINE

MAN UTD
10 REASONS WHY 68.5 PER CENT OF
FANS NO LONGER HATE MAN U (AND
WHY THE REST JUST CAN'T HELP IT)

SHARP

SCOTLAND
CUDDLY CONNIVER IN
OF THE TARTAN ARMY –
IN LOVE WITH KYLIE?

KE
OMEDIAN

SPECIAL
OUR FOCUS ON THE
MENTS THAT MADE
LAST MONTH'S
HEADLINES

WHSmith
EXCLUSIVE
OFFER
ONLY
£1·00

PLUS FREE
INSIDE
YOUR VOUCHER TO
SAVE £1·00
OFF EACH OF THE
NEXT 3 ISSUES

MANCHESTER UNITED
OFFICIAL YEARBOOK 1999
CELEBRATE THE UNIQUE TREBLE-WINNING 1998-99 SEASON

MANCHESTER
UNITED

JRNSTILE

OCK
44
NCHESTE

£17.00

Banking on
SHEARER
The hopes of a nation and millions of
pounds have been invested in him.
Is it all too much for one man to
bear? England's captain talks
exclusively to MOTD

9 771364 452019

BECKHAM
Will he grow to

1990s

Who could forget it: Pavarotti singing 'Nessun Dorma', David Platt's winner in the dying seconds against Belgium, Gazza's desperate tears and the anguish of that penalty shootout? This was the closest England ever came to winning the World Cup on foreign soil. Sadly, it was not to be.

Even though they failed, Bobby Robson's creative team restored the feel-good factor to our national game. For purists, though, this was one of FIFA's most uninspiring tournaments. The flair which had characterised Mexico four years earlier was sorely lacking, particularly in an Argentinian team which somehow stuttered to the final with just two victories in open play. Cameroon, the first African team to reach the quarter-finals, were a notable exception and their veteran striker Roger Milla became a world star with four goals and a hugely entertaining celebration dance routine.

Below: A ticket for England's quarter-final match with Cameroon at the Stadio San Paolo.

England's start was typically underwhelming, although their 1-1 draw against Jack Charlton's Republic of Ireland side looked better as the admirable Irish progessed. Robson was pilloried by the UK tabloids and his switch to a sweeper system – uncharted territory for his squad – for the second game against Holland was seen as a gamble. But Mark Wright proved

a natural in the sweeper slot and England looked competitive in their 0-0 draw against the fancied Dutch. When Wright's header decided the ensuing tense encounter with Egypt he put his side through as group winners.

The second round tie against Belgium in Bologna was an over-cautious affair which, by the 119th minute, looked nailed-on for penalties. But then Paul Gascoigne, one of the tournament's truly eye-catching players, floated in a cross from the left. Platt let the ball drop over his soldier and, with immense technical skill, swivelled to despatch a sweet volley.

Platt also put his team ahead in the quarter-final against Cameroon. The Africans were easily the best opponents England had faced, the introduction of Milla at half-time producing a dangerous new threat. Kunde equalised from the penalty spot and then Ekeke snatched the lead before a Lineker penalty late on, and another in extra-time, rescued the day. These were the first penalties England had been awarded in four years; soon a whole lot more would be heading their way.

Above: There was an abundance of merchandising at Italia 90, including England wristbands.

Right: Paul Gascoigne battling against Cameroon in Naples.

The semi-final against Germany proved a classic. The Germans went ahead on the hour when Andreas Brehme's strike looped over Peter Shilton via a lucky deflection off Paul Parker, but Lineker equalised with ten minutes left to set up a nerve-shredding climax. Extra time produced one of the images of Italia '90 as Gascoigne, realising that a booking had ruled him out of the World Cup final, burst into tears. Pitchside cameras showed a grim-faced Lineker, pointing to his eyes, urging Robson to watch the player closely.

Both sides could have finished it (each were foiled by the woodwork) but in the end it was all about penalties. When Stuart Pearce missed his side's fourth, and Olaf Thon netted for the Germans, England needed to score to stay alive. 'Would you want to be Chris Waddle now, or even Stuart Pearce?' asked BBC commentator John Motson. Waddle fired high and wide. Neither he, nor any of his team-mates, would play in another World Cup.

West Germany went on to defeat Argentina in a niggly final settled by a Brehme penalty. It was scant consolation for English fans when Brehme later insisted England's 'exceptional group' would have been champions if the shoot-out had gone their way. Describing a 'horrible' final he claimed the South Americans didn't create a chance, or even a corner. 'Argentina had a terrible World Cup but a lot of luck,' he added. 'Would England have beaten them? Definitely, 100 per cent.'

Right: 'Would you want to be Chris Waddle now?'

Opposite: The German players celebrate after defeating Argentina in the final.

It was the story no-one in football had seen coming. Least of all the Liverpool players who on Friday 22 February 1991 reported for training to be informed by Kenny Dalglish that he'd quit as manager. After 14 successful seasons at the club, King Kenny's shock abdication would leave the red half of the city gripped by conspiracy theories.

Below: Arsenal and Manchester United both lost league points after their players brawled on the pitch at Old Trafford.

Opposite top: Teenager Lee Sharpe scored a hat-trick against Arsenal at Highbury.

'We were just sat in the dressing room in silence,' Ian Rush recalled later, 'and [assistant coach] Ronnie Moran said, "OK let's go training now", and we all got on the coach. All the lads were talking about it on the way and no one had a clue it was coming or why he'd done it.'

The previous day Liverpool's board had spent ten hours trying to persuade Dalglish to change his mind. It made no difference. The final straw was unclear – in fact no one could even be sure there was a final straw particularly since the club sat top of the table. True, Everton had just fought back to 4-4 in an epic Merseyside fifth-round FA Cup replay but that was hardly a 'plank-walker'. At a press conference later Dalglish insisted he'd not made a sudden decision; the pressure he'd placed on himself was just no longer bearable.

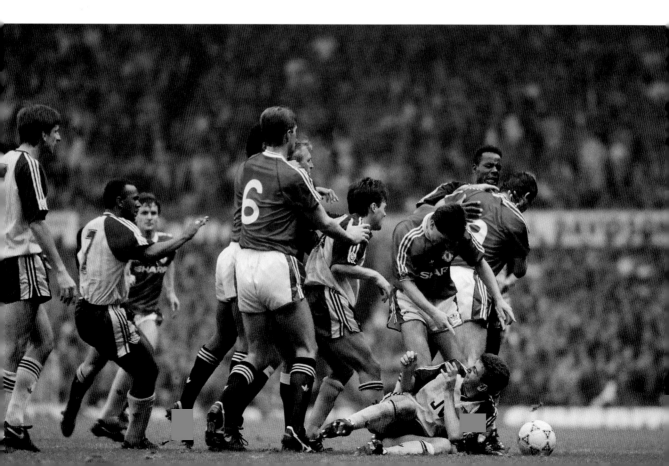

 Match of the Season
Arsenal 2 Man United 6

No one could have predicted this one. Almost four months into the season Arsenal had conceded just two goals at home and hadn't lost a game. For their part United were having an indifferent league campaign but in 19-year-old Lee Sharpe possessed that most dangerous of managerial weapons – a teenager playing without fear.

Indeed, it was Sharpe who scored the goal of the game, darting infield from the left to place a 25-yard curler over the flailing David Seaman. That put United 3-0 up at half-time and although Alan Smith's two goals got the Gunners back in contention their push for an equaliser inevitably opened defensive gaps which the speedy Sharpe ruthlessly exploited on the break. He duly netted two more for his hat-trick while Danny Wallace added a sixth

to inflict Arsenal's heaviest home defeat in 70 years. It says much for the Gunners' mental attitude that they recovered to beat Liverpool 3-0 at Highbury the following weekend to keep title ambitions firmly on track. United went on to lose the Rumbelows Cup final to Sheffield Wednesday but had the consolation of beating Barcelona to take the Cup Winners' Cup – a particularly sweet moment for Camp Nou reject Mark Hughes.

Above: Souvenir badge for Arsenal's championship win.

Among his team the effect was predictable. Some 28 hours after that dressing-room bombshell they travelled to Luton and lost 3-1. Their title challenge was foundering and pundits began asking whether Dalglish's departure meant the end of Liverpool's domination. The answer is now clear although it would be facile to blame two decades of domestic decline on one man's decision.

For Liverpool's main rivals, Arsenal, the sight of Fortress Anfield crumbling was akin to a points handout. On 3 March the Gunners gleefully accepted all three in front of a stunned Kop, their momentum a stark contrast to their hosts' stuttering title defence. Runaway leaders before Christmas, Liverpool now looked like also-rans. Yet for Arsenal the reverse was true. They had been docked two points in November over their players' part in a mass brawl at Old Trafford and then suffered the indignity of a 6-2 Rumbelows Cup defeat to Manchester United at Highbury. Now, their season was coming up lollipops. They deservedly cruised to a tenth title seven points clear of Liverpool.

Squaring Things With Jimmy – Des Lynam's Heart-to-Heart

At the end of the eighties, BBC Sport bosses decided to freshen-up flagship programmes by re-shuffling presenters. Des Lynam was asked to leave *Grandstand* to front *Match of the Day* and *Sportsnight*, with Tony Gubba taking his old job. The move meant more of a punditry role for *MotD*'s long-serving anchorman, Jimmy Hill.

At first, Des was worried about his colleague's reaction. But the pair had a heart-to-heart chat and it was clear there were no recriminations.

'I thought I'd better OK this with Jimmy,' Des recalled, 'because Jimmy was an old friend. I didn't want to upset the guy and I would have to work with him. He said: "I'm OK with it. I'd rather you did it than somebody I don't like." So I did it and Jimmy became the leading pundit and we worked for years like that very successfully and happily.

'In fact, doing [the programme] with him and Terry Venables were some of the highlights of the shows because they argued all the time. It wasn't stage-managed – they actually did see the opposite point of view about everything. But they were great friends, of course.'

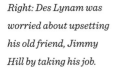
Right: Des Lynam was worried about upsetting his old friend, Jimmy Hill by taking his job.

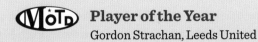

Player of the Year
Gordon Strachan, Leeds United

With his devilish body swerve, nimble footwork and low centre of gravity, Gordon Strachan's wing wizardry during the 1990–91 season cemented his position in the Scottish wide-men hall of fame.

In 1989 he was signed by then Second Division Leeds for £300,000 from Manchester United after being convinced to drop down a league by Howard Wilkinson. Strachan duly captained the Elland Road outfit to the title and a place in the top flight.

The following season he showed his most consistent, match-winning form. Instead of struggling, as many had predicted, Leeds enjoyed a terrific return season in which Strachan was the catalyst. The Whites finished fourth and reached the semi-finals of the League Cup with Strachan contributing seven goals and many assists.

A natural leader on and off the pitch, few were surprised to see him enjoy a generally successful career after his playing days. He managed Coventry, Southampton, Celtic and Middlesborough before his current role – manager of the Scottish national team.

Above left: Strachan shows off his Player of the Year trophy.

Left: Gordon Strachan was never anything less than passionate on the pitch.

It had been 18 long years since Leeds United took the First Division championship but Howard Wilkinson's flair-packed side began the season with high hopes. In just four years Wilkinson had transformed Leeds from Second Division strugglers into a force comparable with the great Don Revie sides.

Above: Souvenir edition of the Yorkshire Evening Post *showing champagne spraying across the changing room.*

In defenders such as Chris Whyte and Tony Dorigo, a magnificent midfield comprising Gary McAllister, David Batty, Gary Speed and, particularly, captain Gordon Strachan, plus a rampant striker in Lee Chapman, Leeds had a squad that commanded respect. When striker Eric Cantona rejected an extended trial at fellow Yorkshire title contenders Sheffield Wednesday in January 1991 Wilkinson moved fast, signing him for £900,000 from Auxerre. It was a canny bit of business.

Cantona scored just three times in his 15 appearances for Leeds during the remainder of the season, often as substitute, but he delivered a huge bang for Wilkinson's buck. His partnership with Chapman was wonderfully symbiotic with the Frenchman providing a string of crucial assists. The sight of him warming up brought an inevitable response from the Elland Road terraces – 'Ooh... Ah ... Can-toh-nah' – while opposition defenders waited nervously for the unpredictable.

For all Leeds' quality and firepower they were up against a Manchester United side which seemed nailed on for the last-ever First Division championship. In mid-April Alex Ferguson's side were two points ahead of their rivals with a game in hand. But the thrilling prospect of a first title in 25 years ratcheted up the pressure with every passing game. The Red Devils faltered, losing at home to Forest and bottom side West Ham before swallowing the bitterest pill of all – a 2-0 defeat to Liverpool at Anfield. They took just four points from their last five games; Leeds took 13.

Some suggested Leeds were just handed the title because Manchester United lost it. Nonsense, of course, as Ferguson sportingly admitted in his 1999 autobiography, citing Wilkinson's 'excellent campaign' and his team's ability to hold their nerve. Wilkinson, by the way, remains the last English manager to win a top flight English championship.

Ferguson's players got some consolation from winning the League Cup 1-0 against Nottingham Forest – the last appearance by Brian Clough as manager in a major domestic final – while Liverpool took the FA Cup with a 2-0 victory over Sunderland. Reds' manager Graeme Souness had been urged by doctors to steer clear of Wembley given that he'd just had heart surgery. That was never going to happen.

Below right: Alan Shearer scored the second of Southampton's goals at Old Trafford.

 Match of the Season
Manchester United 2
Southampton 2
(3-4 on pens)

This was one for the trivia nerds as it was the first time a Division One side had been knocked out of the FA Cup on penalties (FA Cup shoot-outs had just been introduced in the main competition to cut fixture congestion). In fact, United were thankful merely to have the chance of spot kicks after going two down within 21 minutes to goals by Stuart Gray and Alan Shearer. Flying Ukrainian winger Andrei Kanchelskis pulled one back just before half-time but it was left to Brian McClair to slot home a minute into added-on time to give United another chance.

Indeed, when Bryan Robson's header seemed to have crossed the goal-line in extra-time Southampton looked destined to lose this fourth-round tie. But this was an era when the Goal Decision System was not even a twinkle in some IT nerd's eye. Robson's appeals were waved away and the tie moved to sudden death. Two United players – Neil Webb and Ryan Giggs – both missed their penalties while Southampton stuck away their first four without even troubling their usual pen-man Matthew Le Tissier. It was the right result for a Saints side that never looked fazed by the occasion.

The Premier League Signs for *MotD*

On 20 February 1991 the break-up of the 104-year-old Football League was confirmed by the FA Council. Starting in August, the new Premier League would comprise 22 clubs, reduced through relegation to 20 by the end of the 1994–95 season.

At first the smart money was on ITV buying up rights. But the BBC and BSkyB had influence and support within the new set-up and in May the clubs' chairmen backed their joint counter-bid. The five-year deal awarded Sunday and Monday live matches to the satellite broadcaster with a Saturday night highlights package for the BBC. *Match of the Day* was back where it belonged – crucially with league action. ITV was left with the remaining Football League (formerly Divisions 2 to 4) and the League Cup.

Opposite top: Lineker in England colours against Finland in Helsinki in 1992. England won 2-1.

Below: The MotD *team with the Carling Premiership trophy. Carling sponsored the league from 1993 to 2001.*

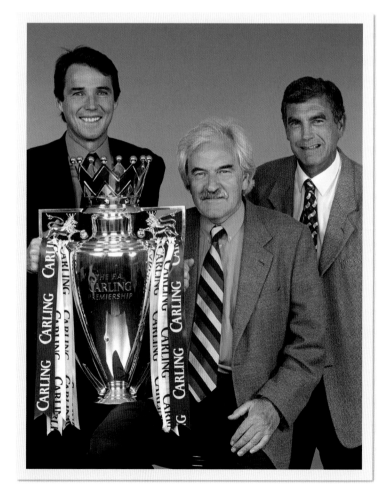

The new-look *MotD* retained the classic formula of the eighties – three main matches – although viewers could now watch goals from every other game. Fronted by Des Lynam, there were debuts for new pundits Trevor Brooking and Alan Hansen, whose contrasting styles proved surprisingly effective. West Ham favourite Brooking, generally acknowledged as one of football's nice guys, would be reluctant to criticize players but Hansen balanced this with his no-nonsense, sometimes excoriating analysis – '... terrrrrrrible defendin' became an early catchphrase. Players could hardly dispute the Liverpool legend's qualifications. His CV read: Been there, done that, won that.

 Player of the Year

Gary Lineker, Tottenham Hotspur

After turning down advances from Alex Ferguson to partner his old Barcelona team-mate Mark Hughes at Manchester United, Gary Lineker returned to English football with Tottenham Hotspur in 1989.

It was as if he'd never been away. He finished as Division One top scorer, helping Spurs to a third-place finish, and during his three years at White Hart Lane bagged 67 goals in 105 league games – a strike rate which speaks for itself.

However, his final season in England coincided with Spurs' disappointing 1991–92 campaign. The north London club could manage only 15th place despite vintage Linker performances illustrating the intelligent movement and ruthlessness that had made him England's most important attacker during the mid-eighties and early nineties. Along with his Player of the Year accolade he was awarded an OBE in the New Year's Honours.

He ended a magnificent career with an injury-prone spell at Japan's Nagoya Grampus Eight, retiring in 1994. Remembered as a gentleman both on and off the pitch, he hung up his boots having never received a yellow card in an 18-year professional career.

Forest's Steve Hodge challenges Lineker during the 1991 FA Cup final.

The birth of English football's brave new world – aka the FA Premier League – coincided with a resurgent Manchester United. Having come so close in 1991–2 they were in no mood to fluff their lines again and with a couple of games left they stood four points clear of Aston Villa, the only challenger still standing.

Above: Eric Cantona holds off Sheffield United's Brian Gale at Old Trafford.

Villa played first on Sunday 2 May knowing they had to beat relegation-threatened Oldham at home to keep their hopes alive. United were not due to play their home tie against Blackburn until the following day and the squad was ordered by Alex Ferguson not to watch the game on TV. Few took any notice and when the Latics won 1-0 players converged on Steve Bruce's house for an impromptu celebration.

Bruce rang his boss to confess that a 'few lads' had turned up. Ferguson, who had heard the news while playing golf, asked: 'OK. How many?' Bruce replied: 'Well, it's more than a few – there's about twenty-five of them round here.' Sore heads there may have been the following day but the players knew it was no time for queasiness. The crowd at Old Trafford to watch the first Premier League trophy being presented included Sir Matt Busby – the last United manager to win a top-flight title back in 1967 – along with the Holy Trinity themselves, Law, Best and Charlton.

It had taken Ferguson almost seven years to win the title. But he now had a side worthy of Sir Matt's legacy. The likes of Schmeichel, Irwin, Bruce, Sharpe, Pallister, Ince, McClair, Hughes, some Welsh kid called Ryan Giggs and the warhorse Bryan Robson: these players were the backbone of United's fourth great squad. Then there was the new kid on the block, striker Eric Cantona, signed from Leeds in November. On the big day they didn't let Old Trafford down, beating Blackburn 3-1 to trigger rapturous celebrations.

For Arsenal it had been a mediocre league season – tenth spot and 28 points off the pace. But they won both cup finals, each against Sheffield Wednesday and each by a 2-1 scoreline. Meanwhile, at the bottom Crystal Palace fans felt seriously miffed to be relegated with 49 points (albeit that

the Premier League initially comprised 22 teams). With a week left Palace were eight points clear only for Oldham to win three on the bounce. Forest finished bottom, marking a sad end to the career of Brian Clough, the manager who gave them so much.

Match of the Season
**Manchester United 2
Sheffield Wednesday 1**

Every season has its tipping point – a particular game trumpeted as the day the title was *really* won. Some such claims are more spurious than others but in the case of Man Utd v Sheffield Wednesday on 10 April there can be few arguments. And, remember, this was way before Fergie time became a terraces' cliché.

United went into the game under huge pressure – hopes of an elusive title tantalizingly within their grasp yet a formidable Aston Villa still in the chase. And the nervousness showed in their passing game even though Wednesday were minus their two most potent players, David Hirst and Paul Warhurst. When the Owls took the lead with a second-half penalty, and with time running out, Old Trafford feared their challenge was collapsing for a second season running. Then, like some character from Roy of the Rovers, a hero answered the call.

First, stand-in skipper Steve Bruce headed an 85th minute equaliser from an Irwin corner. Then in the 96th minute – yes, 96, count 'em – he nodded home a second to give United a crucial three points. Assistant coach Brian Kidd's knee slide on to the pitch said it all and United never looked back.

Above: Premier League arm patches appeared on the sleeves of players' shirts.

Right: United skipper Steve Bruce headed both goals against Wednesday.

Gubba the Dubber

The late Tony Gubba was a BBC football commentator for 40 seasons, the third longest-serving on British television, and an occasional *MotD* presenter. However for much of his career he handled second-string matches with Messrs Motson and Davies taking the marque fixtures.

His former *MotD* colleague, now ITV lead commentator, Clive Tyldesley recalls how one Saturday evening task was to overdub commentary onto videotape highlights biked in from those less glamorous games. No ground commentator would have been assigned to them but Tony and Clive still had to make the soundtrack sing – especially for Goal of the Month candidates.

'When I arrived at the BBC in 1992 John and Barry were fully established as number one and two,' said Clive. 'Tony was the number 3 commentator and I was the young upstart coming to maybe challenge for that role.

Below: The much admired Tony Gubba was an expert at predicting events on the pitch, especially after they had happened.

'Tony was lovely to me from the beginning and we became close friends. He also became Gubba The Dubber because whenever there were goals that had been filmed but not commented on it would be either Tony or I who would be called in to give them 15 seconds of authenticity.

'Tony got quite cheeky with these commentaries – almost as if he knew what was going to happen. "He might just try it from here, you never know" he'd say before somebody lashed one in from 30 yards. Tony was the wisest man after the cvent in British television … and we loved him for it.'

Opposite top: Waddle had an immediate impact on arriving at Wednesday.

Opposite bottom: Waddle won Player of the Year at the age of 32 and was still playing football twenty years later.

Player of the Year

Chris Waddle, Tottenham Hotspur

Before tormenting Division One defences with his inimitable body swerve and inventive approach play Chris Waddle worked at a sausage and meat-pie factory, playing for non-League Tow Law Town between shifts.

He was signed by Newcastle United for £1000 in 1980 and alongside Peter Beardsley and Kevin Keegan was instrumental in the Magpies' 1984 promotion from the Second Division. A successful spell at Tottenham followed but it was at Marseilles and Sheffield Wednesday that he really found the top of his game.

At Les Phocéens he was a key man in an exciting four-pronged attack comprising Jean-Pierre Papin, Jean Tigana and Abedi Pele, helping secure three championships in three seasons. He also appeared in the 1990 European Cup final in Bari where Marseilles were beaten on penalties by a particularly strong Red Star Belgrade team.

Waddle was brought to Wednesday by Trevor Francis in 1992 and had an immediate impact, striking a potent understanding with forward pair Mark Bright, also a new signing at Hillsborough, and David Hirst. It was his pivotal role in Wednesday's run to the FA Cup and League Cup finals, however, that won him Player of the Year, his free-kick in a semi-final derby showdown against Sheffield United a particular highlight.

Waddle retired from professional football in 1998. Despite his penalty shoot-out miss in the Italia 1990 World Cup semi-finals he is celebrated as that most cherished of talents – a thrilling and effective English winger.

MoTD 1993-94

In successfully defending their title and completing only the fourth double of the twentieth century, Manchester United gave notice that the nineties would become the greatest decade in their history. They were not yet a truly dominant force but they remained the country's outstanding side.

Above: Britain's most expensive footballer, Chris Sutton, grappling with the Steinkejer defence in Norway.

Right: A Man United scarf as worn by their legions of fans.

Opposite top: Everton's David Unsworth hails the final whistle.

Perhaps equally interesting for the neutral was the performance of United's main rivals. Blackburn had been promoted to the new Premier League only the previous season yet still eased themselves into fourth place. Now they were runners-up under the revitalized coaching of Kenny Dalglish and the vision of ambitious chairman Jack Walker. When Chris Sutton became Britain's most expensive footballer at the end of the season, signed from Norwich for £5 million to partner Alan Shearer, they looked ready to rip up some trees.

Managerial merry-go rounds provided plenty of red meat for sports editors, particularly the departure of England boss Graham Taylor at the end of another humiliating World Cup campaign. Taylor was subjected to outrageous vilification – one back page had his face transposed on to a turnip – but his international record could no longer be defended and Terry Venables took control. Meanwhile, Graeme Souness's disappointing tenure at Liverpool was ended three years into a five-year contract.

In Europe it was George Graham's Arsenal who carried the torch for English clubs. They were undisputed underdogs for the Cup Winners' Cup final in Copenhagen against a Parma side boasting the brilliant Gianfranco Zola, Colombian target man Faustino Asprilla and the Swede Tomas Brolin. Arsenal were without their suspended leading scorer Ian Wright, Jensen and Hillier were injured and David Seaman needed pain-killing injections just to warm up.

Despite this, the Gunners proved tactically superior and when a bungled bicycle kick from opposing skipper Lorenzo Minotti fell to veteran striker Alan Smith he calmly chested it down to hit a sumptuous left-foot volley in off the near post. The goal secured Graham his sixth major trophy in eight seasons at Highbury.

![MotD] Match of the Season
Everton 3 Wimbledon 2

For sheer bottom-squeaking drama there was only one candidate. On 7 May 1994 Mike Walker's Everton faced the sixth-placed Dons knowing that relegation beckoned. Confronting the drop is a nightmare for any fan but for Toffees-lovers, whose team boasted the most consecutive appearances in top-flight football, it was unthinkable.

The permutations were, naturally, complex. A win would keep Everton up unless any one of Southampton, Ipswich and Sheffield United won away. A draw would be no good unless Ipswich lost at Blackburn. Things didn't start well.

Wimbledon, whose *raison d'être* was to stick two fingers up at 'big clubs' quickly took a two-goal lead – the first a penalty following a baffling Anders Limpar handball, the second a Gary Ablett own goal which took so long to happen that some home fans grew visibly old in the process. At this point

Everton's grave had been dug and the coffin lowered. They were about to be buried.

But oh, it's a funny old game. Graham Stuart's penalty made it 1-2 at half-time then Barry Horne's 30-yard blaster – let's be kind, a rarity – brought Everton level. It would still not have been enough but then nine minutes to go Stuart's toe-poke sent the ball bobbling benignly towards goal. Hans Segers' attempted 'save' looked more like a 'lie-down' – so farcical that it was later scrutinized in a match-fixing inquiry (Segers was cleared). But the goal gave Everton their most important victory for 40 years and sent spadefuls of earth over Sheffield United.

Graham Stuart celebrates an unlikely goal with fans and pitch marshals joining in.

MotD Memories: Fashion Tips for Pundits

Arsenal legend Ian Wright, now carving out a new career as a TV and radio pundit, believes *MotD* analysts are often as controversial and captivating as the action itself.

Below: Ian Wright rarely sees eye-to-eye with commentators and analysts.

'I remember scoring a nice goal against Everton [at Highbury, August 1993] when I flicked it over [defender Matt Jackson's] head, and over Southall's head, and scored and Alan Hansen just said; "It was bad defending"', says Wright.

'I was so disappointed. I thought, when I see him I'm going to absolutely slaughter him. Bad defending from Matt Jackson? For me, that was the best goal I'd ever scored. I just watched in horror.

'As for John Motson's sheepskin. You'd think, look at the thickness in that sheepskin. It was so thick. Massive old thing, it was beautiful. That's one of the memories that will stay with me forever – Jimmy Hill looking like Robin Hood and John Motson's sheepskin.

'If I could change one thing now it would be Lawro's shirts. There must be a mate who's making them for him. If he sells one of those shirts off the back of Lawro wearing them then I'd say; "well done."

'They are the worst shirts I've seen – how many collars are on there? I'm not hearing the analysis because I'm still looking at what's going on with the collar. This is what I'd change. He's not allowed to wear those shirts on *MotD*.'

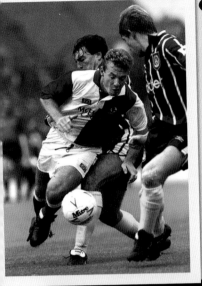

 Player of the Year
Alan Shearer, Blackburn Rovers

By far the greatest goalscorer in Premier League history, it's astonishing to think that Alan Shearer won only one major honour at club and international level – the 1995 Premier League title with Blackburn Rovers.

He began his career at Southampton as a 15-year-old apprentice and spent two years with the youth squad before making his professional debut. He then unveiled his abilities with some panache, smashing a hat-trick against Arsenal on only his second appearance.

Performances with the Saints attracted the attention of Blackburn boss Kenny Dalglish and Shearer moved to Ewood Park in the summer of 1992 for £3.3 million – rejecting Manchester United among a host of other suitors. Critics who questioned the price tag were soon put in their place as Shearer bagged a double – including a screamer – against Crystal Palace on his debut. However, his first Rovers campaign ended in disappointment when he was sidelined with a snapped cruciate ligament.

In typical fashion he bounced back, scoring 31 times in 40 matches the following season to ensure shoe-in status for Player of the Year. Of many special moments his spectacular flying volley against Southampton stands out; a mid-air twist to smash the ball home.

Shearer won his sole medal in 1995, helping Blackburn pip Manchester United to the line on a dramatic last day, and later headed back to his Geordie roots with Newcastle United. He finished his career with 260 Premier League goals, 72 more than his nearest rival Andrew Cole, and 30 from 63 international appearances.

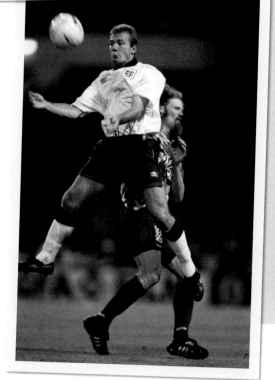

Top: Shearer takes on Man City's defence.

Bottom: Shearer outjumps USA's Alexi Lalas at Wembley.

It is a rare and precious thing for an English football stadium to be united in glee, both sets of supporters singing the same songs, chanting the same hero's name. For this to happen at Anfield, for the scoreline to be irrelevant, for the glee to be focused entirely on events 200 miles south – this was surely an unrivalled piece of sporting theatre.

Above: Blackburn Rovers souvenir pennant.

Opposite top: Cantona demonstrates his martial arts skills at Selhurst Park.

Opposite bottom: Pogs became the collectors' obsession in the mid-nineties.

All season Kenny Dalglish's Blackburn Rovers had been outstanding ambassadors for the English game. Chairman Jack Walker had shown how a small, family-friendly club could, given enough financial muscle, battle with the best of them to produce exciting and effective football. Theirs was a genuine team effort but in Alan Shearer and Chris Sutton – Rovers' SAS – they also possessed two of the Premier League's most feared strikers. Shearer hit 34 league goals, a record he still holds jointly with Andy Cole, while Sutton, in his first season at Ewood Park, contributed 15.

Even so, Blackburn went into their final match needing a win at Anfield to be sure of the championship. Emotions were running high all round, not least because any sighting of King Kenny at Anfield was never going to pass without loud approval from the Kop. Liverpool themselves were well off the pace and their fans faced a quandary. They didn't want to lose the game but neither did they want Kenny to lose the title. Especially if the beneficiaries were despised rivals Manchester United playing simultaneously at West Ham.

It was John Barnes and Jamie Redknapp who nearly spoiled everything. Their goals in response to Alan Shearer's trademark opener meant that a late winner for United at Upton Park would give them the crown. When the whistle blew at Anfield agonising seconds passed before the title's destination was confirmed. Ferguson's side had drawn 1-1. Blackburn had won by a point. The party could start.

All sides of Anfield echoed to the guttural chant of 'Dalglish', 'You'll Never Walk Alone' and the Monty Python classic 'Always Look On the Bright Side of Life'. United went on to double despair, losing the FA Cup final to Everton while Liverpool at least had the consolation of the League Cup.

Off the field grim headlines abounded: George Graham sacked over 'bung' allegations (which he always denied), three players arrested over match-fixing allegations and Eric Cantona's kung fu antics at Crystal Palace. Whatever criticisms could be made of the Premier League, dull it wasn't.

Match of the Season
Crystal Palace 1
Manchester United 1

This was certainly no classic. But in terms of terraces talking points it was gold-standard. It showed how the best elements in our national game can also be its worst and why players at all levels occasionally need reminding that football isn't above the law.

It's never good to be sent off for kicking an opponent but when seconds later you start kicking and punching a supporter – who, by the way, has paid to watch you – it smacks of anger-management issues. Certainly the actions of Eric Daniel Pierre Cantona during Manchester United's visit to Selhurst Park on 25 January were fully deserving of the headline: 'Off, over the top and out'.

Cantona had been red-carded for kicking Palace defender Richard Shaw following some shirt-pulling. On his way back to the dressing room a fan ran forward to berate him from the sideline. Cantona responded with a kung fu kick to the chest and a battery of punches. He was later sentenced to two weeks in prison, though this was reduced on appeal to 120 hours' community service.

He was fined £20,000 by United who also voluntarily banned him for four months. At his first press conference following the whole shameful business his only comment was a piece of baffling pseudo-nonsense: 'When the seagulls follow the trawler, it's because they think sardines will be thrown into the sea.'

MotD Memories: Paolo's Push

Rap star and music entrepreneur Lethal Bizzle is, like Piers Morgan, another north London celebrity who crossed his family's football rubicon – he supports Arsenal despite his dad following Spurs.

Below: Devlin and Lethal Bizzle were involved in the 'Battle of the Bands' to find an official FA Cup anthem.

He enjoys *Match of the Day* as much for off-the-ball incidents as classic goals, singling out Paolo di Canio's push on referee Paul Alcock during Sheffield Wednesday v Arsenal in September 1998. 'I thought the ref made a bit of a meal of it though,' says Lethal. 'He definitely earned his money with those stumbles; I thought he was going to do a back-flip while he was at it.'

In a *MotD* 50th anniversary interview with the BBC di Canio admitted his mistake but insisted: 'It wasn't violent conduct – it was silly and stupid conduct.' He also played down the praise he got in December 2000 for sportingly catching the ball to stop play when Everton goalkeeper Paul Gerrard was injured in a challenge with one of his West Ham team-mates. 'There was too much praise,' said di Canio. 'Someone was on the ground screaming in pain so it was easy for me. I had already switched off. I was just respecting an opponent.'

Below: Spurs boss Alan Sugar brought Jürgen Klinsmann to north London from sunnier climes in Monaco.

Lethal – real name Maxwell Ansah – has family roots in Ghana and ranks the 25-yard missile of a volley by Ghanian Tony Yeboah for Leeds against Liverpool in August 1995 among his favourite goals. '[In Ghana] we've got really strong feet,' he says. 'A lot of my cousins used to play barefoot on gravel pitches.'

MotD Player of the Year
Jürgen Klinsmann, Tottenham Hotspur

The 1994–5 season started under a cloud for Spurs after they were deducted 12 points, fined £600,000 and banned from the FA Cup.

That punishment, linked to financial irregularities during the 1980s, was at the time the heaviest ever meted out to an English club and although the points deduction and cup embargo were eventually revoked it clearly affected the team. Despite boasting a wealth of attacking talents such as Darren Anderton, Teddy Sheringham and a certain Jürgen Klinsmann, they got off to a slow start.

Spurs boss Ossie Ardiles was replaced by Gerry Francis in November and by this time Klinsmann was starting to show why owner Lord Alan Sugar had splashed the cash to sign him from Monaco. The 'Golden Bomber' was a shining light amid the Lane's doom and gloom, exhibiting the sort of creativity and technique that was years ahead of English football at the time.

His 20 league goals helped guide Tottenham to seventh place and their highest finish for five years. Although it was a brief sojourn in north London – he signed for Bayern Munich at the end of the season before rejoining Spurs on loan in 1997 – Klinsmann won his place in fans' hearts with clinical finishing, an admirable work rate and his famous goal celebration – the wonderfully self-mocking 'Klinsmann Dive'.

'I will love it if we beat them. Love it.' So concluded Newcastle manager Kevin Keegan's incandescent rant on live TV in response to Alex Ferguson's claim that Leeds players tried hard only against Manchester United. As sporting spats go this was up there with the most ludicrous which, of course, made it even more enjoyable.

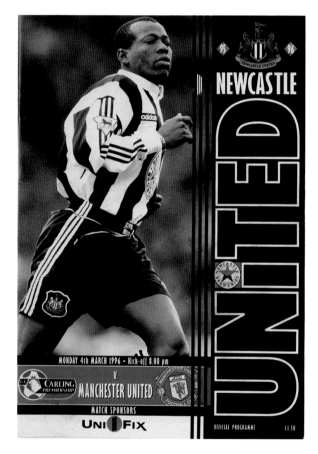

Above: Programme for a match the Magpies lost 1-0 with a war of words between managers raging in the media.

Later Ferguson would be dubbed master of mind games and Keegan lampooned as a buffoon. These notions were travesties of the truth yet somehow came to define the 1995–96 title run-in.

As ever it was all about context. Since replacing Ossie Ardiles at Newcastle, Keegan had guided the Magpies back to the Premier League and won respect in the process. In the summer of 1995 he bought wisely – winger David Ginola, goalkeeper Shaka Hislop, striker Les Ferdinand, defender Warren Barton – and it showed. By early February Newcastle held a 12-point lead and the Toon could almost taste the title. But that ramped up pressure. And in a string of early spring defeats the pressure also showed.

But not only on Newcastle. Manchester United were far from convincing and their stuttering 1-0 home win against Leeds on 17 April immediately followed defeat at Southampton. Leeds played with 10 men for 73 minutes and even had to stick defender Lucas Radebe in goal after Mark Beeney was sent off.

Whatever Ferguson said afterwards in the dressing room – and it was unlikely to be pleasant – his post-match comments were all about diverting attention from a parlous performance. He observed that Howard Wilkinson deserved better from his players. 'If they had played like that all season they'd be near the top,' he fumed. 'They raised their game because they were playing Manchester United. It was pathetic.'

True, Leeds' next opponents were Newcastle at Elland Road. The media assumed, because it was a good story, that Ferguson wanted to fire them up but the idea that professional players might respond to a rival manager's roasting is questionable to say the least. Whatever, it didn't work. Newcastle won 1-0 but then drew both their final games to see United finish four points clear. True, Fergie's rant may have got to Keegan. But the Toon's real downfall was their spring form not Ferguson's storm.

Below: Keegan was bitterly disappointed with his team's performance during the spring season.

At Wembley Man Utd's young guns notched up the 'double double' – the first club in history to complete league and FA Cup doubles in consecutive years – with captain Eric Cantona lifting the cup following a 1-0 victory over Liverpool. In the Coca-Cola Cup Brian Little's excellent Aston Villa outplayed Leeds to win 3-0.

 ## Match of the Season
Liverpool 4 Newcastle 3

Nothing summed up the agony of Newcastle's collapsing title ambitions better than this game. But it was also one of the truly great rollercoasters; attackers all at their best,

defenders all at, well, sea. The Premier League later named it 'Match of the Decade'.

Going into the game Roy Evans' Liverpool had begun to rediscover some form while Newcastle, as we now know, had peaked too soon. Goals apiece from Ferdinand and Ginola and two from Fowler set up a fascinating final third but when Asprilla scored in the 57th minute it seemed the visitors might prevail. Step forward Stan Collymore – along with Fowler superb throughout – for Liverpool's third and then two minutes into injury time it was Collymore again completing an intricate passing move with a far-post Exocet of a shot.

Amid Liverpool's celebrations the camera suddenly, brutally, switched to Keegan: forehead resting in despair on the Carlsberg advertising hoarding. Yet afterwards he remained defiant: 'If we stop playing this way, I go.' Evans was more realistic: 'Great for the fans but realistically nobody will win the championship defending every week like these teams did tonight.'

MotD Memories: Winning With Kids

It was the comment which would haunt Alan Hansen for 19 years as *MotD*'s leading pundit: 'You can't win anything with kids.'

The date was 19 August, 1995 and Aston Villa had just beaten Man United 3-1. Alex Ferguson's team featured six players of 20 or under, including Beckham, Scholes, Butt and the Neville brothers. As fans never tire of reminding Alan, they went on to win the double.

United keeper Peter Schmeichel (who also played that day) says some younger players felt intimidated by the remark, though it didn't affect motivation. 'It wasn't like, "oh, he's said that, we'll go and try even harder" because you were at the try-very-hard club anyway,' he said. 'If you don't try hard at Manchester United you're not going to make it.

'It made Alan Hansen and it's kind of funny. But it was a special crop of kids. Alan wasn't to know – you're a few years on and you haven't seen them playing. But we knew at some point they were all going to come good. It just took everyone by surprise that it [happened] so early.'

Paul Scholes agrees. 'At the time I probably thought [Hansen] was right,' he says. 'We'd had a disappointing day, been hammered at Villa, 3-0 down after 20 minutes and really struggling. But [his comment] acted as a kind of motivation throughout the season really and from that day onwards we improved and managed to prove him wrong.'

Right: Peter Schmeichel in the MotD *studio.*

Opposite top: Cantona was crucial to United's success.

Opposite bottom: The Frenchman fires home a penalty for United.

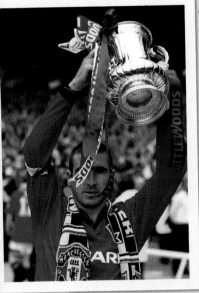

MOTD Player of the Year
Eric Cantona, Manchester United

Surprisingly signed from then First Division champions Leeds United in 1992, Eric Cantona is credited as one of the main architects of Manchester United's 1990s' revival.

Enigmatic, philosophical and talismanic, he had all the skill and passion the Stretford End loved, although the latter of these attributes also caused a few headaches for his club – particularly that kungfu kick on a Crystal Palace fan in the 1994–95 season.

After weathering the subsequent media firestorm, and serving the ban imposed by his club, Cantona had serious doubts about his future in England. But Alex Ferguson persuaded him to stay and the manager's private and public display of faith was repaid in style.

In 1995–96 Cantona hit 19 goals in all competitions, including a vital winner away at title rivals Newcastle on 4 March, which swung momentum Fergie's way, and a stunning FA Cup final-winning volley over Liverpool at Wembley.

His tendency to contribute when it mattered most meant he was selected captain for the following season. It would prove to be his last – he retired aged 31 – but his legacy at United is hard to overstate. Rare is the December home game when the Stretford End doesn't sing the 'Twelve Days of Christmas', substituting Cantona's name for each gift.

Three lions on a shirt,
Jules Rimet still gleaming,
Thirty years of hurt
Never stopped me dreaming ...

So ran David Baddiel and Frank Skinner's lyrics in the chart-topping 'Three Lions' summer anthem of 1996. And, for three glorious weeks in June, Terry Venables' lions really did roar. Not at first, admittedly. The tournament opener against Switzerland started brightly enough with Alan Shearer ending his international goal drought (he went on to claim the Golden Boot) after 23 minutes. But the second half saw a Swiss fight-back and a fatigued-looking England bereft of ideas. A bad result against bitter rivals Scotland, up next, would put the hosts in danger of elimination.

The first half of the Scotland game was a typically nervy affair but, after the break, England stepped up. Jamie Redknapp orchestrated midfield while his Liverpool colleague, Steve McManaman, suddenly looked a real threat following a switch from left to right wing. In the 53rd minute, McManaman released Gary Neville on the overlap and the resulting perfect cross was meat and drink to Shearer.

England kept creating chances but frustratingly failed to finish. In fact, but for the outstanding David Seaman they could easily have gone behind. The Arsenal 'keeper brilliantly clawed out a Gordon Durie header, then saved a Gary McAllister penalty. Seconds later, the game was over.

Below: The England figurines set lines up to take penalties.

Gascoigne ran on to a bouncing through-ball, flicked it over the head of Scottish defender Colin Hendry with his left foot and, in the same motion, volleyed home with his right. Noone needed Gazza's bizarre 'dentist's chair' celebration to realise that this was pure class.

Next came Guus Hiddink's Holland, not the force of old but still a major test. England took them apart in a ruthless 12 minutes after the break. Already one up from a Shearer penalty they doubled the lead through a Sheringham header then scored a wonderful team goal culminating in an unerring finish from Shearer. Sheringham then got a second before Kluivert's late consolation. It was England's best tournament result since Wembley '66.

Below: Steve McManaman outwits Germany's Stefan Reuter.

In the quarter final against Spain, England were fortunate to see Salinas' goal wrongly ruled out for offside. With a 0-0 deadlock at full time, and no golden goal (first to score wins) scored in extra time, a penalty shoot-out beckoned. England won it, thanks to the cussed mental strength of Stuart Pearce, who put his kick away despite the memories of Italia 90, and a David Seaman save. It meant a semi-final against Germany ... and yet more penalties.

The Germany game ranks among the finest internationals ever staged at Wembley. BBC commentator Barry Davies later admitted that 'if somebody told me you are going up to heaven and you can take one game with you, I think I would take that England game. I'd try to get the result changed when I got up there, though.'

England's early lead courtesy of Shearer was quickly cancelled by Stefan Kuntz. But Venables' side dominated the latter stages as Sheringham had a shot cleared off the line and Darren Anderton hit the post. Still more excruciating was Gazza's inability to connect with Shearer's cross eight minutes into extra time. A toe-poke could have settled things.

It was not to be. Eleven of the subsequent shoot-out penalties gave neither 'keeper much chance but Gareth Southgate, whose tournament performance had been outstanding until then, had his tame shot saved. Germany went on to become champions with a 2-1 win over the Czech Republic. For England the hurt would continue but the dreams would at least be sweeter.

Right: Kuntz equalises for Germany putting a penalty shoot-out on the cards.

Opposite: Gascoigne found the going tough against the Germans.

Another year, another Manchester United title. And another runners-up spot for Newcastle. In fact *déjà vu* ruled at the top with third to fifth places occupied by the same names as last season – Arsenal, Liverpool and Aston Villa – only in slightly different order.

Top: David Beckham grabbed the headlines by scoring from the halfway line.

Right: Glenn Hoddle left Chelsea to take over as England manager.

That said, it was a far from dull campaign and while David Beckham's stunning goal from the halfway line against Crystal Palace on the opening day proved a foretaste of things to come, United again proved vulnerable to humbling lapses. Among the best was an autumn blip in which they conceded 11 goals in three games, including a 6-3 loss to Southampton and a 5-0 defeat to Newcastle. It is no urban myth that on Tyneside a video of the latter was produced titled 'Howay Five-0'.

Alan Shearer scored in that game and Kevin Keegan's decision to sign him for a world record £15 million from Blackburn in the close season looked worth every penny. Shearer would go on to score 25 league goals in 31 appearances but his working relationship with the manager was short-lived. Keegan quit Newcastle on 8 January 1997, insisting he had 'taken the club as far as I can'. The Toon Army converged on St James' Park, many in tears, but the surge of support would not change Keegan's mind and Kenny Dalglish took the hotseat.

It was not the only key managerial change. By far the most important would be the arrival of Arsène Wenger at Arsenal to replace Bruce Rioch (given barely a year in the job). *Arsène Who?* screamed the *Evening Standard*. They would soon find out.

Over at Chelsea Ruud Gullit took the helm following Glenn Hoddle's departure for England. Chelsea fans had endured a difficult start to the season – their popular vice-chairman Matthew Harding died in a helicopter crash in October – and they lacked the consistency of true contenders. However, in January 1997 their fourth-round FA Cup tie against Liverpool provided the perfect tonic.

This was a great cup fightback. Two-nil down at half-time Gullit called Mark Hughes into action. It was like sending a hungry tiger out for dinner. Hughes scored within five minutes and caused such mayhem in the Reds defence that Zola and Vialli ran riot. Chelsea won 4-2 and went on to win the FA Cup final against Middlesborough. Poor Boro also lost the League Cup final (to Leicester City) and were relegated by two points having been docked three earlier in the year for failing to fulfil a fixture due to sickness.

Below: Steve Ogrizovic was the hero of the hour for Coventry.

Match of the Season
Tottenham 1 Coventry 2

They are English football's kings of escapology. Which is why, as yet another drop-beckoning fixture unfolded at Spurs, Coventry fans kept the faith. Having avoided final-day relegation nine times in 30 years, even the most pessimistic among them was convinced God didn't want it to happen. At least not yet.

That said, it was an unusually nervy climax even by Sky Blues' standards. Having to win at White Hart Lane was a tough enough prospect but survival also depended on both Sunderland and Middlesborough dropping points. A further frisson was added when heavy traffic delayed the kick-off by 15 minutes.

This was both a curse and a blessing. On the one hand Coventry knew that with 15 minutes left holding their 2-1 lead would do. The whistle had blown at Leeds where Boro, minus an unfit Ravanelli and dogged by an uninspiring Emerson, had been held 1-1. Sunderland had obligingly lost 1-0 at Wimbledon. The curse, however, was 15 minutes of torture as Spurs did their duty and threw everything at a packed defence. In the end Gordon Strachan's side held out thanks to the goalkeeping heroics of Steve Ogrizovic.

Gary Lineker Joins *Football Focus*

Below: The new MotD *line-up – Hansen, Lineker, Crooks, Lawrenson and ... Blair? Lineker joined in the mid-nineties. Tony Blair visited ten years later.*

It's like this. If you're the player who equalises for England in a World Cup semi-final against the Germans, after obliterating their defenders with pace, then no amount of bizarre crisp adverts are going to stop the nation loving you. True, England went on to lose that 1990 match on penalties but ... oh, let's not go there again.

When Gary Lineker joined *Football Focus*, first as a pundit and then, in 1996, as presenter, it seemed a natural fit, especially for an ex-striker who had always wanted a media career after he hung up his boots (a decision forced upon him in 1994 after two seasons of persistent injuries). Indeed, in a *Guardian* interview years later, he admitted he'd never even considered management.

'I never really liked training that much,' he said, 'and the thought of watching other people train ... I just think to be a manager you've got to live and breathe and have this incredible enthusiasm for football, the whole thing. And while I love the game, and it's been a large part of my life, it's not the only thing in my life.'

Lineker presented *Football Focus* – the BBC's Saturday lunchtime football magazine – for three more seasons, also appearing as an occasional pundit on *Match of the Day*. He guest-fronted his first *MotD* shows in 1998 before taking the lead role full-time a year later.

Below: New Chelsea signing Gianfranco Zola meets the press with manager Ruud Gullit.

 Player of the Year
Gianfranco Zola, Chelsea

At the end of a less than spectacular 1995–96 – they finished 11th in the Premier League, were knocked out in the semi-finals of the FA Cup and lost their manager Glenn Hoddle to the vacant England job – there was an understandable air of pessimism at Stamford Bridge.

The appointment of Ruud Gullit as player-manager at the fans' behest raised morale, however. The Dutchman dipped into the transfer market to sign exciting new continental players such as Roberto Di Matteo, Gianluca Vialli and, particularly, Gianfranco Zola, who arrived from Parma in November for £4.5 million.

If the mood on the terraces was on the rise in the early stages of the campaign it positively shot through the roof after Zola's home debut for the Blues against Newcastle United. The diminutive Italian displayed impudent touches and mesmerizing skill, including an outrageous dummy against David Batty that had *Match of the Day* pundits purring that night.

After contributing several assists in his first few matches, he opened his personal account in December with a magnificent curling free-kick against Everton – the first of twelve goals in 1996–97. His back-heel flick to set up the FA Cup-winning strike for Eddie Newton against Middlesborough is one of the enduring images of a season which saw him become the first player ever to win the FWA Player of the Year award despite having not spent a full season in English football.

There's an argument, even among some Arsenal fans, that Arsène Wenger was fortunate to inherit a good side in September 1996. He certainly inherited a great defence along with, crucially, Dutch maestro Dennis Bergkamp and veteran striker Ian Wright. Yet one league title and two domestic cups in seven years was barely par for a club of this size. The defensive fortress wasn't enough. Arsenal needed a shake-up.

Below: Ian Wright celebrates becoming Arsenal's top goal scorer in April 1997 in a match against Bolton Wanderers.

Wenger was the man to do it. His great strength was innovation and it's hard to think of any manager anywhere who has transformed a club so quickly. In his signings, his training methods, his scientific approach to nutrition, his attacking philosophy and, yes, in his trophies, *Le Professeur* raised the bar for every English club. Not for nothing do the Gunners faithful still raise the banner 'Arsène Knows'.

Even before officially taking over Wenger had advised his friend and Arsenal board stalwart David Dein to sign Patrick Vieira. After missing out on a Champions League place on goal difference he strengthened further for 1997–8 with Nicolas Anelka, Marc Overmars and Emmanuel Petit, the latter forming an instant and crucial partnership with Vieira.

In Manchester nobody seemed to notice. Not even when Arsenal won a 3-2 thriller against United at Highbury in November (see Match of the Season), a game which solidified the players' belief in their potential. One bookmaker paid out on United retaining their title as early as Christmas and indeed in December Ferguson's side sat 13 points ahead of the sixth-placed Gunners.

Emmanuel Petit and Tony Adams close down Everton's Duncan Ferguson.

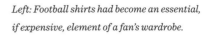

Left: Football shirts had become an essential,
if expensive, element of a fan's wardrobe.

But then a scintillating run-in saw Arsenal record 15 wins – including a 1-0 victory at Old Trafford – and three draws to pocket the title with two games to go. This achievement was in no small part due to Wright, who at 33 beat Cliff Bastin's long-standing club scoring record by slotting his 179th in a Highbury hat-trick against Bolton.

The final word came, rightly, from the inspirational Tony Adams. With his side already 3-0 up in the title-clinching home game against Everton he stole forward to volley home a superb flighted pass from back-four partner Steve Bould. There could have been no finer demonstration of Wenger's attacking philosophy. Arsenal went on to complete a second double, only the second club to do so, with a 2-0 win over Newcastle. But spare a thought for Middlesborough whose 2-0 League Cup defeat to Chelsea was their third Wembley disappointment inside a year.

Below: Arsenal's
Patrick Vieira
against Man Utd.

Match of the Season
Arsenal 3
Manchester United 2

The visit of the defending champions to Highbury was the biggest test of the Wenger revolution to date. Any early nerves on the North Bank were calmed when 18-year-old Nicolas Anelka notched his first Premier League goal but it was Patrick Vieira's stunning opportunistic 20-yard strike, doubling the lead inside 30 minutes, which triggered an outbreak of general ecstasy.

Going two down away at Highbury would have seen many a lesser side crumble. But this was a Manchester United buoyed by self-belief. Teddy Sheringham, always obliged to play the panto villain at Arsenal because of his Spurs links, dampened the home fans' enthusiasm with a brace before half-time and Gunners fans feared the worst. But with just seven minutes to go David Platt popped up with a header to thrillingly settle an outstanding game.

The win moved Arsenal within a point of the top. More importantly, it provided the springboard for an irresistible title challenge that would ultimately restore the club's league and cup credentials.

If Only *MotD* Did Poetry Corner

France '98 was to be Des Lynam's last World Cup as *MotD* presenter and – bizarrely – it would provide him with a brief career reciting poetry. The tournament had been an emotional journey for England but the tension which enveloped hosts France as they faced Brazil in the Paris final was pure football theatre.

'At the end of World Cups the BBC always have a review, a nice piece of five-minute videotape, and they put music to it,' said Des. 'Well, it was the World Cup where Michael Owen scored that brilliant goal and Beckham got sent off and a story about triumph and disaster occurred to me. I thought of *If*, Kipling's famous poem, so I said why don't we get a reading of that and put it to music.

'Niall Sloane was editor at the time and they got recordings of all these famous actors reading *If*. But they were all too theatrical. They said: "We need someone common. You're common, Des, you do it."' And so as coverage of the final ended viewers heard Des intoning: '... If you can meet with Triumph and Disaster. And treat those two imposters just the same ...'

Des said: 'We got a huge reaction to it, so much so that the BBC's poetry and music department asked me if I would read *If* for them and do a CD. It made the top 40.'

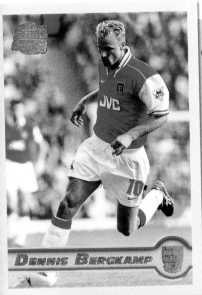

 Player of the Year
Dennis Bergkamp, Arsenal

Arsenal had agonizingly missed out on a Champions League spot the previous season (a slightly inferior goal difference) and perhaps Dennis Bergkamp felt partly responsible. He was sent off for a high tackle, against Sunderland in the 33rd minute of a January 1997 encounter, in a match the Gunners eventually lost 1-0.

Whatever drove him during the subsequent campaign the 'Iceman' was inspired from the off. Arsène Wenger's decision to make him the fulcrum of a thrilling attacking unit proved inspirational and of many highlights to drool over his hat-trick against Leicester stands out.

His first was a curled effort into the top corner; the second a one-on-one finish that ballooned off Kasey Keller. But the third was simply a thing of beauty. Bergkamp controlled a through ball landing over his right shoulder with his right foot, turned a defender with his left – the ball still having not touched the turf – and clinically finished in the far corner. These were goals which exhibited the technique, finishing ability and pure panache that Gunners fans revered for the rest of his playing days.

Not only was Bergkamp the club's leading scorer, FWA Player of the Year and a double winner, he also had the distinction of having his strikes voted first, second and third in *Match of the Day*'s prestigious Goal of the Month competition – a feat yet to be equalled.

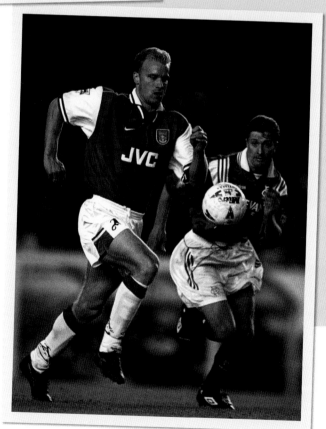

WORLD CUP – FRANCE 1998

Glenn Hoddle's only World Cup as England manager began with a good, old-fashioned media maelstrom. His appointment of faith healer Eileen Drewery as 'advisor' – part of the so-called Hod Squad – was always going to be pilloried on the back pages but the axing of Paul Gascoigne was even more controversial.

Gascoigne was dropped on injury and disciplinary grounds, although many fans felt their Euro '96 hero still had a role, a view emphatically shared by the player himself. There were reports of a hefty damages bill for Hoddle's hotel room when Gazza got the news.

England's opening match produced a 2-0 victory over Tunisia but it hardly inspired confidence and the second match, against Romania, was a

Below: Michael Owen shrugs off Argentina's Jose Chamot.

Above: England souvenir pennant from France '98.

dire 2-1 defeat. It wasn't until the third, crucial, qualifier against Colombia that Hoddle's team gave glimpses of its potential with a 2-0 win. England finished second in Group G, pitting them against an Argentina side which had beaten all three of its Group H opponents.

There are fewer tastier encounters in international football and this one delivered in bucketloads. Both sides won a penalty within the first ten minutes; Batistuta netting for Argentina and Shearer replying for England. Then, in the 16th minute, Beckham floated a ball to Owen five yards inside the South Americans' half.

What followed was seven glorious, jaw-flooring seconds which made every watching England fan feel good to be alive. The fresh-faced Owen, looked like he'd been plucked from the under 14s by mistake. Perhaps the Argentine defenders thought his pace was over-hyped; that he lacked big-match experience. Owen was already moving fast as he took the pass in his stride but when he touched the throttle it was like Roberto Ayala and Jose Chamot had lead in their boots. The youngster showed strength too, shrugging off an initial attempt to muscle him off the ball. As to the finish, an 18-yard screamer into the far corner – nervy it was not.

From that point on Owen's mere presence in his opponents' half was a tactic in itself, but an intelligent, creative Argentina side was never going to lie down easily. Shortly before half-time, a cleverly-worked free kick saw Zanetti equalise and it was game on. Or, in David Beckham's case, off. During a great international career Beckham would be England's saviour on countless occasions but his kick at Simeone, right in front of the referee, just after half-time was childish and costly.

Above: Beckham's retaliation for the harsh treatment he received from Simeone earned him his marching orders.

Opposite: Lilian Thuram looks on as French keeper Fabian Barthez clashes with Brazil's Ronaldo.

England now faced a daunting rearguard action but, to Hoddle's credit, you'd never have guessed it. He switched from 3-5-2 to 4-4-1, bringing Anderton into midfield and pushing Scholes and Owen out to the wings where defensive duties would be minimal against an Argentine attack reliant on intricate close-passing. It may have seemed counter-intuitive but it said everything about Hoddle's ability to read a game. It also worked.

In the 80 minutes that followed Beckham's dismissal, Argentina dominated possession but never broke the English defence. David Seaman made no saves of note. Paul Ince was magnificent; David Batty, on for the exhausted Anderton, immense. For most of this time England were prepared to counter-attack and might even have snatched victory had Shearer's foul not cancelled Sol Campbell's headed goal. And had the referee spotted Chamot's clear hand-ball in the penalty area, who knows?

Unfortunately, this colossal commitment counted for nothing. England lost 4-3 in the shootout with Batty (replacing Beckham as penalty taker) missing the final kick. Argentina went out in the quarter finals to Holland but the tournament was deservedly won by France, who outclassed Brazil 3-0 in the final.

Attention all non-Man Utd fans. Throughout the nineties, for obvious reasons, it's been hard not to keep mentioning them. We've tried to balance things because football has never been just about winners. But, actually, in 1998–99 it was. Again and again and again.

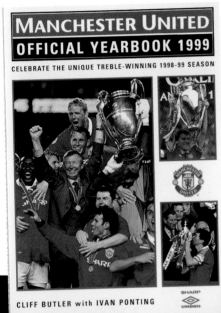

There's no luck involved in winning a title. Not over 38 games. And while a club might need a smidgeon of luck to win one cup in the same season, winning *two* of the toughest knockouts in world football – the European and FA Cup – does rather point to a pattern emerging. Let's be clear: there was nothing *lucky* about Manchester United's treble. In a sport rife with hyperbole, this was an astonishing achievement by astonishing players. For their fans it was also payback for six weeks of mental torture.

At times all three treble trophies looked lost. The FA Cup semi-final against Arsenal at Villa Park on 14 April saw Roy Keane sent off and Dennis Bergkamp presented

Above: Celebrations galore on the cover of the Manchester United yearbook.

Ryan Giggs slots the winner in the FA Cup Final.

 Match of the Season
Manchester United 2
Bayern Munich 1

In his diaries, published in English as *The Burning Brand*, the Italian poet Cesare Pavese writes: 'We do not remember days, we remember moments.' In the Camp Nou, Barcelona, on 26 May, the moment for Manchester United fans was 90.36 on the referee's watch.

Up until then the English champions were drifting out of the Champions League final. Behind to a magnificent swerving first-half free-kick from Mario Basler they were badly missing midfielders Paul Scholes and Roy Keane and the best second-half chances had fallen to the Germans. Alex Ferguson sent on strikers Teddy Sheringham and Ole Gunnar Solskjaer but only in the 80th minute did United's first clear chance come – a Solskjaer header. Even then Bayern hit straight back as Jancker's overhead kick hit the bar.

The fourth official had signalled three minutes of injury time as David Beckham hurriedly prepared to take a corner. The ball was nodded back by Dwight Yorke; Giggs' weak effort was poked home by Sheringham. Against the odds – and the run of play – United had somehow forced extra-time.

Except they hadn't. In the final minute they won another corner and again Beckham delivered. Sheringham headed down, Solskjaer stuck out a foot, the ball flew high into Oliver Kahn's goal. The moment on the ref's watch was 92:17.

It was a moment that said everything about this famous old club. It wasn't skill, tactics, luck or physical prowess that saw them home, vital though all these can be. Staring at defeat in those dying seconds, not a man among them blinked. They just never gave up.

Above right: Solskjaer is ecstatic after scoring the winner against Bayern Munich.

with an injury-time penalty to seal it for the Gunners. But Peter Schmeichel pulled off a superb save to hold the score at 1-1 and set up perhaps the greatest individual goal in cup history.

In the 110th minute Patrick Vieira inexplicably passed the ball to substitute Ryan Giggs ten yards inside United's half. Giggs hit the afterburners – weaving here, dropping a shoulder there until, on the edge of the box, he was surrounded by four of the world's finest defenders. It was, as the Americans used to say of the Viet Cong, like boxers fighting the wind. Giggs drifted through and with the thirteenth touch of seventy mesmerising yards buried the ball in the roof of Seaman's net. Cue his Celebration of the Year: a shirtless pelt down the touchline.

Opposite top: Ginola outstrips the Everton defence at Goodison Park.

Opposite bottom: Battling with Paul Merson and Gareth Southgate at Villa Park.

Below: Des Lynam's departure for ITV meant that Gary Lineker took on the lead role in MotD.

The FA Cup Final itself on 22 May was never going to rival this game and United emerged comfortable 2-0 winners over a below-par Newcastle. But only now did fans dare to mention the treble. Six days earlier the Premier League title had been restored to them in the most nerve-shredding manner as midweek fixtures saw Fergie's side lose at Leeds only for sole rivals Arsenal to blow the opportunity with a draw at Blackburn. On that final Sunday, 16 May, Les Ferdinand opened the scoring for Tottenham at Old Trafford, prompting the unlikely chant 'Come On You Spurs' down at Highbury. But goals from Beckham and Sheringham rendered Arsenal's 1-0 win over Villa irrelevant. The stage was set for Barcelona's Camp Nou in ten days' time.

Gary Lineker Signs for *MotD* – 1998-9

When he first began guest-presenting *Match of the Day* in 1998 Gary Lineker was already a familiar face on TV. In addition to *Football Focus* he'd been a team captain for three years on the sports game show *They Think It's All Over*. But, though the media had dubbed him a 'national treasure', Lineker knew the *MotD* hot seat was not a given.

In those early days he would watch recordings of every programme for a post-show analysis with his editors. 'I told them to be brutal with me,' he revealed later. 'I just really wanted to learn.' He also hired a voice coach to help get 'enthusiasm and light and shade into my voice.'

It proved time well spent. Des Lynam, lured by ITV's promise to wrest back exclusive Premier League TV highlights, resigned two weeks before the start of the 1999-2000 season and Lineker was thrust straight into the lead role.

Des recalled later: 'I knew he'd always wanted to [anchor *MotD*]. Gascoigne used to call him Des because he'd admitted wanting to be a sports presenter. He came into it, learnt the ropes, and I could see he was going to be good. But who is brilliant to start with? Did you see my first television appearances? I certainly wouldn't want to look back on them – I was frightened as a rabbit.'

 Player of the Year
David Ginola, Tottenham Hotspur

When you don't line up for Manchester United, winning Player of the Year in the Treble season takes some doing. But David Ginola's first campaign for Tottenham was so eye-catching and enthralling that there were few arguments about the Frenchman's worthiness.

Ginola signed for Tottenham from Newcastle in 1997 and instantly endeared himself to the Lane crowd with the sort of classic dashing and dribbling wing-play that marked out the classic Spurs sides of yesteryear.

Among many captivating moments in the 1998–9 campaign his FA Cup goal against Barnsley sticks in the memory. Beginning on the touchline, he jinked this way and that into the area at high speed before unleashing a textbook finish. If it hadn't been for Ryan Giggs' memorable solo strike to knock out Arsenal in the semi-finals, the goal of the season would surely have belonged to the Frenchman.

Quick, skilful and imaginative with the ball at his feet, Ginola became the first player in Premier League history to win the FWA award while at a club finishing outside the top four.

They were both ex-England managers returning to the club fold ... but with markedly different back stories. Bobby Robson, Italia '90 mastermind, was hailed at Newcastle as Saviour of the Toon. Glenn Hoddle, an equally big beast, had a rather more controversial baptism at Southampton.

Opposite top: The West Ham players celebrate at Upton Park, but further drama was to come.

Opposite right: Joachim and Margas compete for the ball.

Below: Alan Shearer performed well with Bobby Robson in charge at Newcastle.

Almost a year earlier Hoddle had been sacked by England after reportedly claiming that disabled people were being punished for failures in past lives. His chaotic debut press conference centred on whether he regretted those words. 'I'm glad you asked me that question because I never said those things,' he said. 'They were not portrayed anywhere near what I was talking about ... those are not my beliefs.' Having survived the media tussle in combative style Hoddle went on to win over Saints fans by saving them from relegation.

For Robson, the problems were all behind closed doors. His predecessor, Ruud Gullit, had not only failed to inspire the club's greatest asset – goal machine and now *MotD* analyst Alan Shearer – he'd left a dressing room in turmoil. Robson calmed the troops, geed up the likes of Speed and Dyer, brought back a revitalised Rob Lee and instantly gained Shearer's respect. His first home game was a jaw-dropping 8-1 victory against Sheffield Wednesday in which the striker netted five. Newcastle went on to reach a respectable 11th in the Premiership and an FA Cup semi-final.

In truth it was hardly a climactic Premier League competition. Manchester United had scraped home by a single point against Arsenal the previous year; now they signed off 18 clear of second-placed Gunners – a phenomenal achievement for the newly knighted Sir Alex. Much more interesting was the desperate scramble at the foot of the table and its effect on European qualification.

On the final day of the season the hot money had Bradford for the drop. Though level on points with Wimbledon, the Bantams' inferior goal difference had pushed them into the bottom three. Worse, the Dons were travelling to Southampton – opponents with nothing to play for – while Bradford entertained a Liverpool side needing a win to secure Champions League status.

It took Bradford just 12 minutes to score through an excellent David Wetherall header, a lead they somehow held to the end. The result catapulted Leeds above the Reds into the Champions League while Wimbledon's 2-0 defeat sent them into the Championship alongside Sheffield Wednesday and Watford.

 Match of the Season
West Ham 2 Aston Villa 2
(West Ham 5-4 on penalties)

There were some memorable tussles between old foes – specifically Chelsea's 5-0 thrashing of Man Utd and Arsenal's fantastic comeback at Stamford Bridge in which Nwankwo Kanu hit a hat-trick in the final 15 minutes to secure a 2-3 victory. But for a sheer, anorak-esque, cor-blimey, football talking point nothing really touched the fifth-round Worthington Cup tie between West Ham and Aston Villa.

The match at Upton Park had ended 2-2 with the Hammers going through 5-4 on penalties. But later questions were asked over 21-year-old Manny Omoyinmi's appearance as a sub during the final six minutes of extra-time. Hadn't Manny already played in the second round for Gillingham while out on loan? Wasn't he therefore 'cup-tied' – the rule that prevents a player turning out for different clubs during the same season of competition?

He had and he was. Omoyinmi had forgotten his Gillingham link, West Ham manager Harry Redknapp pleaded a 'genuine mistake' but the Football League insisted on a rematch. This was the stuff of Sunday leagues, where the fielding of illegal players gives many a club secretary sleepless nights.

Villa won the replayed game 3-1 after extra time and two Hammers' administrators later resigned. The cup was eventually won by Leicester City for the second time in four years.

Ray Stubbs and the Stand-Ins

No, not a retro-rock band, but an impressive cadre of sports broadcasters who have all acted as guest presenters on *Match of the Day*. Stubbs was actually a bit more than a guest – he appeared on the programme for 17 seasons from the start of the Premier League in 1992 until departing for ESPN in 2009.

A former professional with Tranmere Rovers, he had hands-on experience of the fragile nature of football finances in the Football League's less fashionable quarters. After retiring as a Rovers' player in 1978, he became the club's commercial director, later securing its first ever shirt sponsorship deal. His television career took off in 1990 after he reported on England fans attending the World Cup for BBC 2's investigative sport series *On The Line*. He became *MotD*'s man-on-the-spot at subsequent England camps, covering off-diary news and features for the show during both Euro '96 and France '98.

Other stand-in presenters over the years have gone on to highly-successful media careers, among them Dan Walker, Gabby Logan, Mark Chapman, Mark Pougatch and Jake Humphrey.

 Player of the Year
Roy Keane, Manchester United

Manchester United's imperious retention of the Premier League crown in 2000 – they suffered just three defeats – coincided with Roy Keane having a point to prove. With his contract negotiations rumbling on, and both Juventus and Bayern Munich reportedly poised, Keane took his game to a new level through his dictation and domination of midfield.

On the afternoon of 8 December 1999 United announced he'd finally signed a new deal and hours later Keane celebrated by firing in the first of his side's three goals in a must-win home Champions League game against Valencia. Old Trafford duly celebrated with its favourite Keane ditty; '... *he didn't sign for Chelsea, or Arsenal 'cos they're ***** he signed for Man United 'cos we're ******* dynamite.*'

Rival fans loved to hate Keane. But the portrayal of him in certain quarters as purely a ruthless – even thuggish – tackler is as ludicrous as it is wrong. Keane's greatest strengths were his footballing brain, his much underrated passing, his positional sense and his constant, unquenchable, will to win.

Keane tackles Markus Schupp of Graz during the 1999 EUFA Champions League match.

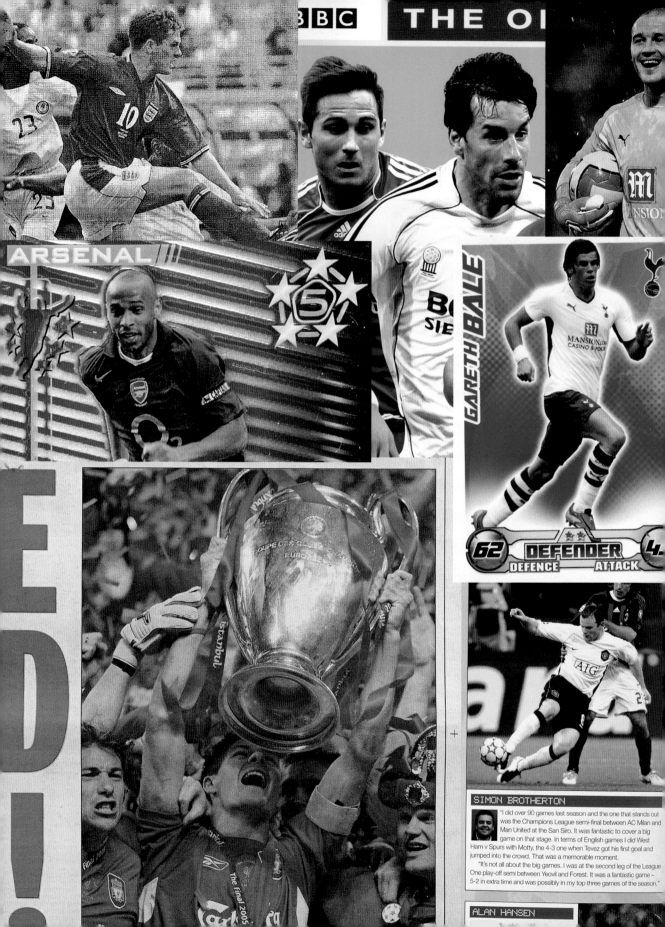

ARSENAL

GARETH BALE

62 DEFENDER **4.**
DEFENCE ATTACK

SIMON BROTHERTON

"I did over 90 games last season and the one that stands out was the Champions League semi-final between AC Milan and Man United at the San Siro. It was fantastic to cover a big game on that stage. In terms of English games I did West Ham v Spurs with Motty, the 4-3 one when Tevez got his first goal and jumped into the crowd. That was a memorable moment.

"It's not all about the big games. I was at the second leg of the League One play-off semi between Yeovil and Forest. It was a fantastic game – 5-2 in extra time and was possibly in my top three games of the season."

ALAN HANSEN

OPORTUNIDADE
DE VINGAR EUROPEUS
DE 1984 E 2000

Brasil 0-1 França

E agora es
franceses!

Págs. 2 a 31

MATCH OF THE DAY

2000s

A new millennium, the first full season of the noughties, but at the top of the Premier League it was same-old, same-old. Fresh from treble glory, Manchester United proved irresistible, nailing another title on 14 April with five weeks still to go. For all the promise at Highbury the Gunners' 6-1 thrashing at Old Trafford in February was embarrassing and Teddy Sheringham took full advantage by miming the lifting of trophies in front of away fans.

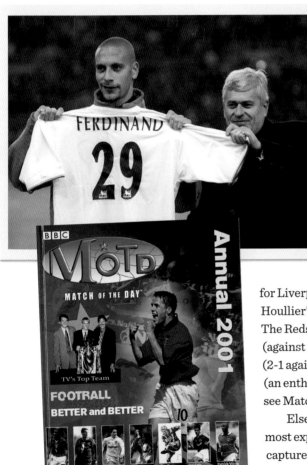

Above: Big prizes were on offer in MotD's *2001 annual.*

At the bottom Coventry City finally waved farewell to top-flight football – a berth they had occupied since 1967 – going down 3-2 at Villa. Having become masters of drop-dodging, they succumbed to their West Midlands rivals in the worst possible way, blowing a 2-0 lead. Joining them in the First Division after a season's sojourn was Manchester City, while Bradford's two-year stay also ended.

With another procession domestically United's rivals looked to the cups for their thrills and for Liverpool, buoyed by French manager Gérard Houllier's transfer frenzy, it was a wonderful year. The Reds scooped a cup treble – the Worthington (against Birmingham City on penalties) the FA (2-1 against Arsenal) and, most notably, the UEFA (an enthralling 5-4 win over Deportivo Alaves – see Match of the Season).

Elsewhere in Europe Leeds, boasting Britain's most expensive footballer following the £18 million capture of Rio Ferdinand from West Ham, proved to be unimpressed by reputations. In the early stages of the European Cup they took four points from AC Milan and memorably held Barcelona 1-1 at Elland Road.

In the second group stage they saw off Sven-Göran Eriksson's Lazio in Rome and then

Opposite top: Rio Ferdinand receives his new shirt from Leeds chairman Peter Risdale.

progressed to the last eight with two wins over Anderlecht, including a 4-1 demolition in Belgium. An equally impressive 3-0 home victory over Deportivo La Coruña saw them to the semi-final but the suspension of Lee Bowyer, easily their most influential player, cost them dear and they were outplayed 3-0 in the away leg against Valencia.

It was a disappointing campaign for fellow English representatives Arsenal and Man Utd, both of whom promised much in the early stages but failed to maintain momentum. Bayern Munich exacted revenge for 1999 by beating United home and away in the quarter-finals while Arsenal succumbed to Valencia on the away goals rule.

Below: Gary McAllister calmly fires a penalty past Alaves keeper Martin Herrera.

Match of the Season
Liverpool 5 Deportivo Alaves 4

This was Liverpool's third UEFA Cup final appearance but their first in a European final since the Heysel disaster. For Alaves it was all completely new. Both teams had much to prove in Dortmund and they did not disappoint.

It was one of those games saluted by neutrals but squirmed over by anyone with a remotely partisan interest. Liverpool started the stronger, going two up through goals from Markus Babbel and Steven Gerrard, before Ivan Alonso responded for the Spanish. Gary McAllister made it 3-1 from the penalty spot before half-time but within four minutes of the restart Alaves were level through a brace from Moreno. Fowler again put Liverpool ahead; again their opponents levelled – this time through former Man Utd striker Jordi Cruyff. And so to extra-time.

But extra-time with an edge.

UEFA had decreed settlement by 'golden goal' so the first team to score would win. Alonso thought he'd done it but was ruled offside; Fowler thought he was the hero until he, too, spotted the dreaded flag. Then in the 115th minute Alaves, already down to ten men, were hit with a second red card after Karmona brought down Vladimir Smicer. McAllister took the resulting free-kick and in a desperate attempt to clear defender Delfi Geli headed into his own net.

MotD Memories: Di Canio's Wonder Volley

The goal that lingers most lovingly in the memory of comedian and West Ham fan Russell Brand is Paolo di Canio's wonder-volley for the Hammers in March 2000 against Wimbledon.

Trevor Sinclair had delivered a high, rangy cross to the far left of the penalty area but as the Dons had four defenders well-placed there seemed little threat. A lesser player might have brought the ball down and crossed, hopefully, back across the box. Di Canio leapt and, with both feet off the ground, produced the sweetest of scissor-kick finishes with the outside of his right foot.

'That was a beautiful goal,' says Russell. 'It was representative of the type of player Paolo was – it required panache, daring, skill and confidence and that kind of stuff doesn't happen too often [in football]. He's someone who wasn't playing by normal rules ... football's about structure and rules and somehow within that you've got to create magic.'

Russell's boyhood hero was Frank McAvennie, who spearheaded West Ham's 1985-6 title challenge. He recalls: 'Frank McAvennie – the girls, the gnashers, the peroxide blonde hair and of course, yeah, he was a bit nippy in the box.'

Player of the Year
Teddy Sheringham, Manchester United

When reviewing such a period of domestic dominance by Manchester United there's a tendency to overlook the unfashionable, but consistently efficient, Teddy Sheringham. Yet his role – in a side containing a host of Fergie Fledglings in their prime – was vital in ensuring a run of three consecutive Premiership trophies.

Sir Alex Ferguson wasn't short of striking talent before the 2000–1 season. The inimitable Dwight Yorke–Andy Cole partnership was still heralded across world football while the instinctive qualities of baby-faced assassin Ole Gunnar Solskjaer meant Sheringham faced a tough task to force his way into the side.

That, coupled with Ferguson's attempts to bring in Ruud van Nistelrooy from PSV Eindhoven (the move collapsed when the Dutchman failed a medical), meant Sheringham's future at United was in doubt before the season began. However, he was awarded a new one-year contract after the van Nistelrooy reverse and stepped up emphatically, displacing Yorke up front and hitting 21 goals in all competitions to finish as United's top scorer. Highlights included a memorable hat-trick against Southampton and the final goal in that 6-1 mauling of title rivals Arsenal.

It would be his last season at Old Trafford – a free transfer to Tottenham beckoned in the summer – but Sheringham's skill, timing, positional sense and any number of important goals ensured his longevity as an Old Trafford favourite.

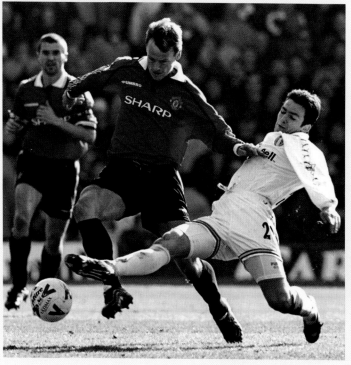

2001-02

Since their last double triumph four years previously, Arsenal had finished runners-up to Manchester United every time. Now at last they were bridesmaids no more, emerging as the dominant force to take their second double of the Wenger era. Sweeter still, the triumph was sealed at Old Trafford with a 1-0 win courtesy of Sylvain Wiltord.

'Hand it over, Ferguson,' sang a delirious away contingent and the United manager could have had few complaints. In the creativity of Pirès, Bergkamp and Ljungberg, the driving runs of Vieira, the work rate of Parlour and the goal machine otherwise known as Thierry Henry (leading league scorer with 24), Arsenal were consistently better than their rivals in every department. They were unbeaten away all season – the first time any club had managed that since Preston in 1888–89 – scored in every game and lost only three times.

Four days earlier, on 4 May, Arsenal had won the FA Cup in a generally dour encounter against Chelsea, a game which, for once, left them looking strangely vulnerable. With Lampard and Petit orchestrating midfield, Chelsea would surely have taken the lead had striker Jimmy Floyd Hasselbaink been fully fit. But the Blues failed to convert chances and in the last quarter of the game Parlour and Ljungberg settled matters with two world-class goals – a 25-yard strike and brilliant solo effort respectively.

Opposite: Beckham hammers home United's fifth at White Hart Lane.

Below: Team shot from Arsenal's year book, featuring Bob Wilson, middle row, fifth from right, as goalkeeping coach.

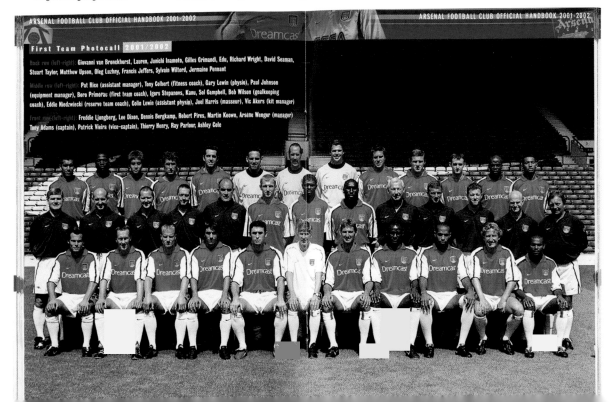

ARSENAL FOOTBALL CLUB OFFICIAL HANDBOOK 2001-2002

ARSENAL FOOTBALL CLUB OFFICIAL HANDBOOK 2001-2002

First Team Photocall 2001/2002

Back row (left-right): Giovanni van Bronckhorst, Lauren, Junichi Inamoto, Gilles Grimandi, Edu, Richard Wright, David Seaman, Stuart Taylor, Matthew Upson, Oleg Luzhny, Francis Jeffers, Sylvain Wiltord, Jermaine Pennant

Middle row (left-right): Pat Rice (assistant manager), Tony Colbert (fitness coach), Gary Lewin (physio), Paul Johnson (equipment manager), Boro Primorac (first team coach), Igors Stepanovs, Kanu, Sol Campbell, Bob Wilson (goalkeeping coach), Eddie Niedzwiecki (reserve team coach), Colin Lewin (assistant physio), Joel Harris (masseur), Vic Akers (kit manager)

Front row (left-right): Freddie Ljungberg, Lee Dixon, Dennis Bergkamp, Robert Pires, Martin Keown, Arsène Wenger (manager) Tony Adams (captain), Patrick Vieira (vice-captain), Thierry Henry, Ray Parlour, Ashley Cole

Match of the Season
Tottenham 3
Manchester United 5

It must have been an interesting half-time team talk. As they trooped into their dressing room 3-0 down the visitors, for all their quality and experience, looked a rudderless and beaten side. Goals from Dean Richards, Les Ferdinand and Christian Ziege had shaken United's self-belief and there seemed no way back.

We may never know whether Alex Ferguson deployed double hair-dryers all round but, whatever was said, it produced a Damascene conversion. Less than a minute into the restart Andy Cole's header gave United hope and then Laurent Blanc notched a second, his first goal for the club. By the time van Nistelrooy headed a third in the 72nd minute the dynamic of the game had been turned on its head. The much-maligned Juan Sebastián Verón hit a clinical low drive for the fourth and then, with Spurs adopting a headless chicken defensive formation, Beckham clinched the points three minutes from time. As Spurs manager Glenn Hoddle succinctly put it: 'God help the rest of us when United start getting clean sheets.'

Blackburn Rovers were the one northern club to see major silverware, celebrating their return to the Premiership with a 2-1 League Cup victory over Spurs at the Millennium Stadium, Cardiff. But at the foot of the Premier League it was a bad year for the East Midlands with both Derby County and Leicester City dispatched to the First Division. For Leicester it was a particularly bitter pill; just 18 months earlier they had been playing UEFA Cup matches. Now their last season at Filbert Street ahead of a move to the new Walkers Stadium had left them 12 points from safety and a shadow of Martin O'Neill's exciting teams of the late nineties.

Whatever the fate of their club side the 2001–02 season will be fondly remembered by most English fans for the extraordinary evening of 1 September. A hat-trick from Michael Owen, plus goals from Liverpool team-mates Steven Gerrard and Emile Heskey, meant the final score in a World Cup qualifying match at the Olympiastadion, Munich, read Germany 1 England 5. It was only England's second competitive victory over their old foes since 1966.

MotD Memories: ITV's Death Wish

When the Premier League opened bidding for a TV highlights rights package in 2000, *Match of the Day*, with eight years' experience, looked nailed-on favourites. But ITV Sport closed the deal with a reported £183 million bid and began its exclusive highlights show *The Premiership* at the start of the 2001 season.

As well as expensive – £1.3 million per programme – it was a ratings' shocker. The original evening slot was unpopular with viewers while critics condemned the lack of match action, too much inept punditry and a fixation on TV technology to analyse decisions (although both Arsène Wenger and Sir Alex Ferguson were generally supportive of this). The programme was axed after three years allowing a re-invigorated *MotD* to resume its place as standard-bearer of the nation's top flight football TV highlights.

Lord Alan Sugar recalls: '*Match of the Day* is a British institution. I remember when the BBC lost it for 3 years; it went to ITV and they completely messed it up.

'ITV put it on at 7pm and it completely bombed out ... it was in the days when I was involved with the Premier League and [TV satellite broadcaster] BskyB and we were all really, really disappointed. Greg Dyke was at the BBC at that time and we worked very hard at BskyB and the Premier League to see if we could deal with it. But ITV had a death wish to take it over. It just didn't work.'

Player of the Year
Robert Pirès, Arsenal

There was enormous pressure on Robert Pirès when he arrived at Arsenal from Metz in the summer of 2000, a £6 million replacement for the popular Barcelona-bound winger Marc Overmars. Such expectation initially appeared to have flustered the Frenchman and he shone only fleetingly as the Gunners limped to second spot ten points adrift of Manchester United.

Yet after adjusting to the hustle, bustle and muscle of English football his second campaign was outstanding and he became a fearsome prospect for defences. Pirès' capacity to run at high speed, the ball seemingly always under his spell, proved a key asset in the trademark counter-attacking style of play that Arsène Wenger had instilled into his side.

He also had the propensity to score spectacular goals ... and there were plenty in the 2001–02 campaign locker. His wonderful lob against Aston Villa inevitably makes the season's highlights reels along with a sweetly struck volley at home to Middlesborough.

A serious knee injury ended Pirès' involvement in March although he'd already done enough to earn the FWA Player of the Year award. By the time he left Arsenal for Villarreal in 2006 he'd scored 84 goals in 284 appearances. Neutrals and Gunners' fans alike still regard him as among the finest midfield talents ever to grace the English game.

2002-03

For so much of the season Arsène Wenger's Arsenal looked a certain bet to retain their title. So certain that by early March bookmaker Paddy Power was paying out any punter who'd backed them. By then eight points clear, and with Thierry Henry dismantling defences for fun, the run-in looked favourable with the likely championship decider a home game against Manchester United.

Above: All smiles on the cover of the United Review, *but Ferguson's foul temper had dramatic consequences.*

Opposite top: Ashley Cole brings down Leeds United's Mark Viduka.

Opposite right: A much-coveted ticket for the FA Cup final between Arsenal and Southampton.

However, this Arsenal side was not yet the Invincibles. Their long unbeaten run of 30 matches had ended in early October when Everton's precocious 16-year-old whippersnapper Wayne Rooney unleashed a jaw-dropping 30-yard drive to beat David Seaman. As the season approached its climax the cracks in Arsenal's defence were widening under pressure. While the Red Devils produced stunning 4-0 and 6-2 wins against Liverpool and Newcastle respectively, the Gunners endured a tame 1-1 draw at Villa Park. The match against United on 16 April had become both showtime and showdown.

This pulsating fixture eventually ended 2-2 but the triumphant body language of Ferguson told its own story. United left Highbury with a three-point lead intact while their hosts contemplated the walking wounded (captain Vieira's dodgy knee) and the suspended (Sol Campbell's red card for elbowing Ole Gunnar Solskjaer). Fergie's team was relentless, winning their next three games against Blackburn, Spurs and Charlton; Wenger squandered a two-goal advantage to let Bolton claim a draw then surrendered the title by going down 2-3 at Highbury to relegation-threatened Leeds.

Arsenal's consolation was a 1-0 FA Cup final victory over Southampton. Perhaps an equally precious memory for Gooners, though, was the sight of Thierry Henry giving Italy's Serie A giants Roma a footballing lesson in November. He became the first Arsenal player to score a Champions League hat-trick – a gentle reminder to Juventus of just how badly they had undervalued his talents – but even Henry could not propel his team further than the second group stage.

Off the field the story of the season was undoubtedly the Old Trafford dressing-room brouhaha in which Ferguson, furious at his team's 2-0 FA Cup fifth-round defeat to Arsenal, kicked a stray football boot into the head

The FA CUP FINAL

ARSENAL F.C. v SOUTHAMPTON F.C.
MILLENNIUM STADIUM, CARDIFF
Saturday 17 May, 2003
KICK OFF 15:00 GATES OPEN 13:00
GATE 3   STAIR 26 LEVEL 6   AISLE 608
BLOCK U9   ROW 1   SEAT 28
         Arsenal F.C.   £80.00

Match of the Season
Arsenal 2 Leeds United 3

This game encapsulated Arsenal's season – flair in attack, fragility in defence. It also had Leeds fans and neutrals scratching heads as to how the visitors could possibly possess such attacking strengths themselves and yet be scrabbling around in the basement. The win all but assured cash-strapped Leeds of another season of Premier League income and handed a reported £500,000 'survival bonus' to manager Peter Reid.

Leeds opened the scoring in the fifth minute, Harry Kewell's exquisite angled drive from outside the box nestling inside David Seaman's far post, but Henry nodded home a rebound off keeper Paul Robinson to level after half an hour. Ian Harte's free kick, diverted by Ashley Cole, restored the lead but then a classically simple Arsenal passing move involving Henry, Pirès and Bergkamp made it 2-2. The final 27 minutes would be season-defining for both clubs.

The 88th minute goal that saved Leeds and turned Arsenal's once-lucid title dreams to dust was fittingly superb. Australian striker Mark Viduka dismissed Oleg Luzhny's challenge on the right before curling the perfect shot into Seaman's far corner. It was the 13th goal of his last nine Premier League appearances – cheered as loudly at Old Trafford as it was among visiting fans in a corner of Highbury.

of David Beckham. The cut required stitches and Beckham made no attempt
to hide the wound at his next training session. Within months he'd signed
for Real Madrid, a move presented as Ferguson's desire to freshen his squad
and Beckham's refusal of a new contract.

MotD Memories: Making the Change

Starring on the pitch is one thing. But converting that experience to effective
punditry or presenting is a whole new ball game for ex-players. As former
Match of the Day, now ITV, commentator Clive Tyldesley often witnessed.

He recalls: 'Our old *MotD* editor Brian Barwick used to tell them: "We
know that you know a lot about football. But your job now is to convey
your knowledge to people who have never been there, never stood on a
touchline, never taken a penalty in a big game. It's not just a simple question
of us thinking you talk quite well, you used to be a footballer. You've got to
embrace our industry."

'That has been a difficult journey for some. I'm sure it was for Jimmy
[Hill], it certainly was for Bob Wilson and it was for Gary Lineker in the
early days. To obtain sufficient broadcasting skills – a brand new skill-set –
in order to bring all that you did as a truly great footballer in Gary's case
and actually look down that black hole [of the camera] and be as good a
presenter ... that's a long, long journey.'

Player of the Year
Thierry Henry, Arsenal

Never is a long time but fans will be extraordinarily fortunate if they ever see a player of Thierry Henry's ilk in English football again.

He set new records, won numerous club and international trophies and collected untold personal accolades – all standard living-legend fare. But what made Henry unique was a concoction of attributes. He combined devastating speed and surprising power with the deftest of touches and great heading ability. Unselfish in pursuit of team success he was, as countless defenders discovered, also the supreme finisher.

Henry burst into European football with Monaco and following a January 1999 move looked set to do great things at Juventus. But his form hit the wall, he struggled to hold a first-team place and by the time Arsenal manager Arsène Wenger arrived to rescue him six months later his confidence had taken a hammering.

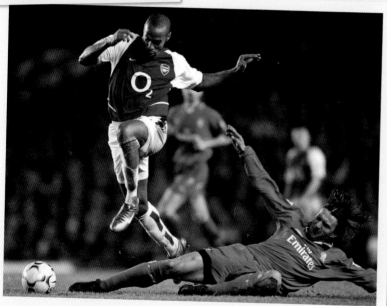

Wenger decided to convert his new signing from winger to striker – a plan Henry himself questioned – and when the player failed to find the net in his first eight appearances it seemed both the positional switch and the estimated £11 million transfer fee were a mistake. Thankfully, both manager and player persevered; by the end of his first season Henry had hit 26 goals in all competitions.

In this, the first of his three Player of the Year award-winning campaigns, he banged in 32 (missing out on the Golden Boot to Ruud van Nistelrooy) and his stunning solo strike in the 3-0 victory over Spurs at Highbury was voted Goal of the Season. He also finished runner-up to Zinedine Zidane in the 2003 FIFA World Player of the Year award and was named Man of the Match as Arsenal claimed a second consecutive FA Cup.

Played 38, Won 26, Drawn 12, Lost 0, Points 90. Rarely, however, do statistics do justice to reality and the achievement of Arsenal's 'Invincibles' – the first top-flight team since Preston North End in 1888–9 to complete an entire league programme unbeaten – was unprecedented in the modern English game. It spoke volumes for the squad's mental strength (an oft-quoted Wenger measure) as well as their passion, commitment and sumptuous football. The 11-point winning margin over Chelsea far from flattered them.

Which is not to say the league was an easy ride. Almost certainly there would have been no Gunner Invincibles had Ruud van Nistelrooy converted an injury-time penalty on 21 September. That miss heralded the notorious 'Battle of Old Trafford' as Martin Keown's dance around the Dutchman – including a forearm bash to the head – sparked a shameful brawl. Parlour, Cole, Lauren, Lehmann and Vieira all waded in and Arsenal were later fined a record £175,000 for failing to control their players.

The Invincibles' great run at first seemed to have validated Wenger's 2002 prophecy of a 'shift of power' in English football. As it turned out the only real shift was from Leeds to Chelsea. The former had sold off many of their 2001 Champions League semi-final stars to service catastrophic debts and were duly relegated along with Wolves and a Leicester side bouncing between divisions. Chelsea had faced a similar glimpse of oblivion despite finishing in the Premier League's top six for seven seasons. But in the summer of 2003 chairman Ken Bates' decision to sell the club to Russian billionaire Roman Abramovich for £150 million proved their salvation.

Wenger would soon see just how much footballing power money could buy. Abramovich clearly had deep pockets while up at Old Trafford an American tycoon, Malcolm Glazer, was said to be preparing a bid for

Above: Match of the Day celebrated its 40th birthday in 2004.

Opposite left: Robbie Fowler shoots wide for Man City.

Match of the Season
Spurs 3 Man City 4

As City manager Kevin Keegan walked down the tunnel at half-time he muttered to number two Derek Fazackerley: 'Where's the nearest Job Centre?' And with good reason. With just one win in 18 games, City were both 3-0 and a man down (Joey Barton foolishly booked for dissent as the sides left the field). In the dressing room a disconsolate Keegan confronted his wretched players: 'We're looking for a miracle,' he admitted.

And along it came. In fact, in sporting terms this was a miracle right up there with some of the best in the Bible. Remember, it was four days before Lazarus was raised from the dead; Keegan's pep talk did the job for City inside 15 minutes.

Spurs eased themselves into the second half confident that goals from King, Keane and Ziege would be more than enough. But City fizzed with panache. The superb Sylvain Distin got one back on 41 minutes, Bosvelt a second on the hour, Shaun Wright-Phillips an equaliser in the 80th and Jon Macken the winner in stoppage time. Like miracles, the thing about comebacks is you just never see them coming.

Above: The Invincibles' Captain Vieira and Manager Wenger.

Manchester United. Both clubs would have replenished transfer war chests which Arsenal's business model could not match. The decade ahead would mean lean pickings for Highbury.

This captivating season was, sadly, not reflected in the FA Cup final – a 3-0 stroll for United against a Millwall team that had, up to then, performed heroically. But Middlesborough's 2-1 Carling Cup win over Bolton provided both emotion and high drama, handing the Teesiders the first major honours of their 128-year history through early goals from Joseph-Désiré Job and Boudewijn Zenden. The trophy justified manager Steve McClaren's teambuilding, particularly the acquisition of Brazilian maestro Juninho, and the huge investment of chairman Steve Gibson.

Stat's Football – *MotD* Statistician Albert Sewell

Opposite top: Man-marking Thierry Henry was every player's nightmare.

Opposite bottom: Not a goal celebration, but a pose for the launch of Arsenal's new away kit.

He was the commentator's crutch and the anchor man's saviour. Step forward Albert Sewell, the man who for 37 years was *Match of the Day*'s statto extraordinaire.

Not for him the bright lights of the studio or the pitch-side manager's interview. Albert was strictly backroom, providing commentators and presenters with statistical jewels that could enliven even the dullest of games. Viewers would discover how one more win would break Bolton's record of successive league victories, or that Liverpool never lost when Ian Rush scored (until the 1987 League Cup of course).

Viewers got to know him through Des Lynam's occasional references to 'our man Albert' and, as former BBC colleague Gerald Sinstadt recalled, '... it became necessary to prove that this was a human being and not a machine. So one Saturday Albert duly appeared in the studio, answered Des's questions modestly, and with his trademark little smile, then quietly disappeared into the background again.'

Albert's first job on leaving school at 16 was a sports-desk messenger boy at the *Daily Sketch*. He later worked for the Press Association before joining *MotD* in 1968.

By the time of his retirement in 2005 his personal records library included 24,000 player transfers and 6,400 managerial changes. John Motson once described his pre-match briefings as 'six pages of editorial gold dust.'

Player of the Year
Thierry Henry, Arsenal

This was the season which perhaps saw Henry at the peak of his powers. The previous year he'd won both the Football Writers' Association and Professional Footballers' Association Player of the Year awards; now both sailed his way again. Hardly suprising given his contribution – 39 goals in all competitions – to the Arsenal Invincibles.

By now it was no longer a case of winger or central striker; Henry was playing everywhere and scoring from anywhere. Tactically, it's hard to know what more Arsène Wenger could have said to his teams other than 'give it to Thierry'. That was certainly standard advice from the home terraces.

Henry had developed many subtle nuances to his game but the sight of him drifting out left to receive possession was enough for many a defence to hit the panic button. It would usually signal a definitive, driving run at phenonomenal speed, backtracking opponents caught between risking a tackle and trying desperately to slow him down. As for man-marking him, it would have been easier to get alongside a ghost.

Henry ended the season with both the Premier League and European Golden Boots (the top scorer's award) and could count himself unlucky to finish runner-up to FIFA's World Player of the Year – Barcelona's Ronaldinho.

2004-05

Roman Abramovich's first season at Chelsea – a league runners-up spot and Champions League semi-final – could be considered reasonably successful. But the owner wanted more bang for his buck. Claudio Ranieri was sacked and a new, charismatic manager unleashed.

Above: José Mourinho arrives at Stamford Bridge.

Opposite: The Liverpool Echo*'s reaction to their team's fifth European Cup victory.*

The arrival of José Mourinho at Stamford Bridge felt like Roman's revolution was finally underway. Football press conferences can be dull affairs in which meaty scoops are as rare as lengthy managerial careers. But Mourinho, who had just steered Porto to their first Champions League win, lobbed a hand grenade into the whole process. 'We have top players and, sorry if I'm arrogant, we have a top manager,' he informed the assembled press corps. 'Please don't call me arrogant, but I'm European champion and I think I'm a special one.' He then set about proving it.

Chelsea did not so much win the Premier League in 2005 as flay the living daylights out of it. They finished with a record 95 points – 12 more than their closest rivals Arsenal and 18 more than Manchester United. In fact the Merseyside clubs, occupying fourth and fifth spot, were closer to relegation in terms of points than they were to the title. But for a solitary off-day at Manchester City, when they lost to a Nicolas Anelka penalty, Chelsea would have become the New Invincibles.

For Arsenal and United, meanwhile, the consolation was an FA Cup final. It ended 0-0, a match dominated by Alex Ferguson's side yet settled by Gunners' keeper Jens Lehmann whose brilliant all-round performance culminated in a decisive save off Paul Scholes during the penalty shoot-out.

Chelsea took the League Cup but again their manager stole the headlines. After being taunted by opposing fans as his side trailed Liverpool 1-0, Mourinho's response to a Steven Gerrard own goal was a 'hush' gesture. He was banished from the touchline but saw his team go on to clinch victory 3-2 and with it his first English trophy. He escaped an FA charge, claiming his actions were aimed at an overcritical press box.

Chelsea's Champions League semi-final second leg was also controversial, hinging on a hotly disputed fourth-minute Luis García goal.

Every TV angle in Anfield screamed doubt as to whether the ball crossed the line but Mourinho went further, insisting that 'the linesman scored the goal'. Whatever, Liverpool were worthy winners on the night. They were nearing the end of a long path back to European Cup glory. Unfortunately it was about to get a whole lot rockier (see Match of the Season).

Match of the Season
Liverpool 3 AC Milan 3
(3-2 on pens)

For the first half of this Champions League final in Istanbul, Liverpool were a stumbling mess. Behind from the first-minute to Paolo Maldini's volley, they had no answer to the Italians' rampant midfield of Seedorf, Gattuso, Kaká and Pirlo and were fortunate not to concede a second in the 13th minute when Hernán Crespo's header was cleared off the line. The Argentinian striker made no mistake in the 39th with a far post tap-in from Shevchenko's cross, then made it 3-0 on the stroke of half-time with a clever dink over goalkeeper Jerzy Dudek. The travelling Kop may have sung 'we're gonna win 4-3' but it was a response born of defiance, not belief.

Belief matters, of course, but often the tactical tweak or sudden inspirational burst turns the tide. Rafa Benítez's decision to introduce Didi Hamann, sidelined until then with a broken toe, re-energised the midfield beyond recognition. And on matters inspirational Steven Gerrard was peerless.

The Liverpool captain threw himself into the fray, first heading home John Arne Riise's cross, then conjuring space to release Vladimir Smicer for the second. It was Gerrard's run into the penalty area which allowed Xabi Alonso to equalize from a penalty and then, after extra-time, Dudek stepped up to save both Pirlo and Shevchenko's penalties in the shoot-out. Liverpool had won their fifth European Cup 21 long years after the last.

Match of the Day Wins Back the Premier League

'We have missed the highlights programme and it feels like we are welcoming back an old and much-loved friend.' That statement from BBC's director of sport Peter Salmon on August 8, 2003 heralded the return of *MotD* to Saturday night, a major revamp of its look and content and – most importantly – a big vote of confidence in its future.

Salmon revealed that in addition to the traditional slot after Saturday's late news the show would be repeated on Sunday mornings (great news for parents with football-mad youngsters). Match footage would also be re-worked into *MotD2*, a second weekend highlights package to be broadcast on selected Sunday nights.

The three-year deal beginning in August 2004 cost the BBC £105 million. But this was dwarfed by Sky's successful £1.02 billion bid for all four 'live match packages' – a total of 138 games per season. Despite concerns by the European Commission that Sky's domination of live football might conceal an uncompetitive bidding process, signed contracts were allowed to stand.

League Managers Association boss John Barnwell described the return of *Match of the Day* as 'terrific, really great news for football' while in its statement ITV said: 'We're disappointed not to win the highlights but we bid what the rights were worth to ITV.'

Opposite: Frank Lampard sprints away from Middlesbrough's George Boateng.

Opposite right: Lampard worries Porto defender Seitaridis and keeper Nuno during a Champions League fixture in Portugal.

Below: Gary Lineker was delighted to see MotD back on a Saturday night.

Player of the Year
Frank Lampard, Chelsea

Signed by Claudio Ranieri for £11 million in June 2001, Frank Lampard was brilliant in his first three seasons at Stamford Bridge. Yet his personal performances were not enough to produce trophies; Chelsea narrowly missed out both in Europe and on several domestic fronts.

However, in his fourth campaign with the Blues, Lampard was the fulcrum of their historic Premier League triumph. He featured in all 38 top-flight games for the third consecutive season and his 19 goals in all competitions represented an outstanding return from midfield. The final two at Bolton were classic Lampard – incorporating powerful running, technical control and deadly finishing – and clinched the title to send José Mourinho's charges into dream land.

Lampard's performances for club and country meant that in addition to his 2005 FWA award he finished runner-up in both the FIFA World Player of the Year and the Ballon d'Or – narrowly missing out to Ronaldinho on both occasions. Adored by Chelsea fans, he became the club's record goalscorer in 2013, topping Bobby Tambling's total of 202 strikes.

2005-06

For Chelsea fans championship trophies must seem like the No. 11 buses that doggedly plough through match-day traffic on the King's Road: you wait for ever then two come along at once. Having won the Premier League in 2005, their first top division title in 50 years, they did it again the following season.

Opposite top: Djibril Cissé scored Liverpool's first.

Opposite bottom: A West Ham cup final flag to fly from your car window.

Below: The ref sends Arsenal's Jens Lehmann packing.

And with similar swagger. By the time they beat closest rivals Manchester United 3-0 at Stamford Bridge they were 12 points clear with two games still to play. Mourinho celebrated as perhaps only he would – by throwing both his jacket and his winner's medal into the Matthew Harding stand. 'One of the reasons we are champions is that we have a very good record at home, and the fans are a part of that, so I wanted to share the moment with them,' he said later.

Chelsea's critics accused them of a drab brand of football yet if goals are any measure the facts suggest otherwise. During their back-to-back league wins the Blues played 76, won 58 and lost only six matches (two of which were after the 2006 title had been won). Over that time they outscored opponents four goals to one, a return few previous champions have matched.

Match of the Season
Liverpool 3 West Ham 3
(3-1 on pens)

This was the last of six FA Cup finals to be played at Cardiff's Millennium Stadium during Wembley's rebuild ... and it proved a classic. The only shame was that 120 minutes of thrilling football, and a great sporting attitude from both sides, had to end in the lottery of sudden death.

West Ham made all the early running and were two up inside half an hour thanks to a Jamie Carragher own goal and a poacher's tap-in from Dean Ashton. Djibril Cissé pulled one back before the break but immediately after half-time only a fabulous double save from Reina kept Liverpool in the game.

When Steven Gerrard levelled things nine minutes into the second half it seemed the Hammers had blown their big chance. But then Paul Konchesky's 64th minute cross-cum-shot floated in and Alan Pardew's young side held firm right up until the PA man began announcing added time. Then the ball fell to Gerrard 30 yards out.

His volley low into the corner of Shaka Hislop's goal was world class. Though the Hammers kept the score to 3-3 in extra-time Gerrard's strike had mortally wounded morale and they folded in the penalty shoot-out 3-1.

Chelsea's celebrations at the end of the season only fuelled the sense of injustice in north London. Both Arsenal and Spurs believed they had lost games which cost them dear both in income and kudos. Arsenal blamed a ref; Spurs, at first, blamed a cook.

Appearing in their first-ever Champions League final, the Gunners were dealt a body blow when Norwegian referee Terje Hauge red-carded Jens Lehmann for denying a clear goal-scoring opportunity. True, Lehmann had caught Samuel Eto'o but Barcelona had gone on to score anyway. If the referee had played advantage the goal would have been upheld and Lehmann would have stayed on the pitch having denied nothing.

To their credit Arsenal rallied and Sol Campbell headed them in front after 37 minutes. They resisted until the 76th minute but then Eto'o scored from a Henrik Larsson pass – a goal Arsenal were convinced should have been ruled offside – and then went behind to the eventual winner from Juliano Belletti in the 81st. 'It's difficult to accept to lose the game on the wrong decisions,' Arsène Wenger fumed later.

For Spurs the final match of the season was almost as painful. A win at Upton Park would have handed them Champions League football but they arrived with ten players violently ill, failed to get a postponement, lost 2-1 and then saw Arsenal snatch fourth place by beating Wigan in their farewell to Highbury. Suspicion focused on a dodgy lasagne but health officials later exonerated the hotel concerned.

Opposite top: Thierry Henry trading card.

Opposite bottom: Henry bypasses Birmingham's Mario Melchiot.

Below: Patrick Vieira liked to make it home from dinner in time to hear himself being discussed on MotD.

MotD Memories: Seeing Red Over *MotD*

Arsenal and Man City midfielder Patrick Vieira says getting home in time for *MotD* was always his plan after games. But he didn't always like what he heard and saw.

'After the game you're going for dinner but you're always trying to get home to watch *MotD*,' he says. 'I have to be honest, I was disappointed with some of the comments about myself when I used to be sent off quite often. But it's a view and I think everyone

has a different opinion.

'Did we discuss it? Yes, of course, on a Sunday morning before training you always have a comment to make.'

Among the outstanding goals he witnessed was Thierry Henry's flick-up and volley past fellow Frenchman Fabian Bartez in October 2000 – enough to secure a 1-0 win over Man Utd – for which Vieira supplied the pass. He also admires Alan Shearer's stunning 22-yarder for Newcastle against Everton in December 2002.

For pure farce he highlights the penalty mix-up between Henry and Robert Pirès during a Gunners' home game against Man City in 2005. Instead of a direct shot Henry wanted Pirès to roll the ball to him. But a baffled Pirès merely wafted a boot and the referee awarded a free kick to City.

'Thierry had tried to speak English,' says Vieira, 'but Robert couldn't understand. It was one of the funniest moments.' Henry tells it differently: 'I didn't touch that ball. I wasn't involved in that. Robert Pirès messed it up – yes Robert, you did!'

 ### Player of the Year
Thierry Henry, Arsenal

The stats behind Henry's glorious career in English football say everything and nothing about the player.

Everything because they bear witness to his consistent brilliance – top goalscorer in the Premier League for a record four seasons, the first player to score 20 goals in five consecutive seasons, third all-time league leading scorer and the best-ever strike rate of 1.46 games per goal.

And nothing because no avalanche of statistics, however impressive, can hope to reflect what it was like to see him in full flight, closing in on a penalty area, fans rising from every seat, the shot from that cultured right foot (he scored only 33 of his 176 league goals with his left) searing unerringly towards its target. He played with a verve, freedom and passion that is sadly all too rare in today's professional game. Little wonder that French car manufacturer Renault made him the face of its Va Va Voom advertising campaign.

Phrases such as 'world class' sometimes trip from the football pundit's tongue too easily. But if anyone was, Thierry was.

WORLD CUP – GERMANY 2006

Yet another World Cup quarter-final exit for England marked the end of an era. Sven Goran Eriksson, the most successful manager since Sir Alf Ramsey, resigned while David Beckham quit the captaincy he'd held for 58 of his 94 caps. Both announcements were expected; the real sadness for England fans was that the FA's 'golden generation' of footballers – the likes of Steven Gerrard, Michael Owen, Paul Scholes, Frank Lampard and Beckham himself – had never fulfilled their potential on the international stage.

Below: Zidane was sent off for a headbutt on Marco Materazzi.

In Germany England's mettle was, to say the least, tarnished. Scholes had retired two years earlier and other golden boys, notably Owen and Beckham, were bedevilled by sickness and injury. But there should still have been enough class in Lampard, Wayne Rooney and Gerrard and the formidable back four of John Terry, Rio Ferdinand, Ashley Cole and Gary Neville, to fire a performance. By the time Eriksson's side tamely bowed out the player who had perhaps most impressed was the one most heavily criticised in advance – Owen Hargreaves.

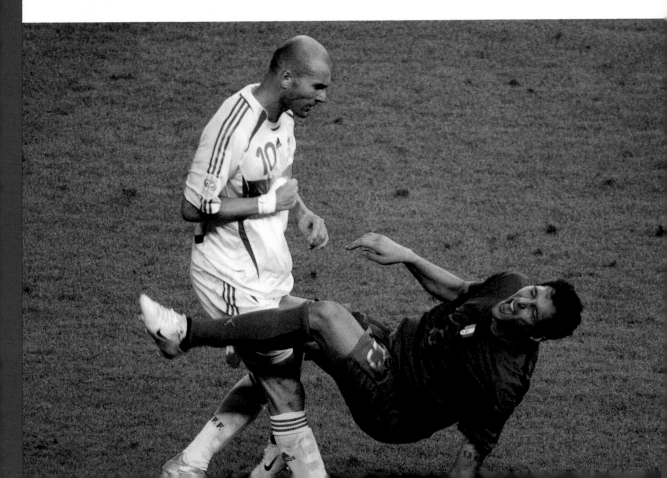

Right: Rooney was sent off for stamping on Portuguese defender Ricardo Carvalho.

In Group B England hardly had the toughest of challenges. Yet they huffed and puffed over Paraquay, squeezing through 1-0 thanks to Carlos Gamarra's own goal, and then toiled against Trinidad and Tobago until late efforts from Peter Crouch and Gerrard. A 2-2 draw with Sweden ensured progression (Joe Cole's dipping volley was the highlight) but Owen's tournament-ending cruciate ligament injury was a big blow to morale.

The second round encounter with Ecuador offered an opportunity to kick-start their campaign. But England flattered to deceive, mixing brief periods of quality with wasteful passing and poor finishing. Once again they were dependant on Beckham's dead-ball prowess – he rolled back the years

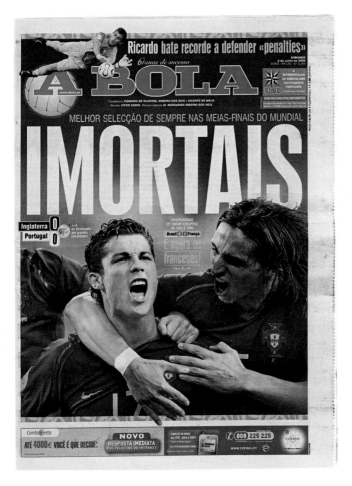

to strike a 30-yard peach – although it couldn't disguise the frailties.

And yet, somehow, England made the last eight. The Portugal side they faced had just beaten Holland 1-0 in the so-called Battle of Nuremberg, a game in which Russian referee Valentin Ivanov issued four red and 16 yellow cards (a FIFA tournament record for a single match). In players like Figo, Ronaldo, and Tiago Portugal had the firepower to trouble any side but they were not at their best and had Wayne Rooney not been dismissed for a stamp on Ricardo Carvalho's groin England might have snatched it. As it was they battled through extra time to a penalty shootout, with Hargreaves magnificent throughout.

In one interview after the game Eriksson insisted 'We have practised [penalties] so much I don't think we could possibly practise them any more.' Unfortunately you couldn't tell. Even by England standards this was penalty-taking at its most

Above: Ronaldo stars on the front cover of A Bola.

Opposite: Peter Crouch gets to the high ball ahead of Paraguay's Denis Caniza.

agonising with Lampard, Gerrard and Carragher seeing their kicks saved and only Hargreaves putting one away. There were brief flickers of hope as Viana and Petit missed but when Ronaldo netted Portugal's fifth it was all over. Once again, the curse of the shootout had struck.

Portugal were knocked out 1-0 by France in the semis – the first defeat in 13 World Cup finals games for manager Luiz Felipe 'Big Phil' Scolari. The other finalists were Italy who overcame the host nation 2-1 with goals from Fabio Grosso and Alessandro Del Piero in the 119th and 120th minutes. Italy went on to take their fourth world championship although their achievement was overshadowed by the dismissal of France's Zinedine Zidane for head-butting Marco Materazzi. It was the 28th red card of the tournament – an all-time record.

2006-07

After their FA Cup heroics at Wembley, West Ham dominated the close-season headlines by pulling off the most sensational transfer coup in years: the double signing of Argentinian World Cup stars Carlos Tevez and Javier Mascherano. It was a deal that would rapidly unravel amid an outcry from rival clubs. It probably also kept the Hammers in the Premier League.

Opposite top: Chelsea souvenir victory pennant.

Opposite bottom: West Ham's Mark Noble and Yossi Benayoun celebrate.

Below: Three players were sent off and both clubs fined £100,000 for the 20-man Arsenal/Chelsea punch-up.

The Tevez –Mascherano affair was mind-numbingly complex but in essence the problem was this. Both effectively appeared under contract to Iranian businessman Kia Joorabchian in breach of strict Premier League rules allowing only clubs to own players. After much administrative wrangling Mascherano was eventually registered with Liverpool in February 2007 but Tevez's contract was rewritten and he was allowed to stay at Upton Park.

West Ham pleaded guilty to charges relating to third-party influence over team policy and failing to act in good faith. They were hit with a massive £5.5 million fine but, crucially, avoided a points deduction. By the spring of 2007 Tevez couldn't stop scoring – seven goals in the final ten games – and aggrieved clubs locked in a relegation battle with the Hammers began instructing lawyers.

Sheffield United, who eventually went down on 38 points along with Charlton (34) and Watford (28), led the chorus of complaints. Tevez's strike in the Hammers' 1-0 final-day win at Manchester United had ensured his side's survival and the Blades argued that his goals, and the lack of any points

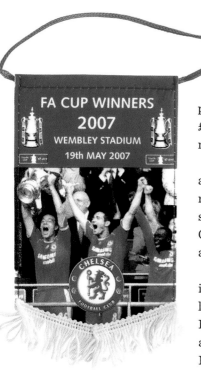

FA CUP WINNERS
2007
WEMBLEY STADIUM
19th MAY 2007

penalty, meant their relegation was a farce. They eventually accepted a £26.5 million out-of-court settlement from West Ham, a sum still being repaid in 2013.

At the business end of the division Manchester United took the title in a season which saw their Portuguese sensation Cristiano Ronaldo really make his mark. Ronaldo bagged almost a quarter of United's 83 goals and slotted home the Manchester derby penalty which sealed the title on 5 May. Chelsea, already languishing seven points behind, could manage only a draw at Arsenal the following day.

The Blues did, though, manage a trophy double; the League Cup (2-1 in the final against Arsenal) and the FA Cup (1-0 against Man Utd). The latter was a turgid game but the League Cup proved a belter in every sense. Both clubs were later fined £100,000 each after a 20-man brawl broke out and three players were sent off. At one point both Arsène Wenger and José Mourinho went on to the pitch to try and calm things down, arguably a spectacle in itself.

Match of the Season
Manchester United 0
West Ham United 1

Manchester United looked a tired team by the final game of the season. With the title secure, and an FA Cup final still to come, they were never going to leap for the Hammers' jugular especially with Scholes, Ronaldo, Giggs and Vidić on the bench. That said, any win for visitors to Old Trafford was impressive and for West Ham it was essential if they were not to depend on other results for Premier League survival.

For almost the entire first half they were ruthlessly battered. Then, as the fourth official signalled two minutes of added time, keeper Rob Green found Bobby Zamora with a long goal kick, his nod down fell to Tevez, a nifty one-two combined with a lucky bounce allowed the Argentine through on goal and the acute-angle finish was perfect.

In the second half, to chants of 'send them down' from the Stretford End it seemed unlikely Alan Curbishley's side could see out the win. But United's edge was gone, passes went astray, key players were thinking ahead to Wembley and the Hammers' counter-attacks proved increasingly effective. At the final whistle there was jubilation all round as Man Utd received the league trophy and West Ham received the adulation of their fans.

MotD Memories: The Essence of 'Lads TV'

Throughout the 1990s Des Lynam was the face of *Match of the Day*. He was by then an experienced and respected sports broadcaster but that didn't stop critics suggesting the real reason for his appointment was a drive for more female viewers.

Lynam's assured presenting style and good-looks may well have appealed to women but according to fellow broadcaster and Arsenal fan Piers Morgan he was never going to demolish the male bastion that is *MotD*.

'Des had that effortless charm which is why he made women watch *Match of the Day*,' says Piers. 'He was very good-looking, very charming and he made it very approachable. [Predecessor] Jimmy Hill was much more of a football man and he had a big chin.

'But, here's the reality, not many women watch *MotD*. It's basically a lads' thing to do; you get home from the pub, you sit down with your brother, your mates, your dad – whoever it is – and you start shouting from the moment it comes on. You shout at what you see and you shout at what the pundits say.

'There are certain sporting [programme] tunes which are completely iconic and the moment you hear it you know what it means; football, passion, a couple of beers, argument. It means all the things you associate with watching football. And it makes you feel better.'

 Player of the Year
Cristiano Ronaldo, Manchester United

When Cristiano Ronaldo came back to England following the infamous 'winking' incident at the World Cup finals in Germany he was perhaps the most hated man in the country.

Facing vitriolic abuse from the stands, dealing with constant speculation surrounding his future (it was the first summer Real Madrid had shown concrete interest) and running at English defenders determined to 'stick one on him', Ronaldo was in a battle to stay on course and fulfil his lifelong dream of becoming the world's best player.

Fortunately he was shielded astutely by Sir Alex Ferguson who once again demonstrated the kind of man-management that made him one of the best British coaches of all time. The Portuguese flyer thrived with this backing, repaying Fergie's loyalty in spectacular fashion.

Having developed physically at an impressive rate during the previous season he now added steel, power and, most importantly, goals to his expanding repertoire. Ronaldo hit 23 in all competitions to secure both the PFA Player of the Year and PFA Young Player of the Year awards alongside his FWA accolade. But the best was still to come.

2007-08

Everyone loves tucking into final-day drama – except, of course, the nervous fans involved – and the Premier League fixtures of 11 May 2008 served up double portions. At the top Manchester United and Chelsea were locked together on 84 points while in the basement Fulham and Reading both had 33, with Birmingham just a point behind. Woeful Derby had long gone; finishing on a record Premier low of 11.

Going into the game United had a 17-point goal-difference advantage but they had to assume Chelsea would win at home to Bolton. That would require them to beat Wigan Athletic at the DW Stadium so when Cristiano Ronaldo bagged his 31st goal of the season from the penalty spot there was much relief among the visiting fans. But not for long.

At Stamford Bridge, Andrei Shevchenko put Chelsea ahead on 62 minutes. United still led the division but Wigan goalkeeper Chris Kirkland was in magnificent form and it seemed the Latics might yet get something from the game. It was, in Sir Alex Ferguson's memorable words, 'squeaky bum time'. Chelsea desperately wanted silverware, having lost the League Cup final 2-1 to Spurs in February.

Below: The Match of the Day *annual celebrated another fantastic year of football.*

With heavy rain rapidly turning the pitch into a pond, Ferguson sent on 34-year-old substitute Ryan Giggs for a record-equalling (with Bobby Charlton) 758th club appearance. For Wigan defenders, leg-weary on a sodden pitch, his must have been the last face – more accurately back – they wanted to see and, sure enough, with ten minutes left, Rooney threaded a ball through the centre for the Welshman to race in and ease the ball past Kirkland.

Match of the Season
Manchester United 1 Chelsea 1
(6-5 on pens)

For 120 minutes this was a thrilling Champions League final although the real drama lay in the penalty shoot-out. The persistent football myth is that John Terry lost the cup for Chelsea by slipping and mishitting the penalty that would have won it. The truth is that United goalkeeper Edwin van der Sar saved the 14th kick, taken by Nicolas Anelka, to bring a third European Cup to Old Trafford. Either way, it spelt the end of Chelsea manager Avram Grant's eight-month tenure following José Mourinho's decision to quit.

United went ahead in the 27th minute when Wes Brown's in-swinging cross allowed Cristiano Ronaldo to head his 42nd goal of the season. Eight minutes later it would have been two but for Petr Cech's double save off Carlos Tevez and Michael Carrick but then, just before half-time, Frank Lampard equalised, latching on to the loose ball which had cannoned between Nemanja Vidić and Rio Ferdinand.

Towards the end of the second half Chelsea twice almost sealed it as first Didier Drogba then Lampard struck the woodwork. But perhaps the cup's destiny was decided when, with just four minutes of extra-time left, Drogba was sent off for aiming a slap at Vidić. This meant Terry was promoted to penalty taker ... and the myth was born.

Above: John Terry sends his vital penalty wide of the mark.

It was all over for Chelsea and Matt Taylor's equaliser for Bolton in stoppage time denied them even the consolation of finishing level on points. United had won their tenth title in 15 years and their manager admitted that, in those final nerve-jangling moments, Giggs was the obvious choice to deliver. 'As soon as it started raining, I was thinking: "how am I going to get Giggs into this game", because he is fantastic on soft ground,' said Sir Alex. 'His balance, his ability to beat a man, are supreme. Maybe it was fate that he scored.'

Back at the bottom Fulham's brave late-season fight, which had included a plucky 3-2 comeback win at Manchester City, looked over. Both Reading and Birmingham were en route to 4-0 victories while the Cottagers remained deadlocked 0-0 at Portsmouth. Then in the 76th minute, Jimmy Bullard's free-kick was met at the far post by the head of Danny Murphy to secure the win and another Premier League season. For Portsmouth an historic 1-0 FA Cup win over Cardiff would soon crown an excellent season.

Peter Schmeichel – Standing Up for Keepers

Opposite top: Ronaldo is brought down by Liverpool's Mohamed Sissoko.

Opposite bottom: Ronaldo takes a hat-trick against Newcastle United at Old Trafford.

Below: Peter Schmeichel rates Motty as the best of the best.

If there's one thing about punditry that really niggles Peter Schmeichel it's former outfield players criticising goalkeepers. He believes the problem is simple; they never see things from the keeper's perspective.

'Most pundits haven't played in goal,' says the treble-winning former Manchester United star. 'You can understand that they don't know how if a ball is deflected for instance you have got no chance. It doesn't matter how close [the shot] is if you are unbalanced. And [they don't see] little things like getting your angles right.

'I know what irritates goalkeepers these days, and back then, "you can't get beaten on the near post"; stereotypes and clichés like that. Or "he's not very good, he's not coming for crosses". In the Premier League who comes for crosses? Not really that many are there – if anyone? It's irritating because they haven't prepared, they haven't asked anybody.'

Schmeichel's favourite commentator is John Motson because 'he's got an incredible voice, a world-branded voice, and his knowledge is incredible. While a lot of what he says is prepared for the occasion he has this back-catalogue of knowledge which not many people in football have.'

Schmeichel adds: 'My personal taste [in commentary] is I like it to be a song – a song that's been sung along with the game; a duet between the commentator and the summarizer. It's what makes me want to listen. Saying every player's name, statistics about every player, that's tiring for me.'

Player of the Year
Cristiano Ronaldo, Manchester United

There are very few athletes in the world capable of maintaining the level of performance that Cristiano Ronaldo produced during his blistering 2007–08 season for Manchester United.

The campaign didn't begin in the best vein – he was sent off against Portsmouth for a head-butt in the second match of the season – but the Portuguese trickster didn't look back after that, hitting 42 goals in all competitions. He was now in the vanguard of a feared counter-attacking trio alongside Wayne Rooney and Carlos Tevez.

Spectacular goals, such as his 30-yard 'knuckle ball' free-kick against Portsmouth, which left David James rooted to the spot, and his audacious back-heel flick at home to Aston Villa became the norm. His trademark, whip-like stepover was impossible for defenders to deal with when performed at pace and his prowess in the air was supplemented by a superhuman leap – perfectly demonstrated by that headed goal in the Champions League triumph over Chelsea.

2008-09

A second hat-trick of titles for Manchester United underlined their dominance of the Premier League since its inception. On only four other occasions had a team won three consecutive campaigns; Huddersfield (1923–26), Arsenal (1932–35), Liverpool (1981–84) and United themselves (1998–2001). The 2008–09 squad was arguably the club's strongest of modern times but it was about to lose its most potent attacker. In June 2009 United accepted an £80 million offer for Ronaldo from Real Madrid.

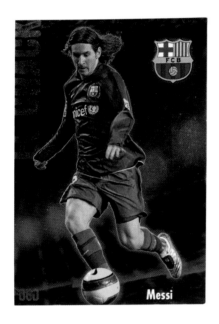

Above: Lionel Messi trading card.

Opposite top: Messi scores the goal that settles the Champions League final at the Stadio Olimpico in Rome.

Opposite bottom: David Bentley opened the scoring for Spurs with a 40-yard shot.

In truth, Ronaldo had come nowhere near his red-hot form of the previous season. His total goal tally of 26 was 16 fewer than 2007–08 and long-running negotiations over the Madrid deal must surely have had an effect. But in Rooney (20 goals), Tevez (15) and Berbatov (14) there was still plenty of firepower.

Many would argue that it was actually a mean defence, particularly keeper Edwin van der Sar and the centre-back pairing of Vidić and Ferdinand, that proved the key to success. United conceded just 24 goals all season – a statistic matched only by Chelsea – though paradoxically this same defence proved uncharacteristically hesitant in the 2-0 Champions League final defeat by Barcelona.

Chelsea fans still insist it should have been their team who faced United in that game. In the home semi-final second leg they lost to the Catalonians after seeing four strong penalty appeals – including a clear handball by Gerard Piqué – turned down by Norwegian referee Tom Ovrebo. For Guus Hiddink, brought in as caretaker manager following Luiz Felipe Scolari's sacking in February, it would have been a fitting climax to his popular three-month spell in charge although he did have the consolation of a 2-1 FA Cup final victory over Everton.

The relegation fight again went down to the final day, producing a 'North East Nightmare' in which four clubs were in danger of the drop. In the fallout, Newcastle United ended their 16 years in the top flight, going down 1-0 at Villa Park, and Middlesborough joined them in the Championship following a 2-1 defeat at West Ham. Those defeats ensured that both Sunderland, who lost 3-2 at home to Chelsea, and Hull City, beaten 1-0 by visitors Man Utd, stayed up. For Hull manager Phil Brown the relief was palpable, inspiring him to lead the Tigers faithful in an impromptu rendition of the Beach Boys classic, and terraces anthem, 'Sloop John B'. Afterwards midfielder Nick Barmby told one interviewer: 'We'll be going out for a few beers to celebrate. But there's no way we're letting the boss near a karaoke bar.'

Match of the Season
Arsenal 4 Tottenham 4

One of those genuinely jaw-dropping games more reminiscent of a schoolyard scoreline than a Premier League derby. At times the eccentricities of both goalkeepers made you suspect the Emirates was a schoolyard – although in fairness there was also some great football on show.

Spurs winger David Bentley set the tone in the 15th minute when he spotted Manuel Almunia off his line and beat the floundering keeper from 40 yards. Fortunately for Arsenal, Heurelho Gomes was in equally eccentric mode at the other end, punching defender Jermaine Jenas in the head while trying to clear a Robin Van Persie corner to present Mikael Silvestre with the equaliser. Gomes was also culpable for Arsenal's second, a William Gallas header, and after Emmanuel Adebayor tapped in a third it looked all up for Spurs. They reduced the arrears when Almunia's fumble allowed Darren Bent a simple tap-in but then the outstanding RVP hit the Gunners' fourth with a minute left on the clock.

You can see why Spurs fans would stream from the terraces at this point but for those who stayed there were rewards beyond measure. First Gael Clichy's slip allowed Jenas to fire home a wicked swerving shot; then with ten seconds remaining Aaron Lennon reacted superbly to convert a rebound off the post. For new manager Harry Redknapp, just five days into the job, there could be only one verdict: 'Amazing.'

The Producers

As *MotD* series producer, Ian Finch has to ensure that the programme's overall look – its set, lighting, on-screen branding and virtual reality graphics – have maximum impact. As the theme tune begins he'll be directing everyone from Gary Lineker to camera and sound technicians, the VT (videotape) team and graphics operators.

Each show is driven by the day's big Premier League stories. That means not only displaying statistics and formations to compliment analysis but, following *MotD*'s 2011 move to hi-tech MediaCityUK studios in Salford, also electronically 'painting' key images onto virtual display panels.

Premier League games are watched simultaneously live on Saturday afternoons with the main discussion points noted. Edit and analysis producers will chip in ideas, together with the commentator, but the script isn't tackled until all results are in and the running order agreed. Only then will Lineker and the editor start 'writing' the programme.

'Because of the pace of our show and the amount of action we have to squeeze in, we generally only have a couple of minutes to discuss each game,' says Ian. 'That doesn't always allow us to go into the same amount of detail as other broadcasters who have more airtime and maybe only one match to discuss.

'Also we have to be aware that *Match of the Day* is a show for everyone – not just the football purist. We have to strike the right balance and while we're keen to offer real insight and tactical analysis, we don't want to alienate the casual viewer with too much intricate detail. We also have a Sunday morning repeat show that is popular with a younger audience, so there's a real emphasis for our pundits to help children better understand the nuances of the game and provide pointers that they can take into their own football.'

Player of the Year
Steven Gerrard, Liverpool

This was the season Steven Gerrard – one of the Premier League's most gifted and consistent midfielders – would come close to winning the title. Starring alongside the likes of Fernando Torres, Fernando Alonso and Javier Mascherano, he contributed 16 goals to the Reds' quest for honours, sometimes hauling his side single-handedly past stubborn opponents.

The tone was set during the first game at Middlesborough which, although it ended 0-0, saw the Liverpool captain in irresistible form. 'Steven Gerrard was awesome today,' Boro defender Gareth Southgate told reporters later. 'We were just laughing in the dressing room that at one stage we thought he was heading his own crosses in.'

In a season of career milestones Gerrard hit his 100th goal for Liverpool against PSV, made his 100th European appearance for the club against Real Madrid and notched a first Premier League hat-trick against Aston Villa. Unsurprisingly he garnered praise from across Europe – not least from Zinedine Zidane who in March 2009 suggested he was the best player in the world. 'He gives the players around him confidence and belief,' said Zidane. 'You can't learn that. Players like him are just born with that presence.'

2009-10

Carlo Ancelotti's first season as Chelsea's manager was also the most successful in the club's history. It marked a new emphasis on attacking play as the club won the Premier League with a record 103 goals – an average of 2.71 per game compared to 1.89 during their previous title win four years earlier. Didier Drogba was instrumental in this, winning the Golden Boot with 29 league goals, but Frank Lampard's contribution of 22 was an outstanding effort from a midfield player.

Above: Lampard congratulates Drogba on scoring against Wigan, having earlier denied him the chance.

Opposite: It's Wigan's turn to celebrate as they bring down Arsenal with three goals in the last ten minutes.

Although they won by a single point, the Blues ticked every box for worthy champions. They won all the big head-to-heads against Manchester United, Arsenal and Liverpool and finished the season with panache, thrashing poor Wigan 8-0 at Stamford Bridge in a game they needed to win to secure the crown. It was a mark of Lampard's professionalism that he shrugged off the Boot-hunting Drogba's pleas to take an early Chelsea spot-kick. Lampard, the designated penalty taker, mouthed forcefully at the striker 'It's 1-0' before duly converting. But when a second penalty was awarded at 5-0 he was smiling as he handed the ball to the Ivorian. Chelsea went on to secure their first ever double with an FA Cup win over Portsmouth.

Among the other 'big clubs' only Manchester United mounted a serious challenge to Ancelotti's side. Perhaps the greatest disappointment was at Anfield, where Rafael Benítez had steered the Reds to runners-up spot the previous season and had just signed a new five-year contract. Liverpool lost two of their first three games and exited the Champions League at the group stage.

Their dismal season was summed up by the infamous 'beach ball goal' which settled Sunderland's 1-0 win at Anfield in October. The Liverpool defence failed to clear a cross and the ball fell to Darren Bent just inside the area. His first-time strike cannoned off a large, red, inflatable beach ball that had just been punched on to the pitch by a Reds supporter. The deflection wrong-footed Pepe Reina but the goal was allowed to stand.

Liverpool's misfortune has since given hours of pleasure to amateur refs and football anoraks everywhere. FIFA's laws state *'that the referee should stop, suspend or abandon the match because of outside interference of any kind.'* That seems clear enough and the game should therefore have been restarted with a drop-ball. But if the referee didn't spot the beach ball in the first place (it was, after all, red) then how could he have stopped play in time?

Match of the Season
Wigan 3 Arsenal 2

It was the game which ended one team's title bid and the other's fear of the drop. No prizes for guessing which was which but the last ten minutes of this encounter encapsulated the agony and the ecstasy of football generally and the Premier League in particular.

Arsenal's title challenge had fizzled out and been relit so many times that they were running out of matches at the Emirates. But a win at the DW Stadium on 18 April really would have given them a fighting chance. Chelsea had lost the previous day at Tottenham and the Gunners could now push to within three points of the top.

With ten minutes to go at Wigan they were cruising on a 2-0 lead thanks to Walcott and Silvestre. Then Ben Watson steered home a Charles N'Zogbia cross, Lukasz Fabianski produced a shocking flap in the Arsenal goal to gift Titus Bramble a header seven minutes later and N'Zogbia himself scored a last-gasp pearler, curling the ball past a motionless Fabianski from the edge of the area.

Then and Now – How Match Commentary Has Changed

The expansion of TV football coverage has coincided with a technological revolution making for a seamless marriage of commentary and action. But it was not always so.

'My set-up at an outside broadcast now,' says former *MotD* and now ITV commentator Clive Tyldesley, 'is a commentary position on the halfway line, monitor here, monitor there, director in my ear and somewhere between 15 and 20 odd cameras.

'I can hear the conversation that the director is having with the VT (videotape) department and so if they're looking at a potential foul I can hear that. So when the replay comes to the screen I've probably had a bit of a preview as to what you're about to see and what I've got to comment upon.

'In the early nineties, when I was commentating on *MotD* there were no replays on site – you commented on the incident then closed your eyes and imagined the replay and tried to come up with words which you hoped would fit that picture. Very often you made it almost impossible for the guy editing to piece together something which fitted those words.

'The master of the art was David Coleman. DC would take a pause, count to four, imagine the start of the replay and then spread his wonderful voice all over 15 seconds of television [often concluding] "... finishing of the very highest order".'

Above: Jacqui Oatley became MotD*'s first female commentator in 2007.*

Opposite top: Rooney concentrating hard during a wintry match against Burnley at Old Trafford.

Opposite bottom: Rooney grabs a goal during the same Burnley game.

Player of the Year
Wayne Rooney, Manchester United

Ever since he burst on to the scene with that memorable winning strike for Everton against Arsenal in 2002, Wayne Rooney has proved time and again to be the nation's most prodigious talent since Paul Gascoigne. It wasn't until 2009–10, however, that fans began to see the best of him.

Five years of ably supporting Cristiano Ronaldo – the main man for most of Rooney's early Old Trafford career – came to an end when the Portuguese star left for Real Madrid in the close season. With Argentinian striker Carlos Tevez also jumping ship, Rooney was tasked with guiding the Red Devils through transition. He grasped the challenge with relish.

Thriving on Dimitar Berbatov's deft touches around the penalty area, and a first-class service from wingers Nani and new signing Antonio Valencia, Rooney netted 34 times in all competitions. Highlights included his 100th career strike for Manchester United, four goals in a match for the first time (at home to Hull) and a headed winner in stoppage time during the Capital One Cup semi-final against derby rivals Manchester City.

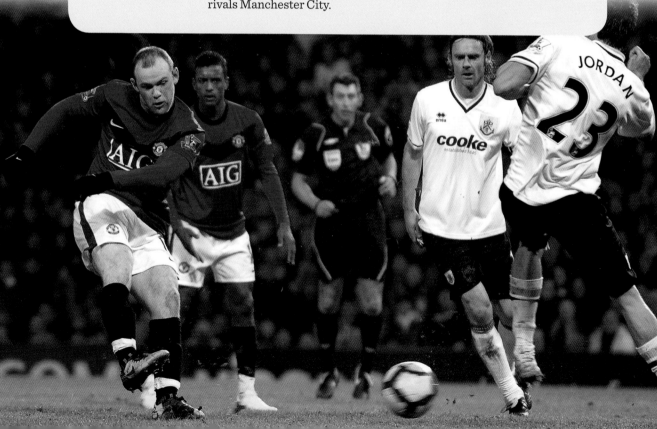

2010s

2010-2011

Any championship-winning season is precious to a club but this one meant so much more at Old Trafford. Despite the trophy-fest of recent years, fans at the other end of the East Lancs Road had always been quick to reference Liverpool's greater top-flight title haul. That taunt had softened with United's 2009 success, placing the clubs on 18 apiece; now it was silenced altogether.

Above: Supporters' badge commemorating Birmingham's first major honour in almost half a century.

Above right: Dimitar Berbatov was key to United's success.

Opposite: Leon Best helps to bring Newcastle back into the game.

United hit the top on 27 November following a 7-1 thrashing of Blackburn (Dimitar Berbatov scored five) and from that moment the coveted 19th title was never in doubt. Sir Alex Ferguson's side maintained top spot through to what was effectively the decider at home to Chelsea – a game they convincingly won 2-1 – and then

squashed any lingering hopes among rivals with a 1-1 draw in their penultimate match away at Blackburn.

The impressive strike rate of Berbatov (20 goals from 24 league appearances) and Javier Hernández (13 from 15) helped United comfortably outscore allcomers and their nine-point cushion at the close did not flatter them. Which says something for the strength of Barcelona, who took the Red Devils apart in the Champions League final a few days later to win 3-1.

While the pressure was off in their final game against Blackpool at Old Trafford, they did have a responsibility to the four other teams battling relegation alongside the Seasiders – Birmingham, Wigan, Wolves and Blackburn. It didn't seem they had taken that responsibility seriously enough as Blackpool went 2-1 up early in the second half but then three unanswered goals sent the visitors down with Birmingham.

West Ham had already been dispatched and wasted little time ending manager Avram Grant's 11 months in charge. He was not the only high-

Match of the Season
Newcastle United 4 Arsenal 4

It may be the weariest cliché in the football reporter's armoury but sometimes it must be said; this was a game of two halves.

Arsenal had gone into the fixture on 5 February with pretensions to the championship. And with ten minutes gone you could see why. Theo Walcott scored the opener after just 42 seconds then Johan Djourou's header from Arshavin's free kick put them two up inside three minutes. Walcott crossed for Robin Van Persie to strike a third and on the half-hour the Dutchman made it four from Bacary Sagna's free-kick. Memo to Gunners fans; at this point, as they say on the news before *MotD*, you should look away.

Once Abou Diaby was deservedly red-carded after the break the wheels came off Arsenal's juggernaut. Warren Barton scored penalties either side of a Leon Best goal and with Toon fans now roaring their side on the Gunners previously assured defence suddenly looked like a car crash. When Chiek Tiote levelled with a scintillating volley three minutes from time, St James' Park was rocking. Arsène Wenger believed his side were 'unlucky' with refereeing decisions but admitted that 'psychologically the damage is bigger [than two dropped points]'. And so it proved.

profile managerial casualty; Roy Hodgson parted company with Liverpool after only six months, to be replaced by Kenny Dalglish, while Roberto Di Matteo left West Brom and Sam Allardyce was sacked by Blackburn.

For clubs seeking an end to trophy droughts there were conflicting fortunes. Manchester City, without a sniff of silverware in 35 years, finally came good in the FA Cup final as Yaya Touré's left-foot volley 16 minutes from time saw off Stoke City.

But for Arsenal, chasing a first trophy since 2005, things went horribly wrong in the League Cup final against Birmingham. With the game tied at 1-1, and two minutes of normal time to go, a communications meltdown between Gunners goalkeeper Wojciech Szczesny and defender Laurent Koscielny allowed Obafemi Martins to tap into an empty net and give Birmingham their first major honours in 48 years.

MotD Memories: The Last TV Social Event

Opposite top: Parker in action against Fulham, for whom he would sign in 2013.

Opposite bottom: Parker challenges Luka Modric of Spurs, for whom Parker would sign in 2011.

Comedian and West Ham fan Russell Brand described his guest appearance as a *MotD* pundit as 'like walking into one of my own dreams.' Here he sums up what the progamme means to him.

'*MotD* is the last, real television social event that people gather round to watch as a unit. I don't think people watch TV like that anymore. It provides the narrative of how top-flight football is perceived and that's a lot of burden on Hansen, Shearer and Lineker.

'It doesn't matter what's going on in your life, what's wrong with work, what's wrong with your relationship at least you can watch the football, you can escape and you can express your emotions – joy, pain, fear, anger, injustice – and all that stuff. It provides a safe forum for men to express emotions that are inexpressible elsewhere. Where else can this happen in our cultural space?

'[The theme tune] conjures up these emotions, the same as when you're going to a football match; feeling a bit nervous, a bit sick, not a straightforward, jolly, fun day out. It is an iconic piece of music and it perfectly captures the spirit.

'*MotD* means I can have an understanding of what's going on in top flight football without having to devote my entire life to it. It somehow captures the truth of football but presents a particular story of football. It is an ever-present and necessary aspect of life.'

Player of the Year
Scott Parker, West Ham United

To win this award with a team fighting relegation is impressive. To be voted ahead of flair players and free-scoring attackers says everything about Scott Parker's hard-tackling, lung-busting performances. As the football writers rightly recognized, every team needs one like him.

The first West Ham player to win the award since Sir Bobby Moore, Parker was signed from Newcastle United in June 2007 for £7 million. He was immediately heralded by Hammers' fans (always appreciative of skilful grafters) for his ability to smother attacking threats and press opponents into mistakes.

He was voted Hammer of the Year in both 2009 and 2010, but it was his fourth and final season in east London that made neutrals across the country sit up and take notice. Parker put in a series of inspiring shifts in a defiant, though ultimately doomed, single-minded mission to retain his side's Premier League status.

His quiet, off-field demeanour masked some enviable leadership qualities and when West Ham clawed back a 3-0 half-time deficit against West Brom to secure a draw at The Hawthorns striker Carlton Cole admitted it 'brought a tear to the eye'. However, Parker's England ambitions could not be served by the Championship and following relegation he moved to Tottenham.

Never has a football team so cruelly messed with their supporters' heads. Nor transported them from agony to ecstasy so quickly. For Manchester City fans present at the Etihad Stadium on the afternoon of 13 May 2012 it is still almost too hard to relive those final moments. Almost.

City went into their match against struggling QPR knowing that, barring heavenly intervention, a win would secure the title on goal difference. Few doubted they would succeed and their only challengers, Manchester United, had gone to Sunderland expecting a runners-up spot.

Yet, extraordinarily, a dismal City were losing 2-1 as the clock ticked into stoppage time despite the fact that Rangers were a man down following Joey Barton's 55th-minute red card. United, meanwhile, were seconds away from a 1-0 win. At the Stadium of Light, Sir Alex Ferguson's players had gone from resigned to expectant. For a few delirious seconds they could all but touch the trophy.

And then it was snatched away. Make no mistake, this was the single most devastating act ever inflicted by one Premier League derby rival against another and in terms of raw drama it transcended even Michael Thomas's last-gasp title-clincher for Arsenal at Anfield in 1989.

With the clock reading 91:15, Edin Džeko headed home David Silva's corner to offer a smidgeon of hope. On the touchline manager Roberto Mancini and his coaches screamed for players to hurtle forward. As the clock ticked into the fourth minute of injury time the ball fell to Mario Balotelli in a crowded penalty area. Somehow he poked it to Sergio Agüero.

The Argentinian beat one defender and from the right of the six-yard box smashed a winner past Paddy Kenny at the near post. Forty-four years after last claiming the title, City had done it. 'We deserved to win this and deserved to win the title,' a jubilant Mancini observed later. 'We were on top for twenty games.'

Above: Celebrations in the Manchester Evening News.

Top: Agüero clinches the match for City.

Match of the Season
Chelsea 3-5 Arsenal

With a remarkable season just 11 weeks old there were already two best-match contenders. Arsenal's abject 8-2 capitulation at Old Trafford represented their worst defeat since 1896 while the 6-1 thrashing meted out by Manchester City in the same stadium was United's worst home loss since 1955. Yet this captivating encounter at Stamford Bridge on 29 October topped both for excitement and entertainment.

The hosts went in front through Frank Lampard after 14 minutes and although Robin van Persie levelled, John Terry restored the advantage with a scrambled goal. Given the obvious fragility of both defences the game looked wide open but Arsenal emerged from half-time the stronger and André Santos showed composed finishing to again equalise before Theo Walcott put the Gunners ahead for the first time, riding two challenges to slot past Petr Cech.

Arsenal held their lead until ten minutes from time when Juan Mata's bending 25-yard strike made it 3-3 – a goal angrily disputed by Arsène Wenger who was convinced Santos had been fouled in the build-up. But it hardly mattered. Van Persie, who had been on fire, form-wise, for months, first took advantage of Terry's slip to round Cech for a fourth and then finished the job by completing his hat-trick; a 28th goal in 27 outstanding Premier League games.

Robin van Persie waltzes past Chelsea goalkeeper Petr Cech.

This thrill-a-second end to the season rather overshadowed Chelsea's historic first Champions League win. Yet the Blues' spirit and dogged determination throughout the competition was truly outstanding – especially given that Roberto Di Matteo had taken over from the sacked André Villas-Boas barely two months earlier.

First they clawed back a 3-1 deficit in the first leg of the knockout round against Napoli (winning 5-4 on aggregate) then held on for a second-leg 2-2 draw in the semi-final against Barcelona, going through 3-2. Finally, following a battering from Bayern Munich in the Munich final, Dider Drogba's 89th-minute headed equaliser allowed them the chance to win a penalty shoot-out 5-4. They ended the season with a cup double thanks to their earlier 2-1 FA Cup final win over Liverpool.

Opposite top: Van Persie was headed for Manchester United at the end of the season.

Opposite bottom: Van Persie nods the ball past Leeds United's Kasper Schmeichel.

Below: High praise for Paul Scholes from Thierry Henry.

Motd Memories: Thierry Henry's Best Goal and Player

Thierry Henry made his final Premier League bow at Sunderland on 11 February 2012. He'd briefly come back to Arsenal on loan from the New York Bulls, ostensibly as 'cover' for Gervinho and Chamakh. To Gooners watching that day, it was a bit like Maurice Chevalier providing 'cover' for The Wurzels.

Coming on late as substitute the Frenchman had just one chance and took it, ghosting between two defenders to volley home the winning goal in stoppage time. It's at times like this that football is both a kind and cruel master. Arsenal fans had seen one last glimpse of Henry magic; now, with three months of the season left, he was heading off across the Atlantic.

Looking back, Henry is in no doubt about his best Premier League goal. It was the second of his hat-trick during Arsenal's 4-2 victory over Liverpool on 9 April 2004, the one where he picks the ball up just past the half-way line and waltzes past five opponents to stroke home. 'It was the first time I felt a stadium breathing,' he told the BBC later. Maybe something was lost in translation but you knew what he meant.

And his best player? 'Paul Scholes. Period. Over. Just his name is enough for me. Watch what he did – he didn't get the credit he deserved. You can ask anyone – a lot [of players] will tell you the same name.'

 Player of the Year
Robin van Persie, Arsenal

When the Dutchman arrived at Arsenal from Feyenoord in 2004 he came with some bad-boy baggage, having fallen out with manager Bert van Marwijk and clashed with team-mates on numerous occasions.

A red card against Southampton early in his Gunners career compounded that reputation and it looked like his time in north London might end early, particularly as he struggled to deal with time on the bench. However, a dose of positive pills from Arsène Wenger encouraged him to focus on developing his outstanding technical, shooting and dribbling abilities. It also helped to be training and playing alongside skill-wizards Thierry Henry and Robert Pirès and by the time the former left for Barcelona in 2007, RVP was hitting a career peak.

Given a platform for his creativity – a natural asset for the son of two artists – van Persie kept threatening to set the Premier League alight only to be frustratingly hampered by injury. In 2011–12, though, he enjoyed a prolonged spell of match fitness and the results were devastating. After being appointed captain following Cesc Fàbregas's sale to Barcelona he took his season's tally to 30 league goals and 37 in all competitions. Despite this, Arsenal's failure to secure a trophy left him frustrated and he joined Manchester United at the end of the season.

As disconsolate Manchester United players headed south after the anguish of winning and losing the title in 15 seconds at Sunderland, Sir Alex Ferguson began working the team coach. His aim was partly to raise spirits. But mostly to hammer home a lesson.

Opposite: Rooney scored two against local rivals Manchester City.

Below: Sir Alex Ferguson shows the Premiership trophy in a Manchester United programme feature.

Bottom right: The Chelsea team surrounds the UEFA Europa League Cup.

Striker Danny Welbeck recalled: 'The manager went round all the young players and said to them: "Never forget this because this will win you titles. This will make some of you into men and be the best you can be."' Ferguson knew words alone weren't enough; his players needed a morale-boost ahead of a season that would be his own swansong. So he produced one. He bought Robin van Persie.

Van Persie arrived at United in August for a reported £24 million, a body blow to Arsenal who had lost not only their club captain and eighth all-time leading scorer (132 goals) but also the Premier League's top scorer from 2011–12 (30 goals). No one player can win a championship but as the season progressed RVP unquestionably tipped the balance. Having scored with his first shot at Old Trafford he added a further 25 as United re-established dominance; winning with four games left, a cushion of 11 points and a goal tally of 86 – 20 more than runners-up Man City.

Two weeks after securing the title, Ferguson announced his retirement. His 26-year career at the club had brought 13 League trophies, two Champions League cups, five FA Cups, a Cup Winners' Cup and four League Cups. In an emotional farewell, delivered after a 2-1 final-day home victory over Swansea, Sir Alex could have spoken for hours about that glorious past. Instead he looked forward, rallying fans behind new manager David Moyes, reminding them that loyalty and perseverance mattered as much as talent.

Match of the Season

Manchester City 2
Manchester United 3

The season was still young but this was the game which reminded Manchester City – Sir Alex Feguson's 'noisy neighbours' – that winning titles is one thing; defending them is the devil's own job. Particularly when the Red Devil you tried, and failed, to sign six months earlier scores the winner in injury time.

City manager Roberto Mancini had freely admitted he'd wanted Robin van Persie at the Etihad so when the Dutchman's injury-time free-kick cannoned off Samir Nasri and over the stranded Joe Hart it must have been a jaw-tightening moment. Mancini had controversially picked striker Mario Balotelli ahead of Carlos Tevez for this game and it proved a stinker of a decision. The Italian was way off the pace and his ludicrous back-heel to concede possession saw him substituted for Tevez soon after the break.

That changed the momentum of the game. In the first half United's sweeping counter-attacking moves had torn through the City defence, with Wayne Rooney's two goals fully deserved. But Tevez's work rate helped put City back on terms and goals from Yaya Touré and Pablo Zabaleta seemed to have salvaged a draw until RVP's late intervention put United six points clear heading into the crucial Christmas period.

'When I had bad times here, the club stood by me,' he said. 'All my staff stood by me, the players stood by me, you stood by me. And your job now is to stand by our new manager.' Ferguson had spoken. Time would tell whether everyone had paid attention.

Elsewhere it was a season of notable competition milestones. After 100 years in business Swansea won their first trophy – the League Cup – with a 5-0 drubbing of League 2 Bradford City (whose brilliant cup run had, incidentally, claimed three Premier League scalps). Wigan claimed their first major honours by deservedly slaying Manchester City 1-0 in the FA Cup final. And Chelsea became the first English club to complete the European grand slam – adding the Europa League (aka the Fairs and UEFA Cup) to previous successes in the Champions League and Cup Winners' Cup.

MotD Memories: The Price of Punditry

Alan Hansen joined *Match of the Day* with the launch of the Premier League and in the ensuing 22 years re-defined the art of punditry. Whereas some ex-pros were overly cautious about criticising former colleagues he told it like it was, explaining criticisms of players and tactics with succinct insight. He was also a fierce defender of the show itself.

Announcing his retirement from *MotD* in 2013 he told the *Daily Telegraph*: 'The viewing figures over the last five years have been absolutely sensational but nobody seems to want to know about that. In terms of audience appreciation figures, they are through the roof as well. The real strength of it – and also its biggest weakness – is that every second is accounted for before you start.'

Hansen regards the main presenters of his *MotD* era – Des Lynam and Gary Lineker – as 'two of the best' and the feeling is clearly mutual. Des says the one big surprise was how jittery the former Liverpool defender would get as the studio counted down to a live broadcast.

'Here was this great star, won everything in football untold times, came on the show nervous as a cat,' said Des. 'Of course it's a different game, television, and tough actually. He told me once he was always nervous before walking out onto the pitch.

'He soon came to terms with it though and he's been a star on the show down the years.'

 ### Player of the Year
Gareth Bale, Tottenham Hotspur

In his short, rollercoaster of a career Gareth Bale has emerged as the most powerful and thrilling winger in world football – no surprise to those who have followed his truncated development.

The Welshman signed professional terms at Southampton, breaking through at left-back at the same time as Theo Walcott, and scored five times in 45 appearances. But there was obviously much more to come and his pace, strength and dead-ball prowess persuaded Spurs to pay £5 million for his services in 2007.

Bale's start at White Hart Lane quickly descended into a nightmare. Despite scoring goals against Fulham, Arsenal and Middlesbrough, he went 24 games without a win while on the pitch and struggled with injuries before losing his place to Benoit Assou-Ekotto for most of the 2008–9 season.

He fought his way back the following year – this time as an attacking winger – and his brilliant hat-trick against Inter Milan during the 2010–11 Champions League served as a wake-up call to the world's top managers. In that game Bale was up against Maicon – then regarded by most observers as the best full-back in world football – but almost dismissively took him apart.

In 2012–13, his last season at the Lane before an £80 million transfer to Real Madrid (a world record depending who you believe) was his most impressive. He scored his first Premier League hat-trick and hit 26 goals in 44 appearances to see off stiff competition from both Luís Suarez and Robin van Persie for Player of the Year.

If the Premier League was a sentient entity it would be an eccentric, lovable uncle - maddening at times but never one to forget a birthday. And for *Match of the Day*'s 50th, it certainly delivered the goods.

Above: Aloysius Paulus Maria (Louis) van Gaal, manager of the Dutch squad, took over as boss at Manchester United.

Opposite top: Arsenal's Polish-born German striker Lukas Podolski goes flying during the FA Cup final against Hull City.

Opposite bottom: Luis Suarez hides his tears as he leaves the pitch.

This was one of the classic climaxes to a top-flight season; the title's destiny still uncertain on the final day, a tense relegation battle, a Champions League semi-final and a managerial sacking that left Twitter in meltdown.

For months it seemed Arsène Wenger might defy his critics and, indeed, for 128 days Arsenal led the title race. But humiliating spring drubbings at the hands of Liverpool (5-1) and Chelsea (6-0) – the latter Wenger's 1,000th game in charge – told its own story. The Gooners did at least silence the trophy-taunters, beating Hull 3-2 in an exciting FA Cup final.

As the Emirates' star faded so Anfield's rose, inspired by Brendan Rodgers' 'old Liverpool' attacking philosophy in which Luis Suarez, Daniel Sturridge and Raheem Stirling emerged as the shock-troops of counter-attacking. Riding the emotional wave which accompanied Hillsborough's 25th anniversary, Liverpool seemed to have done the hard part by beating title rivals Manchester City 3-2 at home. Yet while the Reds were then out-thought by José Mourinho's Chelsea, losing 2-0 at Anfield, and collapsed horribly at Crystal Palace, City's nerve held.

Rival fans accused them of 'buying' the title (as though their own clubs would never do something so despicable). And certainly an £85.4 million transfer war chest made City far and away the season's biggest spenders. Yet it is ludicrous to suggest they needed only to turn up and win. Stars like Fernandinho and Alvaro Negredo still had to gel with the established world class 'spine' of Joe Hart, Vincent Kompany, Yaya Touré, David Silva and Sergio Agüero. That this was achieved was largely down to a calm, tactically astute and thoughtful manager in Manuel Pellegrini.

The prospect of a City title would normally guarantee glum faces at Old Trafford. Yet despite United's dire season, and the sacking of 'chosen one' David Moyes after just ten months, there was a cheerier mood with the appointment of Ryan Giggs as temporary manager. His use of 'Class of 92' former team-mates Paul Scholes, Nicky Butt and Phil Neville as assistant coaches hardly proved transformative ... but it did boost morale.

Match of the Season
Crystal Palace 3 Liverpool 3

With 11 minutes to go, and Liverpool rampant at 3-0 up, there must have been some tense silences in Manchester City households. Not only would City now need to win their last two games to be sure of the title, their goal difference suddenly didn't look quite so superior.

Yet Palace under new manager Tony Pulis were a very different prospect to the hapless and hesitant side which had looked relegation-bound earlier in the season. Pulis's Stoke City rarely lacked fight; now his new squad proved they'd also got the message.

As Liverpool pressed relentlessly forward to build on goals by Joe Allen, Daniel Sturridge and Luis Suarez they revealed the one, major flaw in an otherwise magnificent season; a creaky, leaky defence.

Damien Delaney started the turnaround for Palace with a speculative shot deflected in off Glen Johnson, then substitute Dwight Gayle bagged two more. At the final whistle Selhurst Park was rocking and a distraught Suarez headed for the tunnel, face buried in shirt to hide his tears.

As Liverpool manager Brendan Rogers conceded the title to City he criticised his team for 'thinking we could play Roy of the Rovers football'. If only Liverpool could have called on the likes of Melchester Rovers' Lofty Peake to shore up the back.

As for Chelsea it was a might-have-been season – losing in the Champions League semis to Atletico Madrid and faltering in the Premier League run-in. Meanwhile at the bottom Sunderland manager Gus Poyet proved a master escape artist leaving Norwich, Fulham and Cardiff to ponder life in the Championship

Below: Data and analysis are no substitute for the drama and atmosphere of a live match.

Whither *Match of the Day?*

So what of the next 50 years? Will the hi-tech bells-and-whistles get noisier? The data-crunching on players ever smarter?

As TV companies invest millions in screening rights, the pressure to unearth innovative new approaches will inevitably increase. Player tracking data is already ubiquitous – hence we know that in 2012 Leighton Baines created more chances than any other European player (a goal-scoring opportunity every 21.6 minutes, since you ask) and that 38 per cent of his crosses were accurate. This is 'big data' – churning vast amounts of information to analyse patterns and make predictions – and it is now standard fare at top clubs.

Data generators, and no doubt many betting companies, know that games are not random and can be converted to mathematical models. Pitches are 'networks' on which players connect through 'channels'. A team's ability to keep channels clear (i.e. completing a pass) can now be deconstructed and analysed to the nth degree. TV pundits will have all this data and more in future. Will *MotD* become part football, part chess?

Opposite top: 31 goals in 33 games made former bad boy Luis Suarez Player of the Year.

Opposite bottom: Suarez celebrates a goal scored by team-mate Daniel Sturridge.

The technology magazine *Wired* once quoted Harry Redknapp telling his data analyst at Southampton: 'Tell you what, next week, why don't we get your computer to play against their computer and see who wins?' You can understand his frustration. However good computers get, they can never create algorithms to replace the human drama, skill, excitement and physical courage that is football's soul.

Match of the Day has nurtured that soul for 50 years. No reason to stop now.

Player of the Year
Luis Suarez, Liverpool

There was never going to be much doubt. Although the season produced several worthy candidates - Steven Gerrard, Yaya Touré and Eden Hazard to name but three – more than half the Football Writers' Association votes went to Liverpool's Luis Suarez.

For the 27-year-old Uruguayan, who also took the Players' Player award, this amounted to the unlikeliest of rehabilitations. He had been vilified in the press following his racial abuse of Patrice Evra in 2011 and the notorious arm-munching affair involving Chelsea defender Branislav Ivanovic in April 2013.

Yet after the latter incident Suarez was a reformed character. He emerged from a ten-match ban to score 31 league goals in 33 games, igniting his side's 2014 championship aspirations. That made him only the seventh player in Premier League history to hit the 30 mark, the others being Robin van Persie, Cristiano Ronaldo, Thierry Henry, Kevin Phillips and Andy Cole. *Match of the Day*'s Alan Shearer managed it three times of course – all with Blackburn Rovers.

Acknowledgements

Nick Constable: Thanks to *MotD* series producer Ian Finch for his time and invaluable insight, Lewis Constable for his Player of the Year research and friends who pointed out what *should* have been written about their club.

BBC Books: The publisher would like to thank Phil Bigwood, Mark Cole, Tom Gent, Paul Armstrong and Ian Finch for their help in creating this book.

Picture Credits:
All of the photographs used in this book were provided by Getty Images apart from those listed below.
Pages 7,8,9,10,11,16,28,36,50 (both), 62,74,79 (both), 82 (right), 100, 146, 150, 162, 182, 186, 208, 220, 224, 246 courtesy of BBC Photo Library.
Pages 15, 19, 24, 31(top), 40 (bottom), 45, 48 (right), 57, 91(bottom), 157, 163 (top), 167, 181, 191, 192, 203 (top), 210, 218, 223, 237 courtesy of Welloffside Sports Photography.

Memorabilia photographed by Karl Adamson.

The author and publisher gratefully acknowledge the permission granted to reproduce the copyright material in this book. Every effort has been made to trace copyright holders and to obtain permission for the use of copyright material. The publisher apologises for any errors or omissions in the below list and would be grateful if notified of any corrections that should be incorporated in future reprints or editions of this book.